Reluctant the Gardener

Gardener

A BEGINNER'S GUIDE
TO GARDENING
IN CANADA

Dinah Shields &
Edwinna von Baeyer

Random House
Toronto

Published in Canada in 1992 by
Random House of Canada Limited, Toronto.

Canadian Cataloguing in Publication Data

Shields, Dinah
     The reluctant gardener

ISBN   0-394-22233-4

1. Flower gardening.   2. Gardening.   I. von Baeyer,
Edwinna, 1947–   .   II. Title.

SB453.S55 1992   635.9   C92-093034-4

DESIGN: Brant Cowie/ArtPlus Limited

ELECTRONIC ASSEMBLY: Dale Bateman/ArtPlus Limited

LINE ILLUSTRATIONS: Al Wilson

Printed and bound in Canada

10 9 8 7 6 5 4

Contents

To my sister, Susan, with love. I miss you. DJS

To my family. EvB

Introduction

As people enter adulthood, they often feel the need to garden. Perhaps even the urge. Moving into first homes, or moving up to a bigger and better one frequently activates this urge. Those without green thumbs are a little surprised, if not dismayed, to see that this nice house comes with a mystifying jumble of lawns, flowerbeds, shrubs and trees. Or if a brand new house has been purchased, they might be faced with a vast expanse of lawn, two spindly maple trees, and nothing else.

These homeowners realize they have not the faintest idea how to maintain any of this. They have either been too busy or too uninterested (no shame in that) to tackle previous gardens. Or maybe they have just moved out of an apartment, where their boldest horticultural venture was a potted African violet.

In any event, the garden presents an intimidating challenge to new gardeners. They want to fix it up, nothing fancy, you understand. If they begin by consulting a few conventional gardening books they can easily come away discouraged, feeling overwhelmed by a barrage of advanced information on acid and alkaline soils, or how many sepals there are on a delphinium flower. They do not much care about such things but, since this is not their field of expertise, they have no way to judge for themselves what is important and what can safely be ignored.

Enter *The Reluctant Gardener*. Not just another beginner's gardening book, it is designed for both beginning gardeners and those who are gardening out of a sense of duty. The book deals only with flowers, lawn, shrubs and trees. No fruits, no vegetables, no herbs — what are grocery stores for? This book is a pared-down guide written for ordinary environmentally-conscious gardeners who take a small size in gardening space, budget, enthusiasm and knowledge.

The book is based on Dinah's successful course for people who hate to garden but have to. Both of us are enthusiastic gardeners who blushingly acknowledge that we have attractive home gardens. But we also acknowledge we have a lazy streak. Our own fervor for gardening tends to go in waves, leaving us with days full of garden chores, but empty of enthusiasm. This is what led us to share our gardening shortcuts — shortcuts that allow us to put our feet up with a clear conscience half way through the morning, knowing that we have done all that really needs to be done to keep the garden healthy and attractive. We know how to do it right, but have been able to modify that knowledge to come up with ways to do it both right and easy — ideas we hope you will, reluctantly or not, adopt in your own gardens.

DINAH SHIELDS

EDWINNA VON BAEYER

OTTAWA, 1991

Acknowledgements

We want to thank many editors, friends and relations who listened, laughed and generally supported us throughout the writing of this book. Both of us heartily thank our bemused agent, Denise Bukowski — a non-gardener who suddenly found herself dancing down the garden path — for her support. We would also like to thank Lorraine Johnson for her meticulous first edit and Anna Cundari at Random House for her patient and helpful editing and counsel during the production of the book. And of course we must thank Claire Harrison, the original reluctant gardener. Edwinna's family once again came through when deadlines loomed and dinner was late. Dinah found good friends and confidants in Jim Brown and Len Burnstein. Although many helped us improve the book with suggestions and corrections, any errors or omissions are only ours.

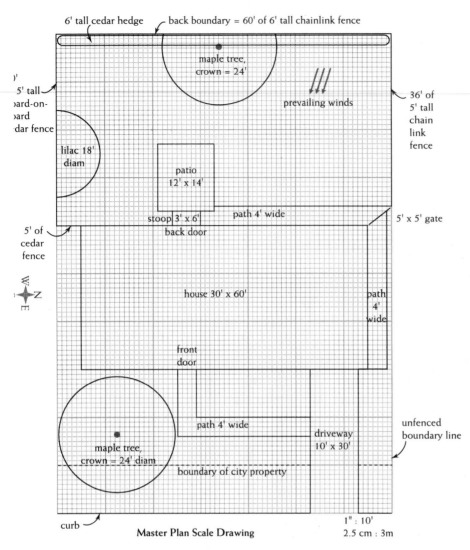

6' tall cedar hedge

back boundary = 60' of 6' tall chainlink fence

maple tree, crown = 24'

prevailing winds

36' of 5' tall chain link fence

)'
5' tall
board-on-board
cedar fence

lilac 18' diam

patio 12' x 14'

stoop 3' x 6'

back door

path 4' wide

5' x 5' gate

5' of cedar fence

W N E

house 30' x 60'

path 4' wide

front door

maple tree, crown = 24' diam

path 4' wide

driveway 10' x 30'

unfenced boundary line

boundary of city property

curb

Master Plan Scale Drawing

1" : 10'
2.5 cm : 3m

Master Plan Elements:
(permanent features on graph paper)

lot – 70' x 100'/21 m x 30 m

house – 30' x 60'/9 m x 18 m

drive – 10' x 30'/3 m x 9 m

paths – 4'/1.2 m wide

back stoop – 3' x 6'/1 m x 2 m

patio – 12' x 14'/3.5 m x 4 m

front maple,
    crown – 18'/5.5 m diameter

back maple,
    crown – 18'/5.5 m diameter

Also:
• no shade from neighbors' trees
• prevailing winds from west
• front 10'/3m belong to city

Ideas for Tracing Paper Overlays:
Back flower beds? 1) along 5 ft./1.5 m chain link fence; 2) along cedar fence; 3) edging three sides of patio; 4) at base of cedar hedge
Front flower beds? 1) along front on either side of front door; 2) one or both edges of driveway; 3) front edge of path

Also:
• placement of a storage shed
• shrubs
• permanent placement of large, heavy planter tubs
• placement of a cast-iron bench
• built-in sandbox
• swing set

CHAPTER 1

Green Dreams: Planning and Designing Your Yard

One of your authors skips guiltily over the design chapter in most of her gardening books, because the whole topic intimidates her. Reading that a well-designed garden is like a poem or a fine painting makes her want to hide under the bedcovers, because she knows she is not, and never will be, a poet or a painter. Reading that the rugged bark of a tree is supposed to make her think of timeless strength only makes her impatient. Talk of balance, unity and contrast sends her looking for chocolate. She will gladly settle for something that just looks nice. Our design chapter is written with the real world in mind, the world in which artistic objectives must be reconciled with the placement of a garage-sale swing set.

Planning and Designing, Part I:
Everything That is not a Flowerbed

Master-Plan Scale Drawing

The first step in de-fanging this intimidating job is to make a line drawing, to scale, of your property. Making this drawing will take a little time and measuring, but it will save time, money and confusion. Also, it only has to be done once — just remember to store it in a safe place. It will be your master plan, and will be referred to many times over the years.

Pencil, paper and tape measure in hand, go outside and measure the length and width of everything *permanent* — house, garage, driveway, patio, paths, flowerbeds, hedges, fences, compost box, diameter of the crowns of your trees and shrubs. Note shady areas. Now measure the perimeter of your yard. As well, measure the distances of the permanent objects from one another and the lot lines. At this point you are just making a list of measurements, remember. These measurements will help you accurately place each object on the final drawing.

Now take out your graph paper and begin to draw a picture of your property. (Decide if your drawing will be in an inch or centimeter scale: 1 in. = 10 ft./2.5 cm = 3 m, or 1 in. = 1 ft./2.5 cm = 1 m, if you have large enough paper.) First draw in the lot line perimeters. Next, sketch in all the permanent things, as though you were looking down on your property from a helicopter hovering overhead. Mark the prevailing winds, and put in a little compass to show N-S-E-W. The results will look like the sample opposite page 1.

This is a good time to remind you of the depressing fact that your lot is not entirely your lot. Check to find out how much of your front yard (bordering the road) belongs to the city, despite the fact that you faithfully mow, water and feed it. The survey drawing made when you bought your place is probably stored with your mortgage or deed papers, and will show where this line falls. Anything you plant or build between this line and the curb, whether you like it or not, can be torn up if the city decides to install gas lines on your street, or to fiddle with the sewers. Draw a dotted line on your plan to indicate the city-owned portion.

Now, the drawing is ready to be used to plan new additions, but you are not going to do this by drawing directly on your master-plan scale drawing. In fact, once it is finished you never ever draw on the master plan.

Suppose you fancy a rose hedge alongside the driveway. Sketch the hedge onto a piece of tracing paper. Lay the tracing paper or a paper cut-out over top of your basic yard drawing. Does it look good? Fine. Now set the whole thing aside and look at it again in a week. Still look good? Hmm. Maybe not. This note of indecision brings us to the next section.

When to Plan

Design and planning are best done slowly, over a period of time. Play with our plan on and off for a few weeks before buying *anything*. Plant in haste, repent at leisure. We like to plan in January, when the ground is frozen solid. Remember that rose hedge? Suppose you had not taken that week to think it over. As well, suppose you had been planning in May, when the nursery was open, and had rushed out and spent hundreds of dollars and broken your back planting this rose hedge. Now the hedge is planted and (a) you are no longer sure you like the way it looks, and (b) to your horror you have finally read the rose chapter in this book and discovered that roses are high-maintenance plants. You find yourself reaching for your hanky. Now, we do not want to sound like your mother, but if you had originally come up with the rose hedge idea during a January planning session you would have had time, before May, to think your decision through.

Similarly, be cautious if you have just moved into a new house. Live with the property for a while, get used to its idiosyncrasies, virtues and drawbacks before committing yourself to any permanent changes.

So, come January, spend some time in front of the fire with your gardening books, your scale drawing and lots of tracing paper. Plan, dream summer dreams, until a workable, affordable design appears, saving you aggravation as well.

Conservative or Daring?

When planning, consider how long you expect to be in this house. Landscaping can enhance the value of your home, but if you are planning to stay only a few years you might not want to add anything too idiosyncratic or labor-intensive that might scare away prospective buyers or that cannot be dismantled and taken with you. A grotto full of concrete elves, for instance, or a fish pond. If you plan to be in this house for years and years, feel free to add all the elves and ponds you please. Many people who plan to be in a house for only a short time invest money and effort solely in container-gardening, which is covered in Chapter 6 on annuals.

 ————————————————————————————————

IT TAKES TIME — Try to visualize how you want your yard to look a few years down the road, and remember that it will not be immediately transformed into its final form. Patiently steer, year by year, towards that goal.

As well, reality will often rear its sometimes ugly head because you are stuck with some of your existing yard elements and must always work around them — the back wall of the house, for instance. Some you can replace — that grungy old patio. Some elements will be added over the years — a new shrub one year, crazy-paving path the next, board-on-board fence the next. Go slowly, let the place develop its own identity.

Although your yard will eventually have all the elements you wanted, it will never really be finished. It is just like furnishing your living room: after several years you finally have the sofa, chairs, tables, lights and bookcases that you wanted. But by that time the sofa, which was bought first, is either worn out or you do not like it any more. So there you are in the sofa department, looking at new ones. By the time your yard is "finished," you may be tired of the old patio, and will be planning a big new deck. This is the way life is supposed to be. Imagine how boring it would be if things stayed exactly the same forever.

 ——————————————————————————

Garden Ingredients

Before we discuss designing the flowerbed, we would like to talk about the other items to be considered when planning your yard, such as trees, shrubs, hedges, fences, patios, decks, pathways, drives, storage, garages, tables, chairs, barbecues, toys, flower containers and water features. We assume that you have a small lot, probably not much more than 150 ft. x 200 ft./45 m x 60 m. The Reluctant Gardener who has a larger lot thinks in terms of landscaping only the area closest to the house, leaving the rest simply to grass, ground cover or wilderness.

No matter the size, there are two yard elements that every owner is stuck with: the house placement and the lot's orientation to the sun and wind. If the house is placed so that there is no front yard, you will have to make the best of it. If the back of the house faces north, plan for shade-loving plantings — there is nothing else to be done about it.

Trees

Picture it: a hot, hot August afternoon. You are in a hammock, sipping something cold, reading that trashy novel you have wanted to read all summer long. Overhead, deep green leaves rustle, dappling the delicious shade that protects you from the sun's rays . . . what we really need now is for an enticing hero or heroine (your choice) to appear, gently take the book from your hand, and then lean down and — excuse us, this is not that kind of book. Let us return to trees, not birds and bees.

Trees are precious things to have in your yard, and few things do more to enhance the value of your home than mature trees. Before planning trees into your ideal landscape, however, there are a few points to consider. Trees cast shade, and their thirsty roots take moisture and food away from anything planted nearby. As well, when planning where to plant a tree, remember that trees grow taller: that thin four-year-old sapling will one day be a mighty oak. So there is no point planting, say, a lilac in what will eventually be the path of the oak's shade. When planning, consider where tree shade will fall. Remember that the shaded areas will expand more than you imagined possible, which is fine for cooling house and yard, but not fine for sun-bathers.

It is possible, these days, to spend a stupendous sum of money on a mature tree, something 30 ft./9 m tall. Large trees can be scooped out of the earth by an amazing-looking truck with a big scoop and trundled over to your house and plopped into a prodigious hole — all in one operation. If you have that kind of money, your place is probably professionally land-scaped and maintained, and you are reading the wrong book. The rest of us need to put a lot of thought into the purchase of a tree, because even a three- or four-year-old tree can cost as much as a fancy restaurant meal for two. Read Chapter 9 on trees carefully, check some tree books out of the library. And a marriage manual while you are at it. Controversies over big purchases are a fine source of spousal ire.

Shrubs

The most common mistake people make when planting shrubs is not believing how much bigger they will grow. Trust us: if the tag says it will grow to be 6 ft./2 m across, it will grow that big, even though it is only one-tenth that size when you plant it. Because many people do not take the mature size into account, they plant far more shrubs than they need. This costs unnecessary money and leads to a nasty, crowded mess of intertangled plants, starved for light, food and water. This sad fact will be avoided when the shrubs are plotted onto your scale drawing. Draw the mature spread measurement on your tracing paper when planning shrub plantings. As well, you will see how tacky, cut up and small the lawn will look if shrubs are planted all over, like polka dots on a dress fabric.

Plot out foundation plantings, remembering the above warning about how big they will grow. A poor little bush squashed up against a wall looks tortured. Also, shrubs planted close up against the house can be green magnets for burglars, who like to have cover while they jimmy the house windows.

Hedges and Fences

Hedges and fences, used for ornamentation or to screen wind or sight lines, cost a lot of money to install, so spend a good part of your planning time playing with the tracing paper, to ensure that the right decision is made.

Ask yourself how tall you want the structure or hedge to be. Will your neighbor share the cost? Many shrubs grow quite wide — do you have room for a 6 ft./2 m wide hedge? Would your neighbors mind if 24 in./60 cm of that hedge stuck out into their yard? Is it needed to keep kids or animals in or out? If you want to contain or keep out cats, forget it. One of us has a close-fenced backyard. The two big, old, lazy cats cannot get out, but the small, young, agile cat goes over five feet (a meter and a half) of cedar or chain-link without, apparently, noticing that it is there. A fencing man tells us, however, that a 5 ft./1.5 m high fence will keep all but the most determined dogs at home. Do remember, though, that after a snowfall, your fence will be effectively shorter.

Consider, while you are planning, that wooden fences must be maintained: staining or painting must be done every few years. Who is going to stain the neighbor's side? Some people find that unfinished redwood or cedar weathers to a nice soft silvery gray — an attractive, no-maintenance fence, but this will not work with pine, which will decay if left unfinished. Brown chain-link is more invisible than green, is ideal for supporting a light- or medium-weight vine, and needs no maintenance.

See? Complicated. So plot it all out before buying one shrub or one board length.

Fence-building Regulations

Everyone has a fence horror story to tell — usually involving boundary-line disputes. Before installing a fence, a survey must be done, or have the bank send a copy of the one done when you bought the place. Also, phone city hall and find out what the rules and regulations about fences are in your area. Some communities have unbelievably restrictive by-laws.

Inform your neighbors well ahead of the arrival of the fence installers about what you intend to put in and where. Make sure everyone is happy about boundary lines. Show the neighbors your garden plan — yet another use for it. If they are, shall we say, awkward types, you might want to inform them in writing. Most by-laws require, if you and your neighbor are not sharing costs, that the more attractive side of the fence face your neighbor and that the fence is placed a certain distance within your own property. If it is not, they can make you take it down. We do not know if good fences make good neighbors, as Mr. Frost says, but putting up a fence can certainly make bad neighbors, if you are not careful.

Sometimes several adjacent neighbors will have fencing done all at once, saving considerable commotion, and sometimes even saving money, since contractors give discounts over a certain footage. If you are a do-it-your-selfer, read up on fence construction, because a crummy fence is an eyesore forever. Remember that fenceposts in cold-weather areas must be rooted in a big glob of concrete. As well, before you begin to design, call the utility company to make sure cables are not buried where you plan to dig.

Patios and Decks

Patios and decks cost a lot of money to install, so think carefully before committing yourself. Read speciality magazines and books for ideas and pictures to help you design your ideal structure. You might want to consider the following when planning these structures: wood needs maintenance, and a large mass of stone will heat up the whole yard — which suits your personality and site? Do you want to build a multi-leveled or a one-level deck? Is there a swimming pool in your future? Does your yard lack trees and therefore could the yard use an arbor of some sort? Do you like the idea of interrupting the hard surface of a patio with planting holes, in which trees or shrubs can be planted? How about built-in benches around the edge of a deck? Higher decks and stairs must have railings for safety. In cold-winter areas deck posts, like fence posts, must be firmly rooted in concrete.

Try to choose low-maintenance surfaces — avoid stain-it-every-year wood, for example. Keep the large area from becoming dull and inhospitable by breaking it up with attractively arranged tables, chairs, loungers, and a planter or two of flowers. Plant a few shrubs around the edge to soften its architectural hardness.

If you are environmentally-minded, you may reject the backyard-as-deck option. Our planet needs all the green space it can get. Also remember that a green space will noticeably cool down the house.

Pathways

Gardening books always note that a path or walk must be wide enough to allow two people to walk side by side, about 4 ft./1.2 m. This is a nice proportion, but if either of your authors built a path of this width, they would have no room left for anything else in their small city gardens. We like the notion of a narrower path, maybe just wide enough for a mower or wheelchair.

You will need to play around with the tracing paper to see where to place a new path. Will it be used primarily for idle strolling, or have a more serious purpose in life, say to get from the car to the door? Strolling paths are pretty if done in crazy paving, but if you are lugging bags of groceries from the car, you will want something level, even and direct.

Scout local supply centers to see the vast array of surfacing materials there are to choose from: concrete, exposed aggregate, crazy paving, gravel, cobbles or other stonework, interlock or other brickwork, and wood. Do a lot of research before deciding on the final material.

Does the path need to be lit? Lights may encourage the family to take an evening stroll through the garden. All kinds of solar-powered lights are available, which avoids the problem of installing wiring. Remember to plot the light fixtures into your plan by drawing little circles to represent how far they spread their light.

Storage

Oh dear. Where to put things — always a problem. If your garage or basement is large enough, a separate shed will not be needed for tools, wheel barrow, etc. If it is not, we beg you not to install one of those dreadful metal sheds. They are easily dented during construction, and thereafter are a magnet for more disfiguring dents. A small wooden shed will look better longer. If you are fortunate enough to have some sort of corner or angle of the house that requires only a screening wall to transform it into a storage area, go for it. No matter what you use, however, try out the most advantageous placement on the master-plan scale drawing and tracing paper before hammering the first nail.

Tables, Chairs, Loungers, Barbecues

Fences, plantings and house have determined the walls and boundaries of your outdoor living room. Now it is time to furnish it. Yes, we know you lust after an umbrella table, but would it look silly, considering your backyard is shaded by three big trees? Plot out the size of the table you want, maybe it will not fit into the space considered.

You will need enough chairs or loungers to go around, which means one per family member. Plus a few easily stored ones for guests. Moulded plastic chairs are cheap, attractive, and easy to move around with the sun. You cannot beat a nice big wooden Adirondack (Muskoka) chair for comfort and convenience (those wide arms!), but they are heavy to move every time the grass needs mowing. Buy a good stout table — rickety dinner tables are infuriating. Do not stint on size, since no one likes to be elbow-to-elbow, but remember that you will need storage space for it all come winter.

If you plan to buy a gas barbecue, design a hidden corner to trundle it into when it is not in use. Do not use it too close to the house for safety and to avoid getting smoke and grease stains on the wall.

Playthings for Kids

If you have children, they will plead for swings, a wading pool and a jungle gym. Your scale drawing will help you decide what can be fitted into the design and space. Consider their age: if the youngest is eleven and is pestering for a swing set, should you give in? Safety first: swing sets must be firmly anchored, to prevent tipping. The shallowest wading pool must be supervised. And a sandbox must have a lid, against cats. Well, all right, against what cats (and dogs) leave behind.

Flower Containers

You will, of course, want to decorate this nice outdoor living room with flowers — see Chapter 6 on annuals for advice on planters and containers. You can visit the garden center and take measurements of standard containers and flower boxes in order to plot them on your plan. This is important only if space is at a premium.

Water Features

Pools, ponds and fountains are expensive, troublesome to install, and require a lot of maintenance. Think twice, three times, about adding water features if you would rather golf than garden. However, water features are delightful — the babble of a small fountain on a hot day is wonderful.

Planning and Designing, Part II: Flowerbeds

Designing

Let's switch from concrete to flowers and think about planning flowerbeds — what varieties to plant and where and how to place them. Most people mix perennials (which only bloom for a couple of weeks during the summer, all at slightly different times) and annuals (which blossom all summer long) together in the same bed. Perennials are described in Chapter 7, annuals in Chapter 6.

All right. Back to the master-plan scale drawing, your tracing paper, pencil, and a list of your favorite plants. If you are very organized use 3x5 file cards, one per plant, to list the name, flower color, height, spread and, for perennials, blooming season. Divide them into three groups: sun, shade and part sun/part shade.

Play around with the master-plan scale drawing and the tracing papers until you know exactly where the new beds will be and what shape they, or your reconfigured existing beds, will have. Do not scatter little flowerbeds around the lawn like coasters, this looks awful and is murder to mow. Do not underestimate the maintenance of all those edges against encroaching grass. (The only thing these authors have ever seen that is more encroaching than grass at flowerbed borders is a cat seeking a lap.) Once you have decided absolutely and forever where the flower beds will be placed, add them to your master plan.

Now it is time to lay out the plants within the bed. Take a few sheets of regular paper to doodle and plan on. Consider one bed at a time. Note where the sun hits it and what trees or buildings shade it. Suppose you are planning the sunny flowerbed first. Take the appropriate cards, the sun-lovers, and spread them out on a table top in three rows. Tall plants in the back, then medium-height plants, then short ones in the front, but do not draw them onto the plan along straight rows. Wiggle the line a little here and there to give the design a soft, unregimented look.

Also, do not put two plants of exactly equal height side by side. A 3 in./8 cm high dianthus next to a 3 in./8 cm sedum next to a 3 in./8 cm *Phlox subulata* will look boring as can be. Try, instead, putting the 3 in./8 cm dianthus next to an 8 in./20 cm ageratum, with perhaps a clump of 12 in./30 cm coral bells on the other side. This will give the bed a textural, visual interest.

Heeding the above basic advice, shuffle the cards around until a color and height combination that you like appears. Do this over several days or weeks, because better combinations will occur to you each time. When your mind is finally made up, draw the plant design into the bed's plain-paper outline. Now do the same for each of your other beds. Combination beds (shady at one end and sunny at the other) are trickier. Just go slowly, do the job over a period of time, and do not become exasperated. It will fall into place eventually.

Groupings

Experienced gardeners often plant in threes. That is, three phlox together and three monarda together and three globe thistles together, rather than dotting one of each around the bed. We know you are in a big sweat to try out all these exciting new plants, but restrain yourself. A jumble of too many different plants, especially in small urban gardens, will result in a tangled mess of shapes, colors and textures that will irritate the eye rather than please it.

While you are at it, remember not to plant your three monarda in a solemn row, shoulder to shoulder. Give the row a gentle curve or even make it a right-angle corner. Plants are soft and round, and to force them into straight lines and boxy layouts is to attempt a trickier design than the average home gardener can pull off successfully.

Your authors prefer to buy single-color flats of annuals, and plant them en masse in flowing, amoeba-like shapes. Imagine an amoeba-shaped area filled with low-growing dusty miller snuggled up to a not-so-low planting of deep pink zinnias, backed by a swirl of tallish white nicotine. Lovely.

Have fun with colors, remembering to note which color goes where on your plan. A sure-fire mix is pink-blue-white-yellow. Yellow and white together is bright and crisp. Pale colors show up wonderfully at night. Or plant a good selection of intensely colored plants together for vibrancy and pizzazz: red-blue-yellow looks fabulous.

While you are planning the summer's floral delights, consider the color of your house. Pale colors against brick, brights against white, or pales against white are attractive. Blues against brick look terrific. A white bed against a stained cedar-clad house would also be super. There is no limit to the pleasing arrangements you can plan. Just remember that the only person you have to please is yourself.

ENCROACHING GRASS — Once you have a flowerbed you will, given the laws of physics, have a flowerbed edge. That is not so bad. What is bad is that right next to that edge will be grass. Mean, nasty, vicious grass, poised to ooze in among your flowers and turn your tidy, neat bed into a weedy tangle. The plain truth is that there is no perfect solution to this dilemma, but there is an imperfect solution: a root barrier. You can sink any number of different materials — bricks, uncreosoted railway ties, plastic strips — into the earth between lawn and bed. If the top edge is flush with the soil surface you will be able to mow over it. See diagram 1.

The barriers prevent grass roots from spreading into the bed, but grass seeds will still fly in — that is where the imperfect part enters. The best way to deal with these interlopers is the old-fashioned way: wait until the soil is moist, then pull them out by hand.

Root Barrier Edgings for Flowerbeds

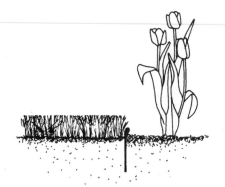

Plastic edging strip, 4" (10 cm).

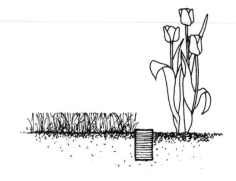

Bricks on edge, laid end to end.

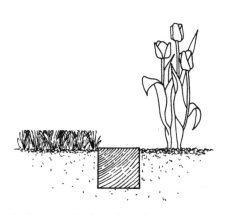

Railway tie flush with soil.

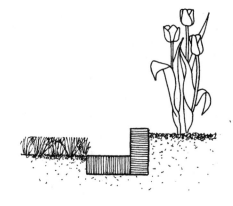

Bricks at right angles to each other, which forms a mowing strip.

Sunken railway tie. Mower will not reach the grass closest to the tie, so extra trimming needed.

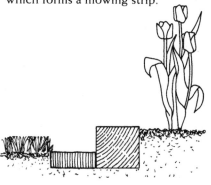

Sunken railway tie used with brick mowing strip.

Are We Having Fun Yet?

Always remember that it is your garden, your house. Its sole reason for existing is to amuse you (remembering, of course, spousal input), so relax and have fun with it. Pencil and paper are cheap, ideas are free. Your only limits are climate, budget and space — let your imagination soar into the horticultural stratosphere.

CHAPTER 2

A Dirty Story: Soil

We know you are itching to start stuffing plants into the ground, but please wait. To give yourself the best possible chance as a gardener, reluctant or not, your first hands-on garden activity must be to improve the soil by adding compost or more topsoil. Unfortunately most house builders haul good topsoil away — assuming there was any on the site in the first place — and sell it, leaving you with an inadequate 3 in./8 cm layer of topsoil with heaven-knows-what beneath. Even if you buy an older house, you cannot be sure that there is decent soil on your lot. There is nothing to be gained from putting perfectly good plants into poor soil. All the fertilizer in the world will not prevent them from becoming weak, sickly and prone to insects and disease.

What Kind of Soil Do You Have?

Unless you are leading a charmed life or have bought a house from a gardening enthusiast, you will often find your soil is either too sandy, or too full of clay. Even if you did have the foresight to buy from a mad gardener, you will have to improve the soil every few years to maintain its health.

Good soil is a mixture of air, moisture, organic matter (decayed greenery), microscopic organisms (tiny critters) and soil particles that are neither too small (clay) nor too large (sand). Good garden soil is often called loam or topsoil. It is crumbly, often dark. It has good drainage, meaning it holds just enough water to be neither too dry nor too wet. The way to transform poor soil into good soil is by adding as much organic material — compost is best — as you can. We are going to beat you over the head with this particular piece of information, because we believe it is the single most important thing a gardener can do, both for their plants and for the planet.

CLAY. Clay soil, often called heavy soil, is the gardener's curse. Its tiny particles are so densely packed that oxygen cannot penetrate down to the plant roots. As well, it contains little organic matter. Roots themselves have difficulty penetrating. Clay is hard to dig, low in nutrients and slow to warm up in spring. In dry weather, it bakes solid. In wet weather it drains badly, becomes water-logged and turns into mire. Plants slowly die as their roots rot from constantly being wet. All in all, not a pretty picture.

SAND. Although there are still problems with sandy soil, it is preferable to clay because its larger particles permit good drainage and air penetration. It, too, lacks certain nutrients, and water drains away practically before plant roots can absorb it. Sandy soil is, however, easy to dig and warms up early in spring. It is often called light soil.

OTHER SOILS. Gravel soil does not need to be laboriously sieved, as some books would have you do. In fact, some gravel is all to the good for it helps aerate the soil. If you have gravelly soil, forget the gravel and concentrate on the soil itself.

Rocky soil will need to be cleared only if the rocks get in your way or on your nerves. If they are large enough, turn them into a virtue and construct a rock garden, or place them in the flowerbed as stepping stones. Again, concentrate your energy on the soil.

Which Is Which?

Murphy's Law being what it is, you will most likely have either too much sand or too much clay. Here are two simple ways to find out:

1. Squeeze a handful of damp soil lightly in your fist. Open your hand and poke. Does it fall apart immediately? Sand. Does it retain the impression of your hand even when poked hard? Clay. Does it fall apart in a leisurely way into small, soft clumps? You are leading a charmed life, this is good garden loam.

2. If you are feeling energetic, dig a hole 24 in./60 cm deep. At bedtime, fill it to the brim with water. If it still contains water in the morning, you have clay soil. If the water vanishes even as you pour it in, you have sandy soil.

Acid and Alkaline

Gardeners use the pH scale to measure the acidity or alkalinity of soil. The scale runs from 0 (very acid) to 14 (very alkaline); 7 is considered to be neutral. Very acidic soil is sometimes called sour, very alkaline soil is called sweet. The reason for keeping track of this figure is that the soil pH influences a plant's ability to absorb nutrients. Most plants (including the ones we recommend in later chapters) are happiest at 6.5 to 7.5. We, however, do not want you to worry about pH levels. It is unlikely that your garden soil is so far away from neutral that you need to do anything about it.

Nevertheless, if your plants are not thriving and you wonder if the soil's pH is causing the problems, there is a simple test to make. You can buy a kit and do it yourself, but various private and government laboratories (listed in the yellow pages under soil testing) will make a much more thorough analysis. Remember to ask them what the labs include in their service, because it varies. They will report on pH, organic and nutrient content, including trace elements such as boron and iron, and sometimes the lab will include suggestions on how to remedy the situation. If you think that your soil has been over-fertilized in the past and might be overloaded with certain nutrients, this is a good way to find out. Soil can be adversely affected by an overdose of certain nutrients just as humans can — for example, vitamin D in large doses is highly poisonous.

If you have any nasty suspicions about toxic substances in your soil, such as particles of lead-based paint, ask the lab to include this in their testing, because you do not want to be growing anything edible in lead-contaminated soil. Tests are best done in autumn, before spring run-off has washed away built-up contaminates. Some government departments of the environment will do this test for free.

We think that it is much easier to balance out-of-kilter soil than to try to grow only acid-loving or alkaline-loving plants. Choosing and finding such specialized plants can be frustrating and complicated. For example, the gardener can make acid soil less so by adding dolomitic lime (quicklime and hydrated lime are too caustic for garden use), bone meal or wood ash to the soil. Half a pound/250 g spread over a sq. yd./1 sq. m should serve. Spread rather more on clay soil, rather less on sandy soil. Better yet, follow the soil analysis lab's instructions. Bear in mind, however, that dolomitic lime and bone meal are fertilizers, rich in phosphorus, and wood ash is full of potassium. These are, respectively, the second and third numbers on fertilizer bags. You will need to adjust your fertilizing program (see Chapter 3 on garden maintenance) to take these additions into account. We do not want to be too picky about this, but acid rain is increasing soil acidity in many areas of North America.

On the other hand, alkaline soil is made more acidic by adding peat moss. Spread a top-dressing 1 in./2.5 cm deep and mix it into the soil with the tip of your trowel or a rake. Water well.

Whatever the pH of your soil, it is important to know that plants growing in organically rich soil will tolerate a much broader range of acidity and alkalinity. So do what we do ourselves: forget pH and think compost.

Improving Garden Soil

The most important thing to add to your garden soil is lots of organic material, that is, decayed plant matter. We cannot stress this enough. Whether you are correcting for sand or clay, the remedy is the same. Addition of organic matter will open up clay soil and make sandy soil more moisture-retentive. A good organic soil, plus a sporadic fertilizing program, will provide an excellent starting point for a trouble-free garden. Even good soil needs regular additions to remain rich and fertile.

Organically rich soil has so many virtues that we begin to sound like snake-oil merchants when we list them:
  • it will have an open, airy structure that plant roots adore
  • it will retain just the right amount of water, thus attaining that
    mysterious state of being "well-drained" that you hear so much about
  • it will be easy to dig
  • the pH will be nicely balanced so that a wide cross-section of
    plants will grow happily
  • earthworms and micro-organisms will move in and stay
  • there is increasing evidence that good soil discourages
    fungal diseases.

Organic Material Explained

Organic material, suitable for gardens, consists simply of decomposed plant matter. It is impossible to add too much organic material to your soil. The most commonly used and easily available types of organic matter are compost and well-rotted manure. Of the two, compost is a little more desirable, because it is composed of a wider variety of materials (leaves, grasses, weeds, soft stems, spent flowers, etc.) and nutrients. Animal manures, especially bovine, contain residue from the chemicals added to modern farm animal food. Peat moss is also an organic soil amendment, but should be used sparingly for the reasons given below.

PEAT MOSS.   Peat moss (finely ground moss) is sold at garden centers in enormous bags. They do not weigh as much as you would think because peat moss is sold in a dry condition. Peat moss is a good organic additive for soil if spread about in small quantities. It does, however, have several drawbacks. When you first open the bag, the fine dry peat moss gets up your nose, makes you sneeze and is generally unpleasant to work with. When first mixed into the soil, the moss takes forever to absorb the first watering. In dry weather, soil mixed with too much peat moss can form a water-repelling crust. Also, adding too much peat moss will create an acid soil. Your authors use peat moss sparingly, confining themselves to throwing in a couple of trowels-full when they plant a new perennial, or half a bucketful when they plant a good-sized shrub. Limiting your use of peat moss diminishes the damage its harvesting does to the wetlands where the peat was created in the first place.

MANURE.   Use only well-rotted manure (WRM) which has not seen a cow or sheep for a few years. Sheep is a little better than cow, because cattle are fed a diet high in chemical additives. WRM is dark, dry, crumbly and does not smell. Fresh (that is, hot) manure must never be used on your garden, because its high nitrogen content will burn the plants, not to mention the neighbors. WRM is like compost in that you can add all you like, knowing it will do nothing but good for your garden. For several years now one of your authors has used nothing but WRM (no topsoil or anything else mixed in) to fill her patio containers and has had excellent results. Buy WRM in a big dirty 30 or 40 litre bag from the garden center, as it is seldom offered by the truck-load.

HOME-MADE COMPOST.   Compost (also called humus or leaf mould) is preferable to WRM because a wider variety of vegetable matter goes into making it, thus creating a more nutritious soil amendment. It can be purchased or you can make your own. It is not as complex and unwieldy as it sounds. Below we describe a method for people with little space and less patience. Once used to the process, it will become an ingrained habit. You will probably find, as we did, that visiting non-composting households gives you the fidgets. "Imagine throwing away this lovely compost!" you will say, holding up a dripping mass of carrot peelings.

Making your own compost is so virtuous we can hardly believe it. It is the ultimate in recycling, reduces the garbage dumped into landfills, and it is pure gold for your garden plants.

How Composting Works

Basically, pile up vegetable matter from the kitchen and garden and let it rot. Mother Nature does this too by making most plants shed their leaves, which then lie on the forest floor until, over the years, they turn into soil. Because humans are often impatient, they have devised a speedier method. How speedy? Once you have created a pile of minimum size in a properly designed box, usable compost will be formed in two to three months.

The key is to maintain a pile big enough to generate its own heat: this is what distinguishes our way of composting from Mother Nature's. A too-small pile will not build up enough heat to break down the organic matter quickly. Well, relatively quickly. When the pile (boxed, for backyard neatness) has a volume of one cubic yard (meter) or more it will begin to 'work,' that is, build up heat at its center. One of your authors has a small cat (Daisy) who, when the weather warms up in the spring and the compost starts to work again, sits on top of the box, warming her fanny.

Choosing a Compost Box

It is possible to compost without spending money on any kind of box — simply pile it up. However, people with a small backyard and an allergy to messy heaps of half-decomposed vegetation within sight of the picnic table will want to consider a discreet container. A well-designed compost box must:
  • hold at least 1 cubic yard (meter) of material
  • have slits or holes in the sides to admit air
  • have an easily removable lid to let in some rain, to easily pile in
    material, and to keep out squirrels and other riffraff
  • sit directly on the earth so worms and soil organisms can crawl in
  • not be too unattractive
  • be convenient to use
  • be durable.
After looking at different kinds of commercially made compost boxes, and at lots of ingenious, laborious-to-construct and downright ugly plans

for compost boxes made from boards and wire mesh, we recommend buying the SoilSaver®, a patented, Canadian-designed box made from recycled plastic. This well-made, long-lasting box costs about the same as four big bags of good-quality fertilizer. Some enlightened municipalities — call your public works department — are making them available to citizens at a fraction of their retail cost.

The SoilSaver® is a dark, matte brown, which makes it visually recessive and its design, as well as the design of other available models, provides the right conditions (see above) for fast composting. It keeps the pile tidy and has a lid heavy enough to keep squirrels out. To fend off more vigorous predators, weigh the lid down with a rock. Set the composter in an unobtrusive corner, in sun or shade, it does not matter which.

A Kitchen Collector

You may not want to trudge out to the compost box every time you peel a potato. What most people do is keep a small covered container by the sink. An old juice pitcher works well. When it's full, take it outside.

Chopping Before Composting

Smaller pieces of organic material break down into usable compost faster than bigger ones. A gardener one of your authors knows puts all his kitchen waste into a blender, purees it, then puts it in the composter. This gives him wonderful, fast compost but is far too much work for the Reluctant Gardener. However, it is a Good Thing to chop waste up as fine as you have patience for. If you have no patience at all big pieces are OK — they will just take a little longer to decompose.

Some people use a lawn mower to chop up autumn garden waste (leaves, clipped-back perennials, yanked-up annuals). Just dump everything on the lawn and run over it a few times with the mower (protect eyes and ankles!), then rake it up and put it in the composter. A loosely stacked pile of about two cubic yards/meters will reduce to hardly more than a bushel or two. Gadget-lovers could buy a small electric shredder to do the same job. They cost about the same as a mid- to low-priced electric lawn mower. If you do not own a mower, use clippers or leaf-mulchers (see Chapter 4 on tools).

What Exactly You Can and Cannot Put In

CAN:
- plants and plant clippings. Nothing too woody, because it will take years to break down. If your non-composting neighbor offers you his herbicide and insecticide-saturated cuttings, just say no.
- weeds. Pull them before seeds set, or the seeds might germinate when you spread the compost next season.
- lawn clippings. Add only a couple of inches at a time, because large amounts of clippings compact into airless mats which take ages to break down.
- leaves. Rake your extra leaves into a big pile next to the composter and add them as space becomes available. This way you will not have to use a bunch of plastic bags.
- potato peelings, tomato skins, carrot tops, get the picture? Knobby things like cauliflower stumps should be cut into small pieces.
- coffee grounds (including the paper filter, but try to use the unbleached ones). Tea bags, if the bag is biodegradable. Make a tear in the bag.
- ashes from a wood fire, but not too much because they are high in potassium. Do not add ashes from fake logs, because there is no telling exactly what is in them.
- egg shells.

CANNOT:
- dog and cat poop (contains parasites harmful to humans, which you may pick up when handling the compost).
- coal and barbecue briquet ashes, because they contain undesirable chemicals.
- anything diseased or bug-infested or covered by herbicide or pesticide residues.
- animal fat, skin, bones, because they will stink and attract rodents.
- anything salty because salt harms the beneficial micro-organisms in your soil.
- dairy products.
- paper, plastic, metal. Newspaper can, technically, be added, but it would have to be shredded, which is laborious work. Also, day after day of adding the local paper would wreck the balance of materials. Better to put it into the recycle box.

Maintaining a Compost Box or Pile

Whatever kind of box you use, you must add both wet (fresh peelings, green leaves, etc.) and dry (dried out leaves, etc.) material to the compost pile. A 50-50 mix will do nicely. Layering used to be the ideal in composting architecture, but new research is showing that all-stirred-in-together is better.

If the pile is too dry, it will not work. How moist should it be? Imagine yourself at the kitchen sink holding a wet sponge. Wring it out enough so it is damp to touch, but no water runs out of it. That's how moist to keep the pile. To moisten the pile, water it with the hose (stick the nozzle right into the middle of the pile), take the lid off during rain or when watering with your sprinkler, or stir in fresh, wet vegetable matter. If you add too much wet material, the pile will stop working and might become smelly. The smell results when aerobic (that is, using oxygen) decomposition stops. A too-wet environment excludes air, giving you anaerobic (without oxygen) decomposition, and thus a dreadful smell. To remedy this, cover the pile during rain, and uncover it when the sun comes out. Also, stir in some dry material. Vegetable matter can be dried before it is added to the pile by spreading it out on the patio or driveway for a day or two. Simply stirring the pile (this adds air) helps a little.

Do not add too much of one thing at one time. Good compost results from a mix of many different materials. For instance, if you have a large amount of lawn clippings, add 2 in./5 cm at a time, not all at once. Vast quantities of autumn leaves reduce in volume if you run a mower over them.

Stirring the pile like cake batter makes it work faster. Doing this (especially to a boxed one) with a spade or fork is damned hard work, but easier if you buy a special compost-stirring stick which is an aluminum pipe, about 1 yd./1 m long, with a handle at one end. At the other end are two hinged flaps 2 in./5 cm long. Shove this end down in the pile — the flaps will fold flat against the pipe. Now pull up — the flaps open out, grab the contents of the box, turn it over. It takes a bit of muscle, so watch your back. We have seen these sticks for sale at about half the price of a spade. Another, simpler stirstick is a fixed, arrowhead-shaped, hand-sized piece of flat metal fixed onto a steel shaft and handle. Pester your local garden center to carry one of both kinds. They are available usually through gardening catalogues or sometimes with the purchase of a compost box.

Throw in a bucket of dirt from your own garden now and then. This helps keep odors down and adds micro-organisms which assist in breaking down organic matter in the pile. A healthy pile will be full of worms, millipedes, sow bugs and other creepy-crawlies. These are good bugs which will also help break things down. Do not bother with commercial composter boosters. They are expensive, and do not appreciably speed up the process.

Working compost loses volume dramatically, making room for more additions. If you start your compost pile in the spring, you may get some nice finished compost by late summer. Remember that a pile is not officially started until it reaches the size of one cubic yard/meter or the box is full.

When Is Compost Ready to Use?

Finished compost is dark and crumbly, composed of a mixture of different-sized particles. It will be found at the bottom of the pile. About once every two months during the growing season, poke around to see if there is enough compost to be worth digging out. The SoilSaver® has two nice little doors you can open to take a look. If the compost is ready, you can stick your spade in and haul it out. Messy, but satisfying, because you are getting such a wonderful soil amendment for free. Load it into the wheelbarrow, throwing anything that has not fully composted back into the box. Gardening fanatics sieve their compost, but this is laborious and Reluctant Gardeners do not do it. If you keep your SoilSaver® topped-up, over the summer and autumn, you will harvest perhaps three to six small wheelbarrows-full, although this will vary according to how finely you chopped up the added material, how often you turned the pile, and what the weather has been like.

How to Apply Compost

The Reluctant Gardener simply spreads the compost over the top of the soil. This is called topdressing. Sidedressing is putting the compost close to, but not actually touching, a plant. This is a good way to use it if you do not have very much. The action of worms and frost-heave will eventually turn it under. However, there is no denying that the best way to apply compost to the garden is to dig it in about 12 in./30 cm down — 24 in./60 cm down is wonderful, but far too much like work. Also, this digging-in business is only possible in an empty bed — such substantial digging in a perennial bed could cause an awful lot of root damage. Isn't it nice to know that something arduous can be bad for the garden? It is, however, permissible to dig it in a little ways, say 2 in./5 cm, with the tip of your trowel. Spread compost over the garden at any time during the growing season. Even good soil must have a steady supply of new compost, year after year, to maintain its condition.

Composting in Winter

In areas where the temperature dips (in our area it does not dip, it plunges) below freezing in December and stays there until spring, the compost pile will freeze and stop working until the weather warms up again. You can, however, still keep your kitchen waste out of the curbside garbage.

If you have an unboxed pile, heap the kitchen waste on top. It will freeze, then begin working after the spring thaw.

If you have a SoilSaver®, you will not be able to add directly to the pile because a frozen pile does not subside the way a working one does — there will not be room for additions. Instead, place a lidded, curbside-sized garbage container, lined with a plastic bag, beside the back door. Put kitchen waste into this throughout the winter, replacing the bags as they fill up. Keep filled bags outdoors in the backyard in the sun, so they can heat up on sunny winter days and the material inside will decompose a little. When spring comes and there is room in the SoilSaver®, dump in the stored waste.

 ────────────────────────────────

GREEN CONE® COMPOSTERS — *During the summer of 1990, a new type of household composter came on the market. The most common version of it is the patented, Canadian-invented Green Cone®, also called the Ecolyzer®. Do you remember Dr. Who and the Daleks? This composter looks like a cross between a Dalek and R2D2 of* Star Wars™ *fame.*

Whatever you call it, and whatever it looks like, it comes in two parts. One part, the digester, resembles a plastic laundry basket and is buried below ground. Attached by screws to this part is a double-walled, tightly lidded plastic cone that stands about hip-high above ground. The seam, where top and bottom are screwed together, is sunk 2 in./5 cm below soil level.

The double walls heat the interior to a higher temperature than conventional compost boxes or piles ever achieve, promoting a fast break-down of the contents. The extra heat also means that this kind of composter can be used for hair, dairy products, small bones and small quantities (the amount that is usually discarded from a home kitchen) of meat, fish and poultry, none of which can be added to conventional composters. One thing that really charms us is this: you know when you are finished in the kitchen after a meal, there is always a handful of sludge (hair, grease, bits of vegetables) in the bottom of the sink? It, too, can go into the Green Cone®. (However, because of parasites, animal droppings must not be added.) Material can be added all winter, because the unit (best placed in a sunny spot) heats up even on cold days as long as there is a little sun. Thus, the heap inside is always subsiding and making room for more material.

Green Cone® compost can be added to the garden, just follow the instructions that come with the unit. Because of the high heat inside the cone, the contents smush down to almost nothing. It only needs to be emptied once every two or three years, and even then you will only get a small amount of compost. Why bother with it, then? Because the Green Cone® will take a LOT of kitchen waste that normally ends up in landfill — sites that we are rapidly running out of.

One of your authors has used a Green Cone® for two years. Her experience convinces her that it has wonderfully reduced curbside garbage — her household of two adults often puts out garbage only one week out of two. It also makes the under-the-sink garbage container much less smelly. Her Green Cone® is just outside the back door, making it very convenient to use.

She does, however, find that the soil level around the seam joining the two cones must be maintained or odors escape from the unit. Once or twice the soil has subsided — sank down into the bottom of the unit, apparently — and needed to be backfilled. Once a cat dug next to the composter, discovered those lovely (to him) smells, and decided to head for China. Putting lengths of firewood all around the composter has put an end to that problem. She has had no trouble with rodents trying to chew their way in, but then there are no determined chewers, such as raccoons, in her area. She does have squirrels, but the tight-fitting lid seems to be tight enough to hide the evidence of its interesting contents.

The Green Cone® is available at many hardware, grocery and department stores, and costs as much as two or three bags of good-quality fertilizer. Some cities are offering them at a fraction of their cost, in an effort to reduce garbage pick-up (which costs taxpayers money) and to reduce landfill (which costs the earth). We think it is an excellent invention. Just remember that skin, bones and fat CANNOT go into conventional composters, only into units like the Green Cone®, with its high-heat, tightly enclosed digesting chamber.

Truly Hopeless Soil?

Suppose you have composted everything in sight, but still do not have enough to make an impression on your impossible soil. You have mixed in purchased manure and peat moss until you are blue in the face and sore in the shoulders and it is still hopeless. You have three options.

1. Soil replacement. Think carefully where to place your flowerbed. Mark the area off with string and stakes, then dig out the old soil to a depth of 24 in./60 cm. Have it hauled away. If you have clay soil, install drainage tiles in the bottom. This is a lot of work, and is usually done by a contractor. If you have sandy soil, lay a sheet of plastic on the bottom of the bed (to help retain water) and slash the plastic here and there so deep root growth will not be constricted. Then fill the hole with good new soil, including as much compost as possible.

2. Raised beds. Buy some uncreosoted railway ties (available at any lumber store) and lay them on the ground, building them up to make a sort of solid-walled corral where you want a bed. Do a proper job of it, fastening the corners together so the whole thing will not fall apart from frost heave. A good handyman's manual will tell you how to do this. A 12 in./30 cm bed will support most annual plants, perennials prefer a depth of 24 in./60 cm. Fill the bed with good new soil. Higher beds are certainly possible, but take a lot of soil. However, a 36 in./90 cm high raised bed can give a lot of pleasure to a person in a wheelchair, or one who has difficulty kneeling or bending.

3. Give up on flowerbeds and lawns completely. Build a big deck or patio and confine your flowers to containers. See Chapter 6 on annuals for more information on container gardening.

Bulk Purchase of Topsoil or Compost

Topsoil, compost and manure can be purchased at the garden center in big, heavy bags. This is fine for the occasional small-scale need, but sometimes larger quantities are needed. In this case call a sand and gravel company. Often, in spring or late summer, these places put flyers in your mailbox. Otherwise, look in the yellow pages. Usually the companies offer topsoil, compost, or a mixture of the two. Compost costs a little more, but is worth it because of the high content of organic matter.

When you phone, they will want to know how many yards you want. Be warned that they mean *cubic* yards. The sand and gravel companies in our area have not yet gone metric, but a cubic yard and a cubic meter are near enough the same size to be considered interchangeable. Calculate how much you will need as follows:

In Imperial measurements a cubic yard measures 3 ft. long by 3 ft. wide by 3 ft. deep, so it contains 27 cubic feet. Three feet long times 3 ft. wide = 9 sq. ft., times the depth of 3 ft., results in a volume of 27 cubic feet, see? Length x width x depth = volume. Now, suppose your proposed flowerbed measures 9 ft. by 18 ft. and it needs a 1 ft. deep layer of new soil. What you need to do is calculate the volume of earth needed and, ultimately, express it in cubic yards. So, 9 ft. long x 18 ft. wide = 162 sq. ft. 162 sq. ft. x 1 ft. deep = 162 cubic feet, this is the volume of earth needed for your bed. To express this in terms of cubic yards, divide this number by 27, which is the number of cubic feet in a yard. 162 divided by 27 = 6 cubic yards.

Express all your measurements in terms of feet, or fractions of feet, and you will do fine. If you wanted a 6 in. (.5 ft.) depth, the calculation would be 9 x 18 x .5 = 81. 81 divided by 27 = 3, so you would order 3 cubic yards. If you wanted a 3 in. layer, 9 x 18 x .25 = 40.5. 40.5 divided by 27 = 1.5, so you would need 1.5 cubic yards.

If you are measuring in metric, it is a little easier, so long as you remember to express all your numbers as meters, or fractions of meters. Suppose your bed is about the same size as the one above, 3 meters by 6 meters, and you want to cover it to the same depth as the first calculation, that is, 1 foot or 30 cm (.3 meters). 3 x 6 = 18 sq. meters, times .3 m deep = 5.4 cubic meters needed. This is near enough to the figure of 6 yards, above, to make no difference. Gardening is an art, not a science, and if you seek precision in any aspect of gardening, you are doomed to frustration and should take up chess instead.

Sand and gravel companies often have a minimum order, usually five cubic yards — awkward if you only need two yards. Adjacent neighbors often go in together on an order. When the truck arrives, the driver will dump half on one lawn or driveway, half on the other, or it can be dumped on the boundary line.

Now, however, you must spread it around. One of your authors once had five yards delivered. It took two adults two weeks (evenings only) of not-very-dedicated work to distribute it. You will need a wheelbarrow, and one shovel per helper. Your children will help for the first barrow-full, but after that the novelty wears off and you are on your own. The hourly rate that children demand for such labor tends to exceed the offered rate. Be sure to cover the heap with a tarpaulin if it rains — water adds weight, remember. Actually, it is a good idea to keep the tarpaulin on it at all times — you do not want the wind to blow your expensive topsoil away.

The truck will leave ruts in the lawn, so if possible, have the soil dumped on the driveway. If you must have it dumped on the lawn, fill in the ruts — they will appear as you get to the bottom of the heap — with soil, which should be stomped down a bit. You can seed the soil patches, or you can let nature take her course: neighboring grass will gradually fill in, just be sure to pull up or mow down any intruding weeds.

Soil Compaction

Soil should have an open texture for optimum root penetration. Walking around on a flowerbed is a sure way to squash the soil down and compact it until it is hard and dense. Stay out of the beds unless you are doing something useful. It is particularly important in spring to stay off the lawn until the runoff has drained out of the soil. Many gardeners dot flat rocks around inside the flowerbed to use as stepping stones.

Worms

One surefire way to tell whether or not your soil is in good enough shape to plant is dig around in it. Do you see lots of worms? Great, get planning. No worms, or very few? Then you do not have enough organic material. Add lots more. Worms will move in when you have enough, and will do a great amount of work to improve it further. Adding worms to poor soil is pointless, because they will migrate to greener pastures.

CHAPTER 3

It's Not as Bad as You Think: General Garden Maintenance

No matter the size of your garden, there are four basic jobs you will need to do over and over again: watering, fertilizing, mulching and digging. We offer the following stripped-down guide to help you pass quickly and, as painlessly as possible, from garden to chair.

Watering — How Much

It is important to soak the soil to a depth of 18-24 in./45-60 cm at each watering. For most soils, this means running the sprinkler between one and two hours. Sprinkle for one hour, then dig down to see how deep the water penetrated. This allows you to calibrate your watering time to the composition of your soil. Use the oven timer to make sure you get it right.

A little half-hour sprinkling does far more harm than good. You see, a light watering will only penetrate the top 2-3 in./5-8 cm of soil, well above the level of root activity. Do this often enough and the roots will head for the surface in search of water. Surface root growth can fry during a period of hot weather, seriously weakening the plant. Similarly, do not be fooled by rain. A short, heavy rainfall will run off more than it penetrates. It takes at least two or three hours of steady rain to really do the garden good.

Watering — How to Do It

Potted plants are watered from a can or the end of the hose (remove any high-pressure nozzles or you will blast the soil right out of the pot). Flowerbeds and lawns can be watered by a simple oscillating sprinkler.

They are easy to use and inexpensive. You will soon discover the best placement which will cover your yard. However, any sprinkler will give up a lot of water (water which took energy to process, and that you pay for) to the atmosphere in evaporation, as much as 30% on a hot day, so try not to water when the sun is out. Overhead watering also wets leaves, which promotes mildew on some plants, although it does wash off smog and dust.

You may also choose from a selection of soaker hoses, seepage hoses, drip irrigators and similar systems which slowly seep water into the soil. Water is not lost from evaporation and none splatters on leaves. Usually, a hose is laid between plants, and left in place throughout the growing season. The soaker hose is connected to the tap by an ordinary hose. Be aware that these hoses are not very efficient — they only water an area about 18 in./45 cm across, so you will need several to cover a wider area. This can become expensive. Also, they are not obviously an option for lawns, so you will still need a sprinkler.

There are many different in-ground sprinkler systems for sale. If you are often away from home during the summer, you might want to research the different systems and choose the one that suits you best.

Watering — When to Do It

There are two "whens" in this question: when during the day, and when do the plants need it?

When during the day should you water? The general consensus is that early morning is best. The leaves can then dry out during the day, which is a good thing because remaining wet in the cooler night temperatures can promote the growth of mildew and other fungal diseases.

However. We find that with jobs, breakfast to fix, and even, occasionally, some serious sleeping-in to do, the plain fact is that we water when we have the time. Your choice. Try to avoid watering when the sun is strong — a lot of water is lost through evaporation.

It is important to check potted plants *every day* for dryness. They have a lot of roots in a small volume of soil, and so dry out quickly.

How do you know when the plant needs water? Take your trowel and dig down a few inches. If only the top 2 in./5 cm are dry, watering is not necessary. If the top 4 in./10 cm are dry, it is time to water.

Over time, you will find that you have one plant that stages a dramatic wilt whenever it is the least bit dry, but revives nicely when watered promptly. Such plants can be used as a bellwether: when they collapse, it is probably time to water everything. Remember, though, that the leaves of many plants will droop noticeabley during a hot summer afternoon. This is because the leaves are losing water faster than the roots can replenish it. If the leaves stiffen again in the evening, watering is not needed.

During a period of sustained drought, it is easy to forget that big trees, too, can dry out. They will not usually show signs of it until they are under considerable stress. Change in leaf color can be a warning. If your garden has had no substantial water for four to six weeks, water each tree by setting the sprinkler to cover its root area (this is the area in shade when the sun is directly overhead), and let the sprinkler run six hours or overnight.

For a word on dry gardening (xeriscaping) see the appendices.

Fertilizing

Garden centers carry many different fertilizers in boxes, bags, bottles and tubs, and they all have a different application schedule. It is all very complicated and discouraging. There is one for roses, one for evergreens, one for flowering shrubs, one for tomatoes . . . we could go on forever. Fanatical gardeners will buy each kind of fertilizer, will use it properly, and will probably have a very nice garden. Unless they are very careful they might over-fertilize, which can damage plants as much as under-fertilizing. They will also spend money needlessly, and will be guilty of adding to the environmentally damaging quantities of nitrogen and phosphates in our soil and waters. Our bottom-line advice on fertilizing is: less is more. The Reluctant Gardener, who has been conscientiously composting, need only apply light applications of fertilizer.

A Simple Fertilizing Program

Organically derived fertilizers are, of course, best. Buy a product that states its organic origins on the bag. We prefer to use good quality, organically derived, all-purpose 20-20-20 or 10-10-10 granular fertilizer. (An all-purpose 15-30-15 water-soluble fertilizer will also do the job, but it tends to be a little more of a nuisance to apply.) All fertilizers must be applied to moist soil, never to dry. During late May or early June, apply it at half-strength (that is, half what is recommended on the bag) on flowerbeds and around shrubs. In late-July or early August, do the same again. That's all.

Use a spreader on the lawn, which is fertilized *only* in September. For shrubs or plants, sprinkle fertilizer around by hand (wear a glove, because some elements in the fertilizer can dry out your skin). Sprinkle thinly, covering the root area, but avoid sprinkling it on leaves, because the fertilizer will burn them. Combined with a program of organic soil enrichment, this is all that is needed. This may sound stingy, but in the last few decades everyone has become accustomed to using far more fertilizer than is necessary.

It is important that shrubs and roses not be fertilized after August 15. A late fertilizing would provoke a rush of soft new growth that will die under the first frost, weakening the plant and wasting money and effort.

THOSE THREE NUMBERS ON THE FERTILIZER BAG — The numbers you see on fertilizer bags are percentages of the three major plant nutrient groups. 20-20-20 means that the mixture is 20% nitrogen (N), 20% phosphorous (P) and 20% potassium (K). The other 40% is inert filler, which is why 20-20-20 costs more than 5-5-5 (which would be 85% filler). An oversimplified breakdown of what does what is this: nitrogen boosts leaf growth; phosphorous, root growth; and potassium, flower development. A mnemonic to remember this by is Little Red Flowers, Leaf-Root-Flowers.

So if you wanted to green-up yellowish leaves you would buy a high nitrogen fertilizer, 20-5-5. To boost flower production on an unwilling annual, give it a 5-5-20. However, if you follow a good program of organic amendments and light, all-purpose fertilizing, it is unlikely the additional fertilizing will be needed.

Mulching

Although it might sound like something a goat would to, mulching is actually just the act of spreading a layer of material over the soil. The choice of mulching material varies, each having some drawbacks.

Winter Mulch

An insulating layer of fresh straw can be spread over your perennial plants in autumn, it is called a *winter* mulch. For a full discussion of this, see the chapter on perennials.

Summer Mulch

A *summer* mulch is a layer of material (we prefer straw) spread over the flowerbed during the growing season. Wait for the soil to dry out and warm up in spring, then spread mulch over the bare soil between plants.

Be sure to keep it far enough back from the plants, either newly emerging perennials or newly planted annuals, so the straw does not touch leaves or stalks, or you will hamper air circulation and promote mildew. We spread fresh straw about 6 in./15 cm thick in spring and leave it there all summer. By the time autumn comes there will be about 1 in./2.5 cm left. During autumn clean-up, it is raked up with all the other garden detritus and composted.

WHY BOTHER WITH SUMMER MULCH? — *A summer mulch takes a little work to maintain, but saves a lot of work in other areas. It is good for both the garden and the environment:*

- *you will water less, because mulch retains soil moisture by preventing evaporation;*
- *it keeps down weeds by shading them out;*
- *the underside of the mulch decomposes over the summer, thus adding organic matter to the soil;*
- *if you walk around on the straw, instead of directly on the earth, the soil compacts less;*
- *erosion during a heavy rain is lessened, because rain is filtered through the straw and lands softly on the soil;*
- *soil-borne plant diseases are fewer, because soil will not, during a heavy rain, bounce back up and cling to the undersides of leaves. This also keeps plants cleaner and therefore more attractive to look at, which is the entire point of gardening;*
- *it keeps soil cooler in the heat of the summer, which both roots and worms appreciate. Worms do not like temperatures higher than 80°F/26°C;*
- *it keeps the soil warmer in autumn, thus extending the growing season a little.*

Our Favorite Summer Mulching Material

Hands down, we recommend straw. It has a stiff, open texture that is too airy to entice most bugs (which like snug, dark hidey-holes) and diseases. As well, it weathers to an attractive silver. We always buy straw at a garden center because it is convenient, relatively seed-free, and has been cut to a civilized length of about 12 in./30 cm.

Summer Mulches We Do Not Like

- those big bark chips are the most aesthetic, but they are too expensive to suit your authors.
- grass clippings add nutrients to the soil, but look terrible as they dry up and begin to fly in the wind. They can also turn into a layer of felt, which harbors mould and resists water absorption. NEVER use grass as a mulch unless you are dead certain there are no herbicide residues (including fertilizer-herbicide mixtures) in the clippings.
- peat moss forms a water-resistant crust during dry weather. It takes two or three hours of rain to soften the crust.
- newspaper mulch adds nutrients to the soil, but it looks dreadful and harbors insects and diseases in its close-packed layers.
- black plastic does a great job of keeping weeds down, but it is expensive and aesthetically repulsive. You need to cut holes for the plants to stick out through. It also overheats the soil, killing worms and roots.
- fancy new types of garden fabrics are always coming on the market, but they usually involve serious money and invariably look awful. They certainly never add organic material to the soil the way straw does.
- leaves left over from last year are not high on our list, because leaves (especially maple) pack down into a tight, damp, airless mat. A vast assortment of bugs and diseases use such cozy places as homes during various parts of their life cycles. Since we do not like the notion of providing pleasant homes for these pests, we rake up all our autumn leaves and compost them.

Slugs and Summer Mulching

About the only drawback we have found with summer mulching is the presence of garden-devouring slugs. To see if slugs are hiding in the mulch, pull back a little of the straw. Do this during the day, when they are hiding from the heat of the sun. If you are not squeamish, you can hand-pick slugs and drop them in a bucket of very hot water. The resulting disgusting mess can be put on the compost heap. If you are squeamish, sprinkle just a little salt (from the kitchen shaker) on them and they will die before your very eyes.

Digging

We do little digging, although we are well aware of all those amazingly elaborate instructions for tilling and digging, and know perfectly well that turning the soil is a Good Thing, since it breaks up clods and introduces air.

We also know, however, that the yearly action of winter frost in any area experiencing below-freezing temperatures does much to break up the soil. We also know that we have added lots of organic matter to our soil, so it is full of worms which industriously do their bit to stir together the different soil ingredients. Isn't it nice to hear that Mother Nature is out there doing all that hard work for you?

However, if we are feeling energetic, we will cultivate the top couple of inches with a hoe or the tip of a trowel. This discourages weeds, breaks up any crust and discourages roots of desirable plants from growing too close to the surface.

At Day's End

All work and no play certainly makes us all reluctant gardeners. But all play and no work creates a weed-infested, insect-thronged, nutrient-starved garden. Be of good cheer, because after the work is completed, what sweeter rest is there than to sit in the shade, drink in hand, surveying your leafy kingdom?

CHAPTER 4

Lead Me Not Into Temptation: Gardening Tools

Anyone who has spent a few minutes browsing through a garden catalogue will soon see that gardening is becoming increasingly fancy. We prefer to keep it plain. No backyard gardener really needs five different kinds of hoes and a pair of kneepads that cost as much as a hardcover book.

Garden tools are like kitchenware — start with the basics and accumulate more and more as time goes on. Most people have an inkling of what constitutes kitchen basics, but do not have the faintest idea about what they really need in the garden and what they can do without.

We have divided garden tools into graduated categories, starting with a list of basics and winding up with a list meant only for gadget freaks. This last list includes stuff that no one really needs, but which some of us cannot resist. You know who you are.

Except for hand-clippers and a trowel, we recommend you buy mid-price tools, the type available at hardware stores or local garden centers. Now and then you will see very expensive garden tools for sale — we know where you can spend $175 on a single spade, no kidding. If this sort of thing amuses you, and you can afford it, by all means go ahead. But your garden will grow just as nicely if you buy less expensive tools, with the two exceptions mentioned.

Beginner's Shopping List

CLIPPERS. Hand-sized, well-made scissors-action clippers are the best.
Do not buy the anvil type which works via two flat surfaces coming

together. This type crushes stems and creates a ragged site where diseases can enter. Buy the more expensive ones, since the cheapies do not work well and will drive you crazy. To keep them in top condition, oil them now and then.

COMPOSTER BOX. See Chapter 2 on soil for a full discussion on composting. A compost-turning stick is a good investment too.

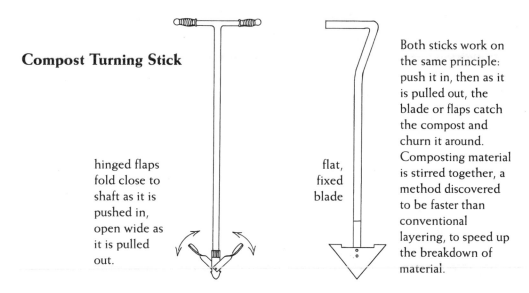

Compost Turning Stick

hinged flaps fold close to shaft as it is pushed in, open wide as it is pulled out.

flat, fixed blade

Both sticks work on the same principle: push it in, then as it is pulled out, the blade or flaps catch the compost and churn it around. Composting material is stirred together, a method discovered to be faster than conventional layering, to speed up the breakdown of material.

GLOVES. Heavy canvas — leather palms are nice, especially if you will be trimming roses. Also, a pair of rubber kitchen gloves are handy to wear when mucking around in the dirt, especially for those squeamish about touching worms. It is a good idea to wear gloves when handling powdered or pelletized substances such as granular fertilizer, bone meal, or lime.

HAT. Protection against the sun, which can make you dizzy with all that bending and stooping. A wide-brimmed one helps keep bugs away from your face. A canvas one can, on hot days, be soaked with water to help you keep cool. A wet cotton bandanna wrapped around your head works just as well.

HOE. Buy the basic model, with a flat blade on the end of a short bent stem. This will be used for shallow digging (scuffling) of the soil surface, to break up crusts and lumps, and to keep down weeds.

MOWER. You have three choices: push, gas or electric. Push, or reel-type, mowers have many virtues but we cannot recommend them. They can only cut grass to a maximum height of 2 1/4 in./5.5 cm, which is too short except for golf greens. This is a pity, because they are otherwise very good for the grass. They are also environmentally correct, and make such an agreeable noise. Gas: well, if you want to wrestle with the filling, exhaust and smell, as well as the draining of the tank in autumn, go ahead. Electric: this we recommend. The only catch is to get the cord organized. Once you have done your lawn a couple of times, a logical pattern will appear, and you will neither run over the cord nor wrap it hopelessly around every tree and shrub in your path. If you do run over the cord, turn the machine off, then go IMMEDIATELY to the wall, and unplug it. Do not touch the cord until you have unplugged it at the power source. Then replace the cord or have it repaired professionally.

To keep the mower running well, scrape the crusted clippings off the bottom and sides of the mower deck a few times during the summer. Sharpen the blade once every season.

Mower size: buy the huge ones only if you have a huge lawn. One of your authors has used a bottom-of-the-line national brand electric, of the smallest size available, for years with no trouble at all. People who have grass-catcher attachments on their mowers say that they are never big enough, so they spend more time emptying them, over and over again, than they would simply raking the lawn.

Mulching mowers are increasingly available. One of your authors acquired one recently, and it was love at first mow. It is simply a regular mower without the discharge chute, so the clippings are forced back over the blade again and again until they are cut up into teeny bits, whereupon they fall to the earth. Because they are already so finely cut up, they decompose quickly, releasing their nutrients into the soil.

NAIL BRUSH. Might as well get some good hand cream too, because gardening is murder on your skin.

PISTOL-STYLE HOSE-END SPRAYER. Or some other type of hand-spraying attachment, the sort you screw onto the end of the hose. We like the pistol type because it can be adjusted to a full, fine spray or a tight, hard jet. Useful for many jobs, from dislodging bugs from plants to washing off the deck to teasing the cat.

RAKES. You will need two: a fan rake and a hard rake. A fan rake, which is the nice springy metal one, is used to rake leaves and dethatch the lawn. (A bamboo fan rake is quaint and aesthetically pleasing, but it breaks too easily.) A hard rake, which looks like a gap-toothed comb, can be used, tines-up, to smooth over the soil. Buy the one with a flat top edge, rather than a bow rake (the one with two gracefully curved arms holding it to the handle).

SPADE. You want the one with a straight, nearly flat blade, a D-shaped handle about 40 in./100 cm long, and a lip (for your foot) at the top of the blade on either side of where the blade meets the handle. Make sure there is a rivet to keep the blade attached to the shaft, and another rivet to keep the handle attached to the shaft. Sharpen it now and then with a cheap file from the hardware store.

SPREADER. Applies granular fertilizer onto the lawn. Very useful if your lawn is larger than about 20 ft. x 20 ft./6 m x 6 m. The cyclone type has a cylindrical hopper with a spinner underneath. It is easier to control and does the job faster than the slightly cheaper drop-feed kind. Plastic-bodied spreaders are more corrosion-resistant than metal ones. Always rinse the spreader well with the hose after each use. Do not try to spread granular fertilizers on the lawn by hand, because you will get pale patches where too little fell, bright green patches where the right amount fell, and burned patches where too much fell.

TROWEL. Buy a good, stout trowel, one with a strong stem attaching the blade to the handle. A cheap one will drive you crazy, because the handle will bend and never straighten properly again. Make sure the handle fits your hand comfortably, because you are going to spend a lot of time using this thing.

WATERING EQUIPMENT. Two hoses of appropriate length, and two plain, cheap oscillating sprinklers. Why two? Save yourself the labor of dragging equipment around — buy one of each for the front and back. If you have a long, narrow area to water, buy a perforated hose, too. You also need a watering can. Gallon-size is useful, larger sizes are too heavy to carry and smaller sizes need to be constantly refilled.

WHEELBARROW. This might at first glance seem inappropriate for a beginner's list, but one of the first and most important things you will be doing is improving the soil, which is another way of saying you will be shlepping a lot of soil, manure and compost around the yard.

A barrow is also useful in other ways. For example, in the morning when you start work in the garden, fill it with everything you might possibly need during the course of the day's work. Trundle it around with you like a faithful dog. This way, you will not become discouraged and quit when you have to return to the garage for the seventeenth time to get the tool you forgot. Wheelbarrows are also great for giving small kids bumpy, thrilling rides.

Nice to Have, But Can Wait a While

BULB PLANTER. Almost a candidate for the gadget list, this is actually a handy tool. It is a metal cylinder, which tapers down a little at one end, attached to either a long or a short handle. The cylinder is 8 in./20 cm long and about 5 in./12 cm in diameter at the larger end. You push it into the earth with your foot, sort of like you would an upright shovel. When it is deep enough, twist the planter, pull it out. A plug of earth comes with it, leaving behind a hole ideally shaped to drop in a bulb. It does not work well in sandy soil because the plug falls apart. Clay is very difficult to penetrate with this doodad, but then you should not be planting bulbs in heavy clay anyhow, they will rot from excessive moisture.

CHAIR. Gardening can be tiring. You will want to have a chair in the yard so you can admire your progress while you catch your breath.

DANDELION WEEDER. A wooden-handled, long, thin, steel hand tool about 14 in./36 cm long. The flat end is sharply notched. You slide the tool down in beside a dandelion root, apply pressure, and ease out the whole root without breaking it. Slightly more effort is required to do the same job with a trowel.

DIGGING FORK. Some people prefer a fork to a spade for turning over the soil or for digging up perennials. Do not apply a lot of pressure on the fork when trying to dig out an underground rock. Once bent, fork tines can never really be straightened again.

ELECTRIC EDGE TRIMMER. One of those noisy power tools. This one whips a plastic string around in a vicious circle, cutting down everything in its path.

The electric trimmer is used to trim the grass where it cozies up to buildings, fences, etc. Keep it well away from your flowerbeds, favorite shrubs and trees. It can slice into bark and cut down things you do not want to lose. The cheap electric ones work perfectly well. This is not a heavy-use item, in fact, you may want to pass it up altogether and use simple, hand-held, non-power grass shears. Many people find the vibrations of a string trimmer most unpleasant, and seldom use theirs except when company is coming. Be sure to wear eye and ankle protection. This small, light-weight tool is often fascinating to small children — keep it securely stored where they cannot get at it.

HEDGE TRIMMER. The power-driven ones are only necessary if you have a huge amount of hedge, or a fast-growing hedge which needs a lot of trimming. Non-power hedge clippers will serve you perfectly well for smaller or slow-growing hedges.

HOSE-END MIX-AND-SPRAY DOODADS. They are an easy, efficient way to apply water-soluble fertilizers, although some people find them too fiddly. There are several different types available. One type is a bottle that screws onto the end of the hose. Fill the bottle with concentrated (follow the directions that come with it), water-soluble fertilizer, attach the hose, and spray.

Another mixer is a bit more complicated. A brass cylinder screws one end onto the faucet, and the other to the hose. A small rubber hose, leading off the cylinder, dangles into a bucket full of high-concentration, water-soluble fertilizer. The force of the water coming out of the faucet pulls the fertilizer mixture through the little hose and into the garden hose, then onto the plants via a regular oscillating sprinkler, or a hand-held pistol sprayer.

KNEEPADS. Take your crummy old gardening pants, stitch patch pockets to the knees, and slide in squares of dense foam rubber. This looks awful, but is very comfortable. Or, buy cheap foam kneepads with elastic to hold them to your knees. These look even worse and are not quite as comfortable.

LADDER. A 6 or 7 foot/2 meters or so step ladder is very useful, for example, when tying long rose canes to their supports. Always be careful when using a ladder, especially if the feet are set into soft garden dirt.

LONG-HANDLED LOPPERS. Useful when you need to trim larger branches
your hand clippers cannot handle. We much prefer loppers to saws
unless we are working on really big branches. The sawing action can
rock a small plant back and forth, and possibly rip off the feeder roots.

For Hopeless Gadget Freaks

This list is for the gardening counterparts of those who keep flossy
camera stores in business. There are endless numbers of garden doodads
out there, joined by new ones every year. It is very easy to spend a lot of
money on stuff you will never use, so think carefully before buying the
latest handy-dandy tool. A good rule of thumb is never to buy anything
until it has been on the market for at least five years.

COMPOST SIEVES. Only for real fanatics. If the compost is too coarse to
suit you, throw it back and let it cook a little longer.

GROW LIGHTS, GROLIGHTS, GROLITES. These fluorescent lights simulate
sunlight and are used to grow plants indoors. Expensive tubes, made
especially for use with plants, provide a broad spectrum of light, but
one of your authors has been growing perfectly nice indoor plants
under plain, cheap, warm white fluorescent lights for years. See seed
starting kits, below.

LEAF MUNCHERS. Actually, one of your authors lusts after a power leaf-
grinder — an electrically powered cylinder mounted on three legs.
Leaves and other vegetation are fed into the top, and then tiny ground-
up pieces fall out the bottom. The finely ground vegetation
decomposes faster in the compost heap. However, these munchers cost
as much as a moderately fancy lawn mower. So your author has
restrained herself, because she knows she can get exactly the same
effect, for a little more work, using her new mulching lawn mower.

MARKERS. Elaborate and expensive plant markers abound and some of
them are most attractive. If they tickle your fancy, fine, but please note
that you can also use builder's shims ($1 a bundle of about two dozen at
the lumber store) and a fat, black felt pen. The print needs to be
refreshed every couple of years, but the wood fades to gray and blends
into the garden nicely. There is lots of room for the plant's name and
the date of planting.

ROTOTILLERS. Rototillers do a wonderful job of cultivating the soil, and are invaluable if you are fixing up a new, empty bed, or one that has been empty for several years. Power-driven ones cost a fortune and are useful only on large expanses of bare ground. Remember that they can be rented by the day. Be sure to wear eye and ankle protection, because pebbles can fly up with great speed and force.

SEED STARTING KITS. The Reluctant Gardener does not start plants from seed — this is advanced gardening, requiring artificial lighting and all sorts of specialized knowledge. Growing flowers from seed might be a little cheaper than using purchased bedding plants, but it can be a frustrating and time-consuming experience. Wait a couple of years until you feel more confident about this whole gardening thing.

SPRAYERS. The shops sell many elaborate solution-sprayers, with pumps, motors and all kinds of attachments. These are meant to spray chemicals, which we disapprove of, and they are only worth their high price to people with acres of fruit trees to protect.

WATERING SYSTEMS. There are all sorts of ingenious watering systems — in-ground and above. If you cannot manage with an oscillating sprinkler, look at all the available systems and choose what suits your situation. New systems come on the market every year. Some are even computerized. The only people who really need elaborate systems are those who are frequently away from home during the summer. Be sure to do your homework, as you would before purchasing any expensive appliance. This homework will probably consist of asking around. We looked in the consumer guide magazines and the only garden equipment they had surveyed was lawn mowers.

All these doo dads must be cleaned and then stored properly, or they will sneak away and hide in obscure places, we guarantee it. To avoid this, you can hang any tool that can be hung on a row of big nails pounded into the garage or basement wall. Most tools have little loops of plastic-covered wire attached to them, or if necessary, you can drill a hole into the wooden handle.

However, you'll know you're going overboard with organization when you start looking speculatively at the wheelbarrow and wondering how big a nail you would need to ...

CHAPTER 5

Buyer Beware: A Plant-Buying Guide

Read This Before You Go to the Garden Center!

There you are, wallet in hand, at the local gardening center. You feel like the new kid in town on the first day of school. Everyone except you is purposefully chugging around clutching grubby pots of greenery, engaged in animated discussions about rhododendrons (which as far as you know is a horrible growth you get on your hands from too much digging) and deadheading (some ghastly new crime sweeping the neighborhood?).

Fear not. Here are a few simple rules of plant purchasing to follow, so you will not return from the nursery thinking that you have just dropped dozens of dollars on plants that even a master gardener could not grow.

Where to Shop

If at all possible, shop only at well-established, local garden centers. Why well-established? Well, you want to be sure they will still be there in two weeks when you go in to complain about the stuff that died. Plant death is not always the gardener's fault — some nurseries will replace stock that died, but not plants that die over winter. Why local? Because local nurseries usually stock plants that will survive in the local climate. Why garden centers and not the supermarket? Because garden centers know how to properly care for plant material.

If your area lacks a garden center, live plants can be ordered from reputable mail-order catalogues. Check gardening magazines for mail-in cards. Most catalogues are free, but some firms charge for them. Never deal with fly-by-night companies that offer such nonsense as six shade trees for five dollars. The general tone of the catalogue will tell you all about the company's quality. Just remember: if it sounds too good to be true, it is.

Make a List

Do some summer-dreaming over the winter, deciding what to buy for next season's garden. Keep in mind the size of your garden and your pocketbook — more on this in Chapter 1 which deals with garden planning and designing. Take this list with you to the garden center. Try to stick to it, but buy some unplanned things, too, or it will not be any fun. Not too many, though, or you will wind up with twenty-seven plants to squeeze into a bed large enough for ten.

AVOID THE CROWDS — *In the cold-winter areas covered in this book, the final weekend of May is usually the official beginning of the gardening season, when it is warm enough to plant out tender annuals. Never go plant shopping during The Big Weekend. Everyone hits the garden centers at once. Line-ups are a mile long, the inexperienced staff feels harassed and so do the customers.*

Do not go just before The Big Weekend, because the centers' stocks will probably be incomplete. Go during the second and third weeks after The Big Weekend. Garden centers are usually open 9 to 9, seven days a week, during the peak planting season. Do not worry the stock will be sold out — a good garden center has full stock at least until mid-June, early July. Do not worry about planting too late. Because the weather will still be cool those first couple of weeks, plants will be growing slowly anyhow. Anything you planted in early June will catch up nicely in two or three weeks.

Make More Than One Trip

Do not expect to buy everything on your list the first time out. Be kind to yourself and plan on making several trips. Expect to visit more than one center, if your area has more than one. It is unlikely that any one center will have everything you want. The plant lists in this book, however, are specifically drawn up to to include only commonly available plants.

If You Are a Gardening Beginner

If this gardening stuff is really new to you, you might even want to make your first visit a dry run. Do not take money or credit cards. Just walk around and familiarize yourself with the stock and the layout. Make notes about what is available at what price. You may or may not want to take an experienced gardening friend with you. Can you trust this friend not to run off at the mouth with all kinds of complicated information that will only confuse you? When you go plant shopping, wear crummy clothes. A potted rose is heavy and dirty, and you may want to balance it on your hip as you heave it into the cart.

Ask Someone Who Knows

Never ask anything (other than "Where's the check-out counter?") of the kids hired on for the rush. When you want to ask things like "Will this grow in a hot sunny area?" the person you need is the lady or gent with dirty fingernails. Look around, find who is in charge of all the kids. (This is another reason to go after the rush: it will be quiet enough for this person to be available.) Befriend this person, since she or he will save you money and, perhaps more importantly, aggravation.

What Is a Flat?

Annuals are most often sold in flats. These are shallow trays made of Styrofoam or peat fiber and hold between six and fifteen little plants whose roots have all matted together. Sometimes annuals are sold in plastic containers that resemble the bottom of an egg carton. Six or nine cells are linked together, each cell containing one plant. Perennials are sold one at a time in pots, ranging in diameter from 3-12 in./8-30 cm.

Annuals are the ones that you plant new every spring (they die in autumn). Perennials are the plants that come up again every year.

Which Flat Is Healthiest?

Buy only short, stocky, well-branched plants. If the flat label says this particular marigold is only supposed to grow to 18 in./45 cm, and the flat you hold in your indecisive hand if full of leggy stretched-out plants that are already 20 in./50 cm tall, you know they have not had enough sun, are stressed and will be slow to establish themselves once planted. Similarly, pale, yellowish leaves indicate that the plant has had too little sun and food, and will be weak and troublesome all its short life. Too many weeds in the pot means a neglectful nursery. Unless you always rescue wounded birds, never buy scraggly plants labelled "reduced to clear" — often found at the end of the selling season. They will either die or take forever to get up to speed.

Containers vs. Bare Roots

Buy perennials, roses and shrubs only when they are growing in containers. You will see some for sale bare-root, especially rose bushes. "Bare-root" means exactly what it sounds like: branches of a rose bush attached to roots free of dirt and container. Container-grown plants, on the other hand, are in a pot full of dirt and so have an established root system, which makes them much easier for the inexperienced gardener to transplant safely. You will see piles of bare-rooted rose bushes at the garden center, lying in a heap, looking like cleared underbrush waiting to be hauled away. Sometimes shrubs have their roots bound in plastic bags filled with peat moss — these, too, count as bare-root.

You can also buy bare-root perennials. These plants consist of a stump that looks much like vegetable trimmings, packaged in a plastic bag filled with wood shavings or peat moss. (Annuals are never offered for sale bare-root.) If an experienced gardener takes these things home and plants them just so, they will grow very nicely. That is fine for the experienced gardener. The Reluctant Gardener buys rose bushes, shrubs and perennials only when they are happily growing in a tub of soil, with a blossom or two showing.

Maintain an Open Flower Policy

Always try to buy a plant with an open flower or two. The ideal plant has one or two open flowers and a zillion unopened buds. There are several reasons for this advice:

1. Plant suppliers use a cheap color-reproduction process for plant tags. A rose pictured as pale yellow might actually bloom closer to orange.

2. You will want to sniff scented flowers before you buy — fragrance is a subjective business.

3. Labels are not always correct. Plants can be mislabeled either by type or color. One of your authors once bought a labeled white alpine poppy, which bloomed bright yellow. Also, pink is not necessarily pink.

You see, there are lots of mauve flowers out there. Some plants started their evolutionary life with dull grayish mauve flowers — Mother Nature just made them that way. Then along came the plant hybridists who set about breeding for pink or blue — with varying degrees of success. However, no one is going to buy a plant labeled "nasty gray-mauve," but they will buy one labeled blue or pink. Watch out for these other, shall we say, optimistic examples of plant labeling: deep yellow = orange; pale yellow = decayed white; red = magenta; red = dark orange; blue = purple; and pink = salmon. Usually red is indeed red, but buying a plant with one open blossom will enable you to be certain.

Latin Names

Please do not faint, but we recommend that you become familiar with Latin plant names at the same time you are learning the common names. Sometimes it is the only way to ensure you get what you really want. If you are looking for a bluebell, you might come home with any old blue-flowered thing. Instead, if you search for *Campanula pusilla*, you will be sure to get that nice little low-growing blue flower your friend has in her garden.

Latin names are very informative too: it is amazing how fast you get your head around the fact that *cardinalis* means red, and that *decumbens* signifies a plant that grows flat along the ground. It is even fun: *crassa* means something fleshy and thick, and *contorta* means something that is twisty. For more on Latin names, see appendices.

After Purchase, Before Planting

Between purchase and planting out, put your plants outdoors sheltered from wind and direct sunlight. Keep them well watered! If the weatherman predicts temperatures of +40°F/+4°C or colder, bring the plants inside for the night. A closed garage will do fine. Take them outside again in the morning (they need the light) unless daytime temperatures continue to be below freezing. Once all danger of frost is past, plant them out. To avoid this rigmarole, we recommend not buying anything until very close to planting time.

CHAPTER 6

Fair Weather Friends: Annuals

Most Reluctant Gardeners will choose annuals over perennials because they find that annuals are easier to grow and bloom long and freely. Give an annual anything close to its preferred conditions and it will flower all summer long. Unfortunately, annuals only return to your garden via the garden center. Unlike a perennial, an annual is planted in late spring, flowers all summer long, and then dies at the first hard frost. It will not survive the winter. The seeds of a few annuals will successfully overwinter and then germinate the following spring although never in a location where you want them.

Annuals, however, have many positive points. Changing the annuals you plant in your flowerbeds can give the beds a completely different look every year. If you have, for example, a brick house, try a cool–looking, elegant, all-white display one year, and then the next summer change to a cosier mix of pink, blue and yellow annuals.

Annual beds require less thought and planning than perennial beds. When selecting perennials, you have to be careful to mix ones that flower in June, with some that flower in July, some for August and some for September. Because annuals bloom all summer long, selection is much simpler. Color coordination is, of course, necessary for both annuals and perennials.

The Reluctant Gardener who does not want to maintain flower beds at all can rely on the annual's happy adaptation to container growing. As well, most annual flowers can be used as cut flowers. Many can be air dried and used in dried flower arrangements. Some can serve double duty as houseplants over the winter.

The second half of this chapter consists mainly of our YES! list, describing the most trouble-free and rewarding annuals, chosen from the ones most commonly on sale.

Buying Annuals

Please read the plant buying guide in Chapter 5 before making any purchases. Nursing weak plants is not the Reluctant Gardener's idea of fun. You do not need to worry about winter hardiness when choosing annuals, since they will all die come autumn anyhow.

Planting Out

Planting out, a term you often hear falling from the lips of enthusiastic gardeners, means the act of planting annuals and other plants into the flowerbed. When the time comes, the Reluctant Gardener should go through the following checklist before planting out:

- You have dug all kinds of lovely, soil-enhancing compost into the flowerbeds.
- You have spent this morning at the garden center buying plants.
- The weather is warmish and, preferably, overcast, so that the plant's system is not jolted into growth activities by the direct rays of the sun before it has established itself.
- The last frost date in your area has passed.
- The flats of annuals were thoroughly watered two hours ago.
- You know where you want to plant everything, that is, marigolds by the fence, portulaca on the south side of the house, geraniums in the window box, etc.

You are now ready for action.

1. Gather up your trowel, kneepads, watering can and a small bucket of compost or well-rotted manure. Carry a flat of annuals to the chosen site.

2. Count how many plants are in the flat, this can range from nine to twelve to fifteen. Check on the tag or our YES! list to see how wide the plant will grow in order to space the holes correctly. The holes will seem impossibly far apart, but have faith, that little seedling will grow much bigger. Dig as many holes as you have plants. Each hole will be about the size of a tea cup. Sprinkle a handful or two of

compost in the hole, then dig it in with the trowel. Fill the hole with water. Follow these steps for as many holes as needed.

3. When, and only when, you have completed step 2, remove the plants from the flat. Spread your fingers out, slide them gently in among the stems of the plants, and turn it all upside down. Shake the flat — one hand on soil, the other gently shaking and pulling the flat away from the soil mat. If the root mat does not come out easily, set the flat down and pry around the edges of the mat with the point of the trowel — rather like easing a cake out of a pan that you did not grease quite enough. If you do not want to save the Styrofoam or peat flat, cut the sides with your trowel and peel them off the soil mat.

    When the soil mat comes free from the flat, you will notice that it is held together by the plant's interwoven roots, which must be carefully separated. To do this, set the mat soil side down on the ground. Holding onto the soil mass with one hand, with the other gently wrestle a corner plant free. Pulling it free of the mat causes less root damage than cutting it out with a knife. Plop the plant into the prepared hole. Remember to handle the newly freed plant by its root ball. NEVER pick up a plant by its stem — it could easily be snapped or crushed.

4. Make sure that:
    • the plant is centered in the hole;
    • the plant stands vertical;
    • the same soil level is maintained around the stem as it was in the flat. In other words, do not bury the plant so low that new soil is heaped around the stem — it may rot.

    Now, with your hands bulldoze the excavated soil back in around the root ball and gently firm the dirt around it. This is important, because it squeezes out air pockets which roots might grow into and then die from lack of water and nutrients. Scoop up some soil to form a ring around the plant to hold water near the plant long enough for it to soak in, rather than running off into the garden. If you have sandy soil, you might want to maintain this ring all summer. Alternatively, put each plant in a saucer-like depression.

5. Pull the next plant free of the mat and proceed through the steps until planting is completed.

6. If you can bring yourself to do it — not everyone can — use your thumb and index fingers to pinch off all the flower buds. Just the bud. You may howl with dismay, but do not worry. The poor transplant-shocked plant has only so much energy, and just now the energy needs to be focussed into making strong roots, not flowers. Flower buds will reappear, we promise.

7. The cutworm is a real hazard to annuals. If you have ever planted a slew of baby annuals and then gone out the next morning only to discover several toppled over, cut clean off at soil level, cutworms have been at work. They are impervious to all but the most horrifying pesticides, so use an old trick: as you plant each new seedling, slide two toothpicks into the soil, closely on either side of the stem. The cutworm does its dirty work by wrapping its loathsome little self around the plant stem at soil level and, doing a boa constrictor imitation, squeezes the life out of the defenseless plant. The toothpicks get in the way and make this impossible.

Planting Out Annuals

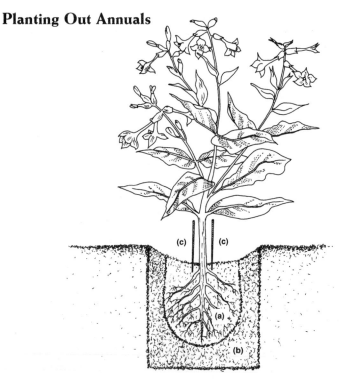

a) rootball, which consists of the mass of roots and soil it came with
b) compost-enriched soil
c) toothpicks to thwart cutworms
Note: this plant has been set in a saucer-shaped depression, slightly below ground level. This is done to hold water over the roots, and is appropriate for average or sandy soil. If you have poorly-draining soil, plant on little hills.

8. Turn the sprinkler on and gently water the newly planted annuals for fifteen to thirty minutes, unless the surrounding soil was very moist when you started planting.

9. For the next week, keep an eagle eye on the plants, do not let them wilt. Keep them really well-watered — at this stage, it is a case of when in doubt, water.

On-Going Summer Care

Once under way, annual plants need little attention besides watering, weeding, deadheading and watching for bug and disease damage. Do pull a weed before it goes to seed or you will weed forever, year after year. Applying a summer mulch (see Chapter 3 on general maintenance) will lessen the amount of weeding needed. A more enjoyable chore is cutting flowers for the house. In fact, the more you cut, the more flowers you will get!

PUTTING ANNUALS TO BED FOR THE WINTER — Good news! This job is much easier for annuals than for perennials. Some gardeners recommend clipping annuals off at soil level, leaving the roots to decompose over the winter. This is a nice theory, however in our experience, roots are very tough. All too often the next spring, you will be aggravated when your trowel thunks into an un-decomposed rootball which then has to be dug and composted anyway. We prefer to wait for a killing frost that wilts the annuals. When this happens, pull the plants out of the ground, shake the soil off the roots and throw them into the composter. That is all.

Gardens in a Pot — Container Gardening

Containers can be anything from hanging baskets to window boxes to patio planters. You are welcome to go out and spend a fortune on ready-made planters — there are some beautiful and expensive ones out there. You can, however, cut costs and use a number of found objects: old bushel baskets, 12 quart wooden fruit baskets, orange crates, shipping crates lined with an old shower curtain, half whiskey barrels and plastic dishpans. Now and then we become real skinflints, you see, and will do anything to squeeze in one more pot of flowers without forking over money for a container.

As you will have guessed, we are very fond of container gardening. Our yards and porches are littered with pots and containers of all descriptions, because it is so much fun to experiment. We like to try grouping pots of red, yellow and deep blue flowers, just to see the effect. One year we might try a pot of all white flowers with, perhaps, one dramatically-trailing red petunia. And the next, for an olfactory experience, we might arrange a mixture of three differently scented flowers.

Container-grown plants are so flexible: if the red-yellow-blue flower-filled container looks less than wonderful next to the house, cart it over beside the picnic table, where it will probably look terrific. We always plant two or three extra containers in case a bare spot in the garden, where something unexpectedly dies, needs to filled in the middle of July. Houseplants which spend their summers outdoors can be press-ganged into the same service.

What to Use for Containers

Anything that will hold soil, yet lets the water drain out, is a good candidate for a plant container. Here is a brief run-down of the virtues and vices of various types of containers, Remember: no matter which material you choose, the container will need a drain hole.

STONE OR CONCRETE. Either works well as a plant container. They are very heavy, of course, so think carefully about siting them. You will not want to shift them every season, especially when they are full of earth. You might want to remove the soil from them in autumn, since damp soil could freeze, expand and perhaps crack them.

TERRACOTTA. Our eyes cross with desire for big terracotta planters, but they cost a fortune, weigh a lot, discolor with age (although many people consider this desirable) and can be brittle. Smart people empty the soil out of the larger ones in autumn if they are to be left outdoors — moist soil expands when it freezes, and can crack the pot.

METAL AND PLASTIC. These containers heat up too much to make really good planters, but if kept well-watered you should not have substantial problems. Recently, some quite attractive terracotta-look plastic planters have come on the market at very reasonable prices. An old cast-iron cauldron has long been a favorite planter.

WOOD. Perhaps our favorite. If you choose redwood or cedar you will never need to paint them, for these woods are rot-resistant. Bug-resistant, too. They will age to a pleasing silver. Still, it is a good idea not to set them directly on the ground — put evenly spaced bricks beneath, to support the weight. This allows air to pass beneath, so the wood can dry out.

PLASTIC BAGS. We have seen people make a lovely show of flowers in a 40 liter soil-filled plastic bag. They poked a few holes in the bottom for drainage, laid the bag flat on the ground, slashed the top open, retaining the side walls, and planted it with impatiens which soon spread to cover the ugly bag. Any spreading plants that are not too tall work fine in this type of container.

Plastic Bag Planter

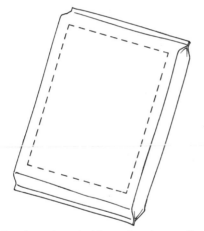

Take an old, pointed breadknife and stab through the soil, down through the bottom plastic, to make several drainage holes. Plant with spready annuals not much more than 12" (30 cm) tall. Impatiens (shade) or alyssum (sun) work well.

Purchased, sealed bag of soil or well-rotted manure, measures 24" x 18" x 6" (60 cm x 45 cm x 15 cm). Lay it flat where it is to lie for the summer and cut along dotted line. Remaining plastic forms a planter with a bottom and four sides.

You can buy ready-planted patio pots and hanging baskets, but for half the cost you can make them up yourself. For instance, empty hanging baskets can be bought for about the price of a mass-market paperback book and filled with annuals (one upright in the middle, four or five cascaders all around the edge). Three flats (one of uprights, two of cascaders) will fill four or five 12 in./30 cm baskets.

Container Soil

One of your authors has, for two or three years now, been using nothing but bagged, well-rotted manure (WRM) in her planter boxes. This, along with a very lax program of fertilizing, has resulted in abundant displays of flowers. Small containers get all new WRM every year, bushel-sized ones get about one-third new WRM. If WRM is not available, use compost or rich soil.

Here is a trick we use for larger containers — for example, half whiskey barrels (which look very smart if painted shiny black). Place the container where it will stay, then put empty annual flats upside down in the container until it is about half full. Now fill in with earth. Run the hose over it after every few inches of soil have been put in, to force the soil down among the crevices. Result: less soil used. As well, you have found a use for those awful Styrofoam flats. With any luck by the time the flats see the light of day again, there will be an ecologically sound way to dispose of them.

Remember to fill your large containers where they will sit. The combination of soil plus water can create a back-straining weight when hefted from the potting area to the front porch, for example.

How to Use Less Soil in a Large Planter

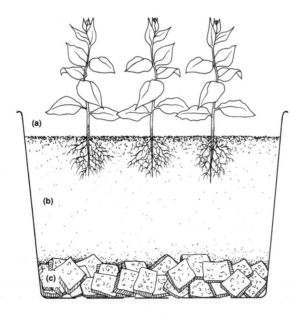

Suppose you have acquired a large planter, say 24″ (60 cm) deep. Most annuals' roots only extend 12″ (30 cm). So why waste 12″ (30 cm) of expensive dirt?

a) 2″ (5 cm) lip for watering
b) soil
c) old annual flats. Broken-up Styrofoam ones work well. A layer of overturned peat or *papier mâché* flats are also good.

Soil Level for Planters

No — water will run off and never soak in. Also, mud will spread all over the patio.

Yes — a 2" (5 cm) depth from lip of planter to soil level means you can fill the top with water and it will happily penetrate down into the roots.

Or — an alternative to watering from the top: a saucer large enough to hold 1 or 2 quarts (liters) of water. Fill it and let the water soak up into the roots. The catch here is that if you have had several consecutive days of rain, the roots will rot from lack of air unless the saucer is emptied.

WHAT TO PLANT IN CONTAINERS — Low- and medium-growing annuals are good candidates for containers. The taller the plant, the more root depth must be allowed for, that is, a deeper, larger pot must be used. If the pot is too shallow, the plant could topple. Also, keep proportion in mind: a 60 in./150 cm plant in a 12 in./30 cm container will look pretty silly. Fuchsias, geraniums (upright and trailing), petunias, lobelia, verbena, marigolds and begonias are just a few annuals an inventive gardener can mix and match.

Perennials and shrubs are not suitable to be grown in year-round, outdoor containers in a cold-winter climate. The roots are above-ground and so can heat up quickly in the winter sun, thaw and then die when the temperatures return to freezing. Perennials prefer to be grown in the ground where they can remain dormant, frozen solid all winter long.

Container Culture

The golden rule of container gardening: *check containers every single solitary day for dryness.* You are asking the plant to grow in a smaller volume of earth than it normally prefers. Roots take up more and more of the soil, nutrients are easily exhausted — altogether a stressful situation. The smaller the pot, the more vigilant you must be about watering, because small pots dry out faster than larger ones. Hanging baskets, which catch more drying wind than earth-bound pots, dry out all the faster. Containers need to be fertilized perhaps twice a month. Top-dressing with compost will not work because there will not be room in the pot. As you can see, container gardening is not suitable for people who go away for the summer.

Introduction to the YES! List of Annuals

Go-ahead-and-give-it-a-try applies much more to annuals than it does to perennials, because annuals are, by and large, less fussy and cheaper. The annuals we have found to be cooperative and easy to find are listed below. But first, here are a few tips and an explanation of the headings under each annual in the YES! list:

Common name: the one everyone uses. Be careful, however, when using common names, because a plant may have more than one and the same name could apply to more than one species.

Latin name: this is the botanical name that specifically identifies a plant.

Height and spread: necessary to know in order to place the plants properly in the bed. Tall plants should be placed at the back, short in the front, medium in between. Knowing the plant spread will help determine the side-to-side spacing.

Description: close-up photographs, so popular in gardening books, give little idea of the plant's habit of growth, that is, whether the plant is tall, skinny, short, mounded or stalky, as well as other details needed when planning a flowerbed. Our description is intended to give you a better sense of the plant's overall looks.

Wild or tidy: tidy-growing plants look fine in wild gardens, but wild ones do not look fine in tidy ones.

Sun: full sun generally means that six or more hours of unfiltered sun will fall on this spot each day. Most shade-lovers will tolerate two or three hours of sun. A plant that is getting too little or too much sun to suit it will put on a poor show of flowers.

Soil: most annuals are not picky about the soil they grow in. However, it is best to dig in lots of compost or well-rotted manure to ensure good performance.

Moisture: some plants need more or less than average moisture. "Average" means keeping the soil as moist as a wrung-out sponge.

Cut flowers: most annuals display well in vases. To prevent rotted leaves fouling the water, strip off any foliage below the water line. Also, holding the stem end under water when you give it its final trim will noticeably prolong its vase life.

Staking: we have tried to avoid listing sprawly plants which need the extra support of stakes and twine. If one of your favorites insists on toppling, simply surround it, when you first plant it, with a miniature forest of

Twig Supports for Floppy Flowers

In spring, when perennial sprouts are 4"-5" (8-10 cm) tall, jam bushy twigs firmly into the soil. They should be not quite as tall as the mature plant will be. The method also works well with newly-planted annuals.

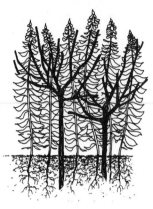

By mid summer, the plant has grown up through the twigs and is firmly supported against wind and toppling.

twiggy branches, of a suitable height. The plant will work its way into these twigs as it grows and be firmly supported all summer long.

Pruning: deadheading, pinching, shearing, cutting back; these are all forms of pruning. Deadheading means clipping off the dead flowerhead, and is done to stop seed production and encourage flower production. Pinch: with fingernails, pinch out growing tip. This will encourage side growth and therefore bushiness. Shear: with scissors, shear away the top inch or two/2.5-5 cm of growth all over, as if giving the plant a brushcut. Usually done in mid-summer when the first flowering begins to look tatty. Cut back: often done in July or early August, when flower production slows down. Cut away one-third to one-half the plant's mass to encourage fresh new growth and more flowers.

Pinching Out

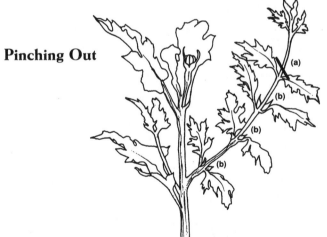

This branch is leggy. To force it to sprout leaves lower down, pinch out the growing tip at (a). This will stimulate the growth of the leaf buds (b) tucked in where leaf stems meet the supporting stem.

Comments: anything we thought might be interesting or useful. For example, if a flower is suitable for air-dried arrangements, we will mention it in this space. To air-dry, simply cut a flower in its prime. Strip off its leaves and hang it upside down (to ensure a straight stem) somewhere dry and airy until the stalk is stiff and dry. Clothespins on a string work fine.

Annuals which are good winter houseplant candidates will be mentioned here. To bring a plant in, dig up a favorite annual and plant it in store-bought, sterilized soil. You want to use sterilized soil to lessen the possibility of disease and bugs which might be hiding in garden soil. (Do not try to sterilize garden soil yourself in your oven, because it will stink up the house amazingly: roast worm, roast centipede, roast micro-organism, ugh.) Care for the plant throughout the winter as you would any houseplant. Most would like to grow under fluorescent lights. Ordinary warm white fluorescents will do, but a mixture of warm white, cool white works well. The light should be no more than 6 in./15 cm from the top of the plant. Pinching out flowerbuds throughout the winter will produce stronger, more compact plants.

Around mid-March, begin rooting cuttings for bedding plants. Cut off a branch containing about six leaves. Trim to just below the point at which the bottom leaf meets the stem, then trim off that bottom leaf. Stick the bottom inch or half inch (one or two centimeters) of the stem into vermiculite (a soil additive made from minerals) or sterile soil. Keep it evenly moist and under lights or in a sunny windowsill. Some plants, such as coleus and impatiens, will root in water. Keep the cutting no more than 2 in./5 cm away from the lights if growing under fluorescent bulbs. Transplant when well rooted.

The Annual YES! List: Twenty Non-Prima Donna Annuals

Common name: AGERATUM

Latin name: *Ageratum*

Height and spread: dwarf varieties are 6 in./15 cm tall and spread out about the same. Taller varieties are 12-15 in./30-40 cm tall and spread about 60% of their height.

Description: flowers are small, fuzzy balls of blue, mauve or pink, as well as a blue and white bicolor. Plant forms a compact, small-leaved mound.

Wild or tidy: tidy

Sun: sun or partial shade

Soil: prefers good soil enriched with compost

Moisture: average

Cut flowers: possible, but the stems are very short

Staking: no

Pruning: maybe a little deadheading needed

Comments: Most people grow the dwarf varieties of this nice little plant. An attractive edging for a bed, it mixes well with annuals such as dusty miller and salvia.

Common name: ALYSSUM, SWEET ALYSSUM

Latin name: *Alyssum maritimum, Lobularia maritima*

Height and spread: height, 10 in./25 cm; spread, 24 in./60 cm.

Description: mounded, with multiple flower heads composed of tiny, scented flowers in white, pink or purple.

Wild or tidy: fairly tidy

Sun: full sun, maybe a little shade

Soil: average

Moisture: average

Cut flowers: yes, but stems are very short

Staking: never

Pruning: may start to develop seeds during July or early August, so shear off faded flowers to promote more bloom late in the summer.

Comments: This is a standard edging plant. Pendulous types are attractive in hanging baskets, but the upright types will also trail effectively. Good in containers. Try white alyssum to contrast with, say, red geraniums or purple petunias. This plant may reseed itself, cropping up in unexpected places the following summer.

Common name: BEGONIA, WAX BEGONIA

Latin name: *Begonia semperflorens*

Height and spread: height, under 12 in./30 cm, spread about the same.

Description: a mound of shiny, waxy-looking heart-shaped, green or red-bronze colored leaves. The waxy-looking pink, red or white flowers have two large petals and two small ones. Pendulous types are available.

Wild or tidy: tidy

Sun: an excellent shade plant

Soil: average

Moisture: average

Cut flowers: not really, the stems are short

Staking: never

Pruning: pinch out dead flowers, for they turn brown and shabby-looking. If plants become leggy, pinch out the growing tip to promote side growth.

Comments: Wax begonias are happy, willing little plants that make an excellent edging for a shady border. Good in containers placed in shady spots, they mix well with coleus or impatiens. Hang baskets of these away from heavy traffic areas, because the stems are brittle. Can be wintered indoors as houseplants.

Do not confuse wax begonias with tuberous begonias which have larger flowers and grow from a tuberous root. This tuber must be dug up in autumn and wintered in pots of vermiculite to keep it from moulding or drying out — a procedure that is more work than the Reluctant Gardener cares to take on.

Common name: CELOSIA

Latin name: *Celosia*

Height and spread: can be found in many heights, ranging from 6 in./15 cm dwarf plants to 40 in./100 cm tall varieties. The shorter ones spread about 75% of their height; taller varieties, less than 50%.

Description: The two commonly grown celosias have distinctly different flowers. The familiar plumosas have soft, feathery flowering spires in reds, pinks or ambers. Cristata types are less commonly grown and have flowers of the same colors as plumosas, but they are shaped somewhat like fat, many-layered rooster's combs. Some people think the flower heads look like disgusting fuzzy brains.

Wild or tidy: tidy

Sun: yes. Does not mind high temperatures, so it is good against, say, a brick wall, which will throw off a lot of heat.

Soil: average

Moisture: average

Cut flowers: yes

Staking: tall varieties might need to be tied to a slender stick

Pruning: deadhead

Comments: Their brilliant colors are sometimes difficult to successfully mix into the flower border. Both types make wonderful dried flowers. Cristata types are good plants for people with a taste for the exotic, but be prepared for some garden visitors to say "Ick!"

Common name: CLEOME (pronounced clee-o-may), SPIDER FLOWER

Latin name: *Cleome*

Height and spread: height, 36-60 in./90-150 cm. A single plant may spread about 30 in./75 cm.

Description: the tall, spiny stem is sticky. The flowerhead, composed of many white, pink or purple smaller flowers, is nearly 6 in./15 cm in diameter. The individual flowers have long stamens, which give the flowers a spidery appearance.

Wild or tidy: a rather wild, yet stiff-looking plant

Sun: full sun, maybe a little shade

Soil: average

Moisture: average

Cut flowers: yes

Staking: can be left to sprawl, but needs to be tied up if you want a tidier look.

Pruning: no

Comments: Do not plant cleome in windy spots. It is an effective plant for the back of a perennial border. Plant several together, about 24 in./60 cm apart in clumps to ensure a good show. Sometimes self-sows its seeds. You can also gather the seeds in autumn and overwinter them in a cool, dry and dark place. In mid-May scatter them where they are to grow.

Common name: COLEUS

Latin name: *Coleus*

Height and spread: dwarf varieties are about 10 in./25 cm tall, taller varieties grow to 24 in./60 cm. Spread will be about 80 or 100% of height for dwarf plants, less for taller ones.

Description: Grown for its spectacular, yet somewhat bizarre-looking, multi-colored foliage — mixtures of cream, green, pink, red, bronze and a grating chartreuse. Leaves are pointed, with edges that range from slightly serrated to deeply divided. Flowers are sad little mauve spikes, which should be pinched out the moment they appear.

Wild or tidy: tidy

Sun: no. This is a good shade plant.

Soil: average

Moisture: average

Cut flowers: no

Staking: no

Pruning: pinch put flowers as they appear. To create bushier plants, pinch out growing tips.

Comments: For a shady corner, few plants are as easy and colorful as coleus. They are usually sold in flats of mixed colors — a glorious riot of variegated leaves. Excellent in containers. Be careful how you mix it in with other plants, however, because the vivid coleus casts other plants into the shade, so to speak. Can be overwintered as a houseplant. Aphids and mealybugs find them a tasty treat, so keep the insecticidal soap handy.

Common name: DUSTY MILLER, SILVERDUST

Latin name: *Senecio cineraria, Centaurea cineraria*

Height and spread: about 10 in./25 cm tall, will spread a little wider than its height. Some varieties grow to 24 in./60 cm and spread about the same.

Description: a nice plant grown for its mounds of silver-gray, slightly fuzzy leaves. Some leaves are very lacy, some less so.

Wild or tidy: tidy

Sun: yes

Soil: average

Moisture: not too wet. A good plant for dry spots, and therefore good for container growing.

Cut flowers: no

Staking: never

Pruning: no

Comments: It is difficult to think of a less troublesome plant than the dusty miller. It makes an excellent foil for brightly colored flowers. A classic combination is dusty miller planted with red salvia. Lovely in containers.

Common name: GERANIUM

Latin name: *Pelargonium*

Height and spread: about 24 in./60 cm tall. Spread is about 80% of its height

Description: a stocky plant, branchy with lots of scalloped, dark-centered leaves. Flower heads — large trusses of small flowers — are held well above the leaves on stiff stems. They come in white, pinks, reds, and oranges. Some bicolors (two colors on one petal) are available. Pendulous types are available.

Wild or tidy: tidy

Sun: full sun. Any amount of shade will drastically diminish amount of bloom.

Soil: average

Moisture: on the dry side. Overwatering will reduce bloom.

Cut flowers: no. Trusses shatter easily and can stain fabrics.

Staking: no

Pruning: remove spent flowers. To stimulate bushiness, pinch out growing tips.

Comments: Where would we be without the trusty geranium? Its preference for dry soil makes it ideal for container growing. It even survives the first few light frosts. The plants are expensive, however, and starting them from seed is only for advanced gardeners. We have found pendulous types to be weak growers, although there is a trailer widely available in a ravishing, deep velvety, burgundy red which we both grow despite its half-hearted performance. Geraniums can be wintered indoors and used for spring cuttings. Although it has never worked for us, some people winter geraniums by unearthing the plants in autumn and hanging them bare naked and upside down somewhere cool and dry until spring, when they can be potted up. Or try simply keeping a couple of favorite plants indoors as houseplants, under lights if possible. In mid-April root cuttings you have taken from the parent plant.

Common name: HOLLYHOCK

Latin name: *Althea rosea*

Height and spread: height can exceed 60 in./150 cm. Spread will be about 24 in./60 cm.

Description: tall, narrow plants with large, round fuzzy leaves. Flowers are single or double, as much as 6 in. (15 cm) across. Reds, pinks, yellows, white.

Wild or tidy: walks a bit on the wild side

Sun: sun, some shade

Soil: average

Moisture: do not let the plant dry out, because it is unlikely to recover from a wilt.

Cut flowers: no

Staking: yes

Pruning: pinch off spent flowers

Comments: Like cleome, hollyhocks are good tall annuals for the back of the perennial border. Its colors mix well with many other plants. Buy *only* the annual varieties, such as 'Pinafore' and 'Summer Carnival.' Biennial varieties are highly susceptible to rust, a disfiguring disease that causes ugly red-brown spots to appear on the leaves. Rust can be treated with sulphur, which is loathsome stuff to work with. Not suitable for container growing.

Common name: IMPATIENS, IMPATIENCE, BUSY LIZZIE

Latin name: *Impatiens*

Height and spread: dwarf varieties, 8 in./20 cm tall, others grow to 24 in./60 cm. Both will spread to their height.

Description: a mounded plant with slightly fleshy leaves shaped like wide arrowheads. White, pink, red or orange flowers are fresh and crisp looking. Double-flowered plants sometimes available.

Wild or tidy: tidy

Sun: excellent shade plant

Soil: average will do, but it will flourish if a little compost is added.

Moisture: do not let it dry out, because wilting will seriously reduce flowering.

Cut flowers: no. Clipping off a branch leaves an unattractive gap in the plant.

Staking: no

Pruning: no

Comments: This is a most obliging and attractive plant for shady areas, which seem to be increasingly common as houses are built closer and closer together. Impatiens has overtaken the sun-loving petunia as the most commonly grown annual. Most bugs and diseases seem to be uninterested in this plant. However, aphids and spider mites will move in if the plant has been stressed. If the soil is kept moist, it does well in containers — try reds, pinks or whites with an edging of blue lobelia. In the flowerbed, white impatiens looks cool and elegant planted alongside perennials such as Solomon's seal and hosta. Impatiens is the first to wilt in autumn — even a mild frost will send its leaves into a dramatic, permanent collapse. Some people say you can winter these as houseplants, but we have never had any luck doing this. New Guinea impatiens grows taller, has stunning variegated leaves, and tolerates more sun than the common impatiens.

Common name: LOBELIA

Latin name: *Lobelia*

Height and spread: height, 4-6 in./10-15 cm. Upright types will make a mound about as wide as they are tall. Trailing varieties have branches about 10-12 in./25-30 cm long.

Description: tiny green or purple-green leaves. Tiny blue (most common), white or pink flowers nearly conceal the leaves when it is growing happily.

Wild or tidy: rather tidy

Sun: shade or part shade. Does not enjoy hot spots.

Soil: average

Moisture: average

Cut flowers: no

Staking: no

Pruning: shear in mid to late summer to promote more flowers.

Comments: It might take a couple of tries to find a location that this pretty little plant likes, but stick with it. Its mass of blue is hard to beat. Hang a lobelia-filled hanging basket beside a shaded doorway to lift the spirits of all passersby.

Common name: MARIGOLD

Latin name: *Tagetes*

Height and spread: comes in all heights, from 10 in./25 cm dwarfs to 36 in./90 cm giants. Spread is generally 50% to 75% of its height.

Description: fern-like, scented leaves, usually dark green, sometimes spotted. Flowers, single or double, come in shades of yellow, orange and mahogany. Some white varieties are available.

Wild or tidy: in between

Sun: full sun

Soil: average

Moisture: average

Cut flowers: yes, if you enjoy the pungent odor of their leaves.

Staking: hardly ever

Pruning: deadhead

Comments: A mainstay of the sunny flowerbed. The marigold is very easy to grow and provides masses of flowers all summer long. Good in borders and containers. In late August, allow a few flowers on your marigolds to go to seed — when the pod is dry and turns downward, pull out the long, narrow seeds and keep them during winter somewhere cool, dry and dark. In spring, when the danger of late frost is over, scatter the seeds over a prepared bed and cultivate the bed lightly, so the seeds are buried about 1/4 in. (less than a cm) deep. Keep the soil evenly moist. This will give you a big, inexpensive marigold display in about twelve weeks. Leafhopper bugs sometimes enjoy munching on the developing buds. Earwigs will snack on the flower petals. But most bugs stay clear of the plants because of their pungent taste and smell. When frost hits your marigolds and the leaves have collapsed, root them up and compost the plants quickly. The frost-bitten leaves quickly turn into the most disgusting, foul-smelling soup.

Common name: NICOTINE, FLOWERING NICOTINE, TOBACCO PLANT

Latin name: *Nicotiana*

Height and spread: some as short as 15 in./40 cm, some as tall as 48 in./120 cm. Spread will be about the same as height, although it is a sparsely branching plant.

Description: the leaves and stalks are fuzzy and slightly sticky. Flowers, clusters of elongated trumpets, are found in reds, purples, pinks, white or pale green.

Wild or tidy: shorter ones are mildly wild, taller ones are quite wild. Give them lots of room, as they are one of the few plants that look attractive rather than messy when they sprawl.

Sun: full sun, or a little shade. Does not mind high heat.

Soil: average

Moisture: average

Cut flowers: yes, very nice for cutting, although masses of them make some people sneeze.

Staking: yes, if you prefer a tidier planting. Use well-branched twigs for best results.

Pruning: some deadheading

Comments: We would like to see more people growing this attractive plant. It is best planted in clumps of at least three plants for a striking effect. The paler colors, especially the white 24 in./60 cm *Nicotiana alata grandiflora* are delightfully scented in the evening. During the day the trumpets will look a little wilted, but as soon as the late afternoon's cooler temperatures arrive, they perk right up and begin to pour out that wonderful scent. A large container, half a whiskey barrel, for example, looks generous and joyful when spilling over with a mix of 24 in./60 cm white and pink and rose nicotine.

Common name: PANSY

Latin name: *Viola*

Height and spread: height, 8 in./20 cm. A single plant will spread about 12 in./30 cm.

Description: forms mounds of narrow leaves and velvety textured, five-petalled flowers. The flowers sometimes measure as much as 2-3 in./5-8 cm across. Flowers are usually combinations of blue, yellow and white. However, orange and even black-hued ones can be found. The black is really black, except when seen in the full sunlight, then it has strong purple highlights.

Wild or tidy: quite tidy

Sun: sun, or a little shade. Does not like hot spots.

Soil: average

Moisture: do not let it dry out

Cut flowers: yes. The more you pick the flowers, the happier the plant is.

Staking: no

Pruning: be certain to keep spent flowers picked, or blossoming will stop.

Comments: The pansy is an old-fashioned, reliable garden favorite. Sometimes reseeds itself. Some are scented. Becomes a bit leggy as it ages.

Common name: PETUNIA

Latin name: *Petunia*

Height and spread: 12-18 in./30-40 cm tall, spreads a little wider than its height. Pendulous varieties are available.

Description: slightly sprawly, branchy plant with fuzzy, sticky stems and leaves. Flowers, large single or double trumpets, appear in every color except black — blues tend to be more mauve or purple. Grandifloras have large flowers, multifloras have smaller but more flowers and make a better overall show, so take your pick if both are available.

Wild or tidy: fairly tidy

Sun: full sun, but if the spot is too hot, they will become leggy. They tolerate a little shade, but not too much or, again, they will become leggy.

Soil: average

Moisture: average

Cut flowers: yes

Staking: no, but if the sprawl bothers you, stick some well-branched 12 in./30 cm twigs in among the plants when you first plant them.

Pruning: If you want to keep petunias blossoming all summer you must pick off the spent flowers, or they will go to seed. Picking off just the faded trumpet, however, is not enough, be sure to also nip off the seedcase, the swelling where the trumpet was attached. In addition, pinch back the growing tips from time to time, or the stems will straggle. If, in August, flower production has slowed down, cut the plant back by about one-third — within a couple of weeks the plant will be in flower again.

Comments: Not our personal favorite, for the reasons given above, but still the petunia is the most popular annual for sunny spots in flower pots, hanging baskets and window boxes. You cannot beat it for choices of color, and they do look lovely in containers. Keep petunias out of the wind, because their big trumpets shatter easily. Prone to aphids — squish or spray with insecticidal soap.

Common name: PORTULACA, MOSS ROSE

Latin name: *Portulaca grandiflora*

Height and spread: less than 12 in./30 cm tall, but spreads about 18 in./40 cm.

Description: a ground-hugging plant with tiny fleshy leaves which look somewhat like soft, short pine needles. Lovely round flowers in the best bright pastels you will see anywhere. Most varieties close when the sun hides behind the clouds.

Wild or tidy: either

Sun: full sun

Soil: likes poor soil

Moisture: dry

Cut flowers: make sure no leaves remain below water level, because they will rot

Staking: no

Pruning: no

Comments: This is another plant we would like to see more widely grown. If you have a hot, dry spot were everything dies, portulaca is probably your solution — and it is as pretty as can be, to boot. It will reseed itself if it is happy. As with most drought-lovers, it will do extremely well in a container. Many people believe that it has different-colored flowers on one plant, but that is not true. Portulaca is almost always sold in mixed-color flats, and the branches of adjacent plants are often entangled. You might then think you have red, yellow, pink, orange and white flowers on a single plant. Single- and double-flowered plants available.

Common name: SALVIA, SCARLET SAGE

Latin name: *Salvia splendens*

Height and spread: height for dwarf varieties, 8 in./20 cm, 30 in./75 cm for taller varieties. A narrow plant, it spreads to no more than 60% of its height.

Description: a small-leaved plant that bears a spiky flowerhead composed of many little flowers. It is commonly available in red, although we have seen a nasty, yellowy white on sale.

Wild or tidy: tidy

Sun: sun, light shade

Soil: average will do, but dig in some compost for better results

Moisture: average

Cut flowers: no, the little flowers drop off so readily

Staking: no

Pruning: cut off spent flower spikes

Comments: This is an undemanding, extremely showy plant. The red is very vivid, so be careful with the colors you plant around it. Salvia looks very smart grown with dusty miller. If you like bold contrasts, combine it with yellow marigolds for a spectacular effect.

Common name: SNAPDRAGON

Latin name: *Antirrhinum*

Height and spread: varieties from 6 in./15 cm to 36 in./90 cm tall are available. Spread measures about 50% to 60% of its height.

Description: a narrow-leaved plant noted for its spikes of velvety flowers. To the great amazement of children, the flowers can be squeezed open and shut — the plant talks! Comes in all colors except blue and black.

Wild or tidy: tidy

Sun: sun, maybe a little shade

Soil: average, but a little added compost is a good idea

Moisture: average

Cut flowers: yes, the taller varieties are excellent. To prevent rot, strip off under-water leaves.

Staking: only the taller varieties which are grown in windy areas — use well-branched twigs

Pruning: deadhead

Comments: It might take of couple of tries to find a congenial spot for them, but once you do snapdragons repay you with a rich show of intense, velvety color. Some are scented.

Common name: SUNFLOWER. Many yellow-flowering plants are called sunflower — we mean the huge tall one called Russian Mammoth.

Latin name: *Helianthus annuus*

Height and spread: There are shorter varieties of 30 in./75 cm, but try the Russian Mammoths, which can grow to 12 ft./4 m, no kidding. There are also some plants which grow about 6 ft./2 m tall. These are narrow plants, so grow them in a mass or a closely packed row.

Description: tall, coarse-leaved, coarse-stalked plants that can scratch. Grown for their edible seeds and for their classic Van Gogh flowers, which look like the biggest yellow daisies you ever saw. Some reds and bronzes are available in shorter (60 in./150 cm) varieties such as 'Autumn Beauty' or 'Color Fashion' Mixed.

Wild or tidy: wild

Sun: full sun, does not mind high heat

Soil: does not mind poor soil

Moisture: does not mind being a little dry

Cut flowers: yes, if you have a tall enough vase and high ceilings

Staking: taller varieties might need to be lashed to something strong, like a fence.

Pruning: deadhead, except Russian Mammoth, which usually produces one enormous flower

Comments: Sunflowers are easily grown from seeds planted no more than 1 in./2.5 cm deep and 3-4 in./8-10 cm apart. Thin the seedlings to 12-15 in./30-40 cm apart. Thinnings can be planted elsewhere — they transplant easily. Once sunflowers are underway, their rate of growth is fantastic — a great favorite with the younger crowd. You can make a little ceremony of going out every Saturday morning to measure and record the plant's progress. Sunflowers produce edible seeds in autumn, but good luck getting there before the squirrels and birds. They also produce substantial stalks and roots, so pulling them up in autumn is quite a performance. Do not plant them too close to perennials because their extensive roots can invade their neighbor's territory, and when uprooted, can pull up the roots of nearby plants.

Common name: ZINNIA

Latin name: *Zinnia*

Height and spread: heights range from 10 in./ 25 cm to 30 in./75 cm. Spreads about 80% to 100% of its height.

Description: a coarse-looking, stocky, bushy plant with stiff, rough stalks. Leaves are narrow and rather scratchy. Flowers are single, or more commonly, double and resemble pom-poms. Enormous color range — everything except blue and black.

Wild or tidy: tidy

Sun: full sun, does not mind being hot

Soil: average, but dig in a little compost

Moisture: not too wet

Cut flowers: yes, very long-lasting

Staking: taller varieties growing in windy areas may need extra support

Pruning: deadhead

Comments: This is a happy, reliable plant that seldom gives any aggravation. Excellent in a hot, dry patch, especially when planted in masses. The colors are intense without being vulgar, but sometimes can be a bit harsh. Some of the taller ones could almost pass as dahlias.

The Absolute Minimum-Maintenance Annuals List

Marigolds for sun, impatiens for shade.

The MAYBE List: Fifteen Annuals for Brave Gardeners

The plants listed below have problems of one sort or another, but are nonetheless attractive and raise the spirits of those viewing them. Some of the listed plants are easy to grow but difficult to find because they are not currently fashionable. Others have one or two drawbacks significant enough to make the Reluctant Gardener think twice before buying them.

Anchusa: looks like an overgrown forget-me-not. We like it because its blue flowers are so beautiful. Reseeds itself a bit too freely. Its million little seeds could have inspired Velcro™ — they stick like burrs to anything that passes by, including your skirt, trousers, child, dog and cat. Try it in a problem area where nothing else seems to grow. Anchusa is not picky about soil, sun or moisture.

Aster: very sprawly, however, it makes good cut flowers, and comes in virtually every color. Does not mind being hot and dry. Plant it in a different spot every year to outwit the soil-borne disease it is prone to.

Balsam: not the tree. This garden annual is closely related to impatiens, except that it is taller and narrower and the delicately pretty flowers are camellia shaped. Does not like to be damp and chilly.

Basil: this is the herb familiar to every cook. In addition to the usual green variety, there are also spectacular bronze and purple varieties which are excellent edging plants. Pinch out growing tips to stop it going to seed. Overwinter as a houseplant. For culinary use, dry by hanging upside down indoors, someplace airy, then crumble it into a jar. Or simply freeze it and cut off a little when needed.

Carnation: very sprawly, and often drags its heavy head in the dirt after a rain. A little too susceptible to bugs to suit us. However, some carnations are deliciously scented and are excellent cut flowers.

Clarkia: a very pretty and delicately shaped flower which cannot tolerate the heat of August. After blooming and thriving during June and July, it fades and vanishes, leaving an infuriatingly bare spot. If you have cool, dry summers, try it in poor, dry soil and full sun.

Cosmos: a good medium-to-tall annual for large areas which need to be filled quickly. It does not so much sprawl as burgeon, making it unsuitable for use in confined areas. However, it is easy to grow and makes good cut flowers. Flower colors are burgundy, pink, yellow, orange and orange-scarlet. Lovely fern-like leaves. Poor soil suits it fine.

Datura: very poisonous, do not grow it if you have children. The exotic, trumpet-shaped flowers feel like the very best satin. Fascinating scent. Sometimes you will find it sold one plant to a pot. Seeds are sometimes offered, but they are difficult to germinate.

Godetia: same problems as clarkia. Has a large, beautiful pink flower rather like a wild rose.

Heliotrope: about 15 in./40 cm tall, this old-fashioned flower is deep purple and strongly scented. Easy to grow, but difficult to find.

Kale, flowering cabbage: very striking — looks like the prettiest white- or pink-trimmed cabbage you ever met. It lasts well after heavy frosts, but is prone to insect invasion. Very stiff looking, kale needs the right place to really shine. Not good to eat though — too tough.

Love-lies-bleeding, tassel flower: an old Victorian favorite, about 24 in./60 cm tall, grown for its long, maroon plush tassels. Grow in a container, so the tassels can drape over the edge. Makes great dried flowers — hang stalks by the bend where stem meets tassel.

Nasturtium: if you like orange flowers, this is for you. We just wish it were more free-flowering. Peppery leaves and flowers are good in salads, but eat only if *certain* no nasty chemicals have been used on them. Prone to black aphids. It thrives, however, in full sun and poor, dry soil. Yellow, red and mahogany varieties are available as well. Climbers are also sold. Both types are easy to grow from seed sown directly in the garden.

Ornamental grasses: many species and varieties are available. Some are most attractive, nodding and swaying gracefully in the breeze. There is a danger, however, that they will go to seed and take over the garden. The common names are delightful: Job's tears, cloud grass, bunny tail, animated oats, quaking grass, love grass.

Snow-on-the-mountain: a foliage plant, 36 in./90 cm tall. Bears many
gray-green, oval leaves edged with white. Lasts a long time in water.
Sap may irritate your skin. Worth a try in poor, dry soil. Also in the
same family is Mexican fire plant or annual pointsettia, which has green
leaves that turn red as the season progresses.

We feel very kindly disposed toward annuals. They remind us of a certain
type of dinner guest — the ones who can always be counted upon to
arrive on time, never outstay their welcome, and in between will listen
attentively and add pleasing and interesting conversational tidbits at
appropriate moments.

Annuals have similar congenial traits. They flower soon after planting,
continuing to bloom all summer long, and buzz off in autumn, leaving the
gardener free to invite them back next spring or try a whole new
combination.

We all have our good, solid old friends — trees, shrubs, perennials —
with whom we go way back. But we are always open to being seduced
into a horticulturally enchanting, although brief, flirtation with an
attractive stranger.

CHAPTER 7

Here to Stay: Perennials

If a magic wand could be waved over your yard, what kind of garden would you choose? Ten to one, it would be full of lush flowering plants — the kind often photographed for glossy garden and architectural design magazines. These gardens always shimmer in mid-summer sunlight, not a weed in sight, the plant masses well defined, artistically matched to their neighbors by foliage, shape and flower color. In short, a picture-perfect garden full of perennials, those miraculous plants that come up again, all by themselves, year after year.

Yes, you think, that is what you want — a flower garden full of lilies, daisies, violets and phlox, a garden where something is in bloom throughout the summer.

But, have you not heard that perennials are more work than annuals? Well, yes, they are, but just barely. Annuals have to be purchased and planted anew every spring, but then perennials have to be divided every few years. Annuals have to be pulled up and disposed of every autumn, while perennials have to be protected from winter cold.

Either choice means work for the Reluctant Gardener, no getting around it. Happily, if you choose the reliable plants we recommend here and avoid those with exotic requirements, the work — and aggravation — will decrease dramatically.

Perennials seem to be miraculous. Every autumn the above-ground parts die, but the roots sleep through the winter. In spring new foliage sprouts from these awakened roots and in time blooms furiously for its alloted time. This sounds wonderful, and is. The catch? Perennials only blossom for two or three weeks during the summer. The rest of the time they remain green and leafy. The trick to creating a satisfying perennial garden is to choose plants so that something will be in bloom throughout the season. Obviously it is important to know when each type will bloom — spring, early, mid or late summer, or early autumn. Remember that annuals are there to mix into the perennials, taking up the burden of bloom when the garden is between flowering perennials.

Buying Perennials

You can buy perennials growing in soil in pots, or, less commonly, as bare rooted plants sold in little plastic bags filled with sawdust or peat moss. The Reluctant Gardener should buy only the potted ones, because they have an established root system and are much less likely to be stressed when transplanted into your garden. Leave the bare root ones for more experienced gardeners.

When choosing from the offerings of potted perennials, buy the biggest potful you can afford — i.e., a 10 in./25 cm diameter pot rather than a 4 in./10 cm diameter pot. Why? Perennials can take a year or two to put on much of a show, so buying a larger one gives you a head start.

Please read through the plant-buying guide (Chapter 5) before making any purchases. Starting with healthy plants is half the battle won.

Planting Perennials

Planting a potted perennial is relatively risk-free. Follow the nine easy steps given below and we guarantee, excluding fate and the condition of the plant when you bought it, success and years of bloom to come.

1. First, buy the plant according to the instructions in Chapter 5. Water it thoroughly the day before planting.

2. Decide where you want to put it: short plants at the front of the bed, tall at the back, everything else in the middle. Remember that three of the same plant in one spot will look more attractive, less patchy, than three different plants in the same spot. For example, three astilbe planted together are more striking than one astilbe, one hosta and one Solomon's seal.

3. Dig a hole a little wider than the diameter of the pot.

4. Throw in a few handfuls of compost or well-rotted manure, and then dig it in a little.

5. Fill the hole with water and let the water drain away.

6. Do not remove the plant from the pot until this point. Knock, pry or poke the rootball out of the pot. (No, you cannot leave those lumpy brown *papier maché* or peat pots in place, you *must* remove them or they will inhibit the development of a good root system.) Never hold any plant by its stem. It is easy to accidently pinch the stem too hard and crush it — this could kill the plant. Try not to break the rootball while knocking it out, but if it does break, it is not necessarily a disaster.

Planting Potted Perennials

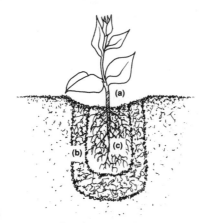

#1. Sandy or regular soil

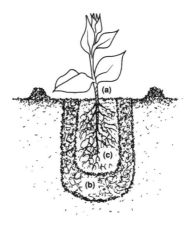

#2. Sandy or regular soil

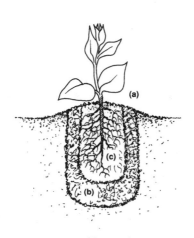

#3. Clay soil

Key

a) in all cases, soil level at the plant's neck is not changed

b) new, compost-enriched soil surrounds c), the soil that came in the pot.

#1 is planted in a saucer-shaped depression, which holds water over the roots. The saucer is always maintained in place.

#2 is planted at ground level, but surrounded by a ring-shaped wall, to hold water over the roots. This wall can be maintained forever (best with sandy soil) or only while the plant is young (if in regular soil).

#3 is planted on a hump, so water can drain away. Clay soil stays soggy, which promotes root rot.

7. Place the rootball in the hole so that the soil level at the base of the stem matches where it was in the pot. This is important, because some stems rot when covered with soil. If your garden contains very sandy or heavily clay-filled soil, see the diagram for more information on soil levels.

8. With your fingers, dribble soil in around the rootball, a little at a time, firming as you go. When the hole is full, water again.

9. For the first week, watch the new plant like a hawk, and water it every day. If you can bring yourself to do it, snip the flowerbuds off a newly planted perennial — this directs food and energy into the rest of the plant. The perennial will be stronger for this.

Perennial Maintenance

DIVIDING PERENNIALS: The major maintenance chore Reluctant Gardeners will have to just grit their teeth and do is dividing perennials. Be of good cheer, though, this has to be done only every three years or so depending on the variety. Perennials obligingly grow bigger every year: the lonesome contents of a little 3 in./8 cm pot of black-eyed Susans will, after a year in the garden, expand into a clump 12 in./30 cm across. The year after that, 24 in./60 cm. Wonderful, you may think! However, there is a catch — by the time the clump is 36-48 in./90-120 cm across, it will (a) be too big for its spot and (b) have stopped blooming in the middle.

You see, the clump grows wider as new shoots sprout around the edges. The stalks in the center become old, cramped, and generally unhappy. They stop flowering. This is your signal to dig the clump up, throw away the too-old parts and put the good parts back. Invariably you will have enough good material left not only to replant the original spot, but also to start a few new colonies. In fact, you can use this opportunity to redesign the flowerbed a little. If you did not like the chrysanthemums next to the bachelor buttons, dividing gives you the chance to dig them up and put them somewhere else.

WHEN TO DIVIDE PERENNIALS: It is generally agreed that if a perennial blossoms in spring, divide it in autumn. If it blossoms in autumn, divide it in spring. Mid-season flowering plants can usually be separated in

Dividing Perennials

In spring, divide when new shoots are 2″ (5 cm) tall. In autumn, divide when leaves have died. Cut stalks down to 4″ (10 cm) stumps.

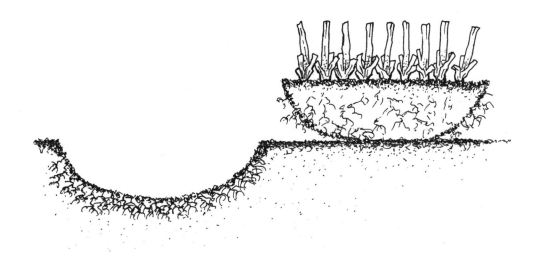

Autumn baby –
stalk and root

Dig up (spade, trowel, fork) as big a clump as you can comfortably handle. Pull, cut or hack it apart. Discard the center, which is too old and tough and woody to flower anymore. Keep the new babies — they are the pieces at the outside of the clump. Plant each baby — it will have a straggle of root and a small piece of stalk or shoot — as you would a new perennial.

Spring baby –
root and shoot

either spring or autumn. We, however, prefer to divide all plants —
unless they are actually in bloom — in September rather than wait for
spring. In fall, our summer garden memory is vivid, we remember what
was wrong with the bed's design, and therefore find it easier to move
things into the right place.

"All right," you may say, "I have decided that some of my plants are
ready to be divided. How do I know when to get the trowel or the
spade out?" In spring, a perennial is ready to be moved or divided when
it shows about 2 in./5 cm of new green shoots. In early autumn, a
perennial can be moved or divided when its leaves turn yellow. That is,
allow at least three to four weeks before the onset of cold weather to
transplant your perennials. This will give the plant time to form roots
before winter arrives.

HOW TO DIVIDE PERENNIALS: If dividing in autumn, cut the stems down
so that 3-4 in./8-10 cm remain. The trimmed-off parts can be composted,
if they are free of bugs and diseases. If dividing in spring, try not to
damage the newly emerged shoots. With a trowel or shovel, dig up the
whole plant, taking as much of the root system and accompanying soil as
possible. Plonk the whole mess down on the ground.

Now, squat beside it and pull it apart. You can usually do this with
your hands, although sometimes you will need a good sharp knife.
Throw away or compost the dead center, and plant the edge bits
wherever you want — back in the same place or in another spot in the
garden. Be sure each division has a piece of stem and a piece of root.
Replant these bits the same way you would a new perennial. Be sure to
plant the clumps before they become too dry — that is, replant in the
same day as you divide. If for some reason there is a delay in planting
of more than a few minutes, cover each division's roots with moist soil
and put them in the shade.

Putting Perennials to Bed for the Winter

TIDYING UP: In the autumn, some perennials wither down to a few sad
brown stalks, others are limp-leafed but green. The best thing to do at
this point is to clip away all the leaves and most of the stalk. Leave
about 3-4 in./8-10 cm of stalk sticking up out of the ground. The stalks
are useful as spring garden markers and as anchors to hold the winter
mulch in place.

Using a fan rake, rake away *all* fallen leaves and any left-over summer mulch, and put it all into the compost or garbage. Do not leave dead foliage lying around in the flowerbed. Rake hard, right over the top of the clipped-back perennials to rake away any dead material. It is amazing how many bugs and diseases can winter over, warm and happy, in that debris. A few gardening books recommend dead leaves as winter mulch, but we can't agree.

Some perennials send up a little thicket of new leaves in late autumn. The new growth will cluster around this year's old, dead stalks. For example, evening primrose forms a rosette of red leaves in autumn, close to the ground. Do not trim this new, fresh-looking growth when you are cutting away the dead stalks. Leave it there all winter and watch its miraculous revival come spring.

Autumn is a good time to mark your plants with name tags. The tags will identify where your plants are so that in spring you will not tread on them before they sprout. As well, if your horticultural memory fails over the winter, you will know exactly what that little green shoot is. This is especially useful if it is one you intended to divide in spring — many perennial shoots will, in this very early stage, look much the same. It also helps to avoid mistaking good plants for weeds.

You will be amazed, come spring, how much time you spend peering at apparently featureless dirt, then begin dancing with glee when you see that your favorite plant has survived the winter.

Winter Mulching

Although the perennials we have included on the YES! list are reliably winter hardy to about -22°F/-30°C (most are worth trying at -40°F/-40°C), we still recommend giving them a layer of straw for winter insulation. This is called winter mulching, or winter protection. Because we have experienced peculiar winters lately, we have learned not to count on an uninterrupted snow cover in winter, no matter where we live.

Why should we go to the trouble of winter mulching? Well, if perennials freeze in late autumn and stay frozen, they will still be alive in spring. But perennials are winter-killed if they are subjected to a repeated freeze-thaw-freeze-thaw cycle. Each time a plant thaws (say, during an exceptionally warm, sunny day in January or February), it rises slightly out of the ground and as it does, many of its teeny root hairs are pulled off. This can be a serious problem because water and nutrients are absorbed into the plant from the soil through these root hairs. So, if they are destroyed, the plant could die. An insulating layer of straw prevents the winter sun from thawing the frozen roots too early.

Gardening, a seemingly peaceful hobby, has its share of contentious debates. When to lay mulch is one of those issues that really riles some gardeners. Some recommend laying mulch early — a couple of weeks after the foliage dies. Others wait until the first day the ground freezes solid. Each school of thought has staunch supporters. Our advice to Reluctant Gardeners is to apply the mulch anytime between leaf brown-off and soil freeze-up.

The Live or Die school occasionally enters the mulching debate. Live or Die gardeners choose only the hardiest plants, and do not apply any winter mulch. If the plants survive, wonderful. If they die, they will be replaced with something hardier. If you are tempted by this notion, you might find the Hardy As Hell List (taken from our YES! list of perennials) at the end of this chapter worth a look.

However, if you decide that your garden could use a mulch, we recommend straw, bought at a garden center (stuff from a farm is likely to contain seeds), as an insulating material. Straw does not compress the way leaves do, therefore the layers retain some air. This provides a less hospitable environment for the bugs and diseases, which love to winter in the tight little places packed-down leaves provide.

Where exactly do you put the straw? Suppose you are covering a clump of black-eyed Susan. You have cut the stalks down to 3-4 in./8-10 cm. Remembering that the plant's spread was about 30 in./75 cm, lay a straw cover on a roughly circular area about 36 in./90 cm in diameter to ensure that the root mass is fully covered.

How thick should the layer be? We recommend that all cold-winter gardeners lay a 4-6 in./10-15 cm layer. In low-snow areas, that will be enough to counteract the warming effects of winter sun. In high-snow areas, this amount of mulch will see you through freak winters when the usual snow cover melts or fails. In either case, your perennials will remain frozen solid until spring.

Removing Winter Mulch in Spring

Do not be in a hurry to lift the garden's straw blanket at the first sign of spring. When the last of the snow has melted, pull back some of the mulch and see what is happening:

- if the top layer of straw has thawed, but the straw farther down is still frozen, put the top layer back;
- if all the straw has thawed and is ice-free but no new green shoots are showing, put the straw back;
- if green shoots are showing, pull the straw back from the new shoots to let the sun in, but push it back in place if there is any chance at all of frost. Check the weather forecast — if temperatures colder than +40°F/+4°C are likely, you should put the straw cover back.
- check the date of the last likely frost in your area. Suppose it is May 17. This is only an average, remember. It means that you should not completely remove the straw before that date;
- if the last frost date has been reached, and if the three or four days beyond it have been frost-free, pull the straw completely away from the perennials. However, you still need to pay attention to weather forecasts for the next little while.

The straw mulch can be composted or used for summer mulching (see Chapter 2).

The YES! List

Gardening books often compile long lists of perennials to choose from (we counted 121 in one popular book). This is wonderful if you know what you are doing, but bewildering, confusing and discouraging if you can barely distinguish between a rose and a marigold.

We assembled our YES! list to include a limited, manageable selection of cast-iron perennials that should survive -22°F/-30°C winters. Many will survive -40°F/-40°C. Hardy, undemanding and pretty, there is not a prima donna in the bunch. A mixture of these will give you a very attractive, no-worry garden.

Remember, if you have not already read the plant-buying guide (Chapter 5) do so before buying any plants.

The YES! List: Twenty-Three Non-Prima Donna Perennials

Common name: ASTILBE, FALSE GOAT'S BEARD, FALSE SPIREA

Latin name: *Astilbe*

Blooming period: late June into early July

Height and spread: dwarf varieties with foliage 15 in./40 cm tall, and taller types with foliage 24 in./60 cm. When mature, flower stalks will be held about the same height above the foliage. The height printed on the tag usually (but not always) includes the height of the flower. The plants will spread about the same distance as the flowering height.

Description: a beautiful, well-behaved mound of deeply cut leaves (dark green, some bronze) topped by white, pink, deep pink or red plumes.

Wild or tidy: either

Sun: shade or part shade

Soil: rich, so add lots of compost and peat moss

Moisture: likes to be on the moist side, but does not grow in standing water

Cut flowers: yes, also makes excellent dried flowers. Simply cut the plumes when they are just beginning to open and stick them in a vase without water. Even the stem dries well.

Staking: no

Pruning: just deadhead — trim off spent blossoms

Division: only when the base if very dense and crowded. This plant can be left in place for years and years. Can be divided or moved in autumn or early spring.

Comments: Astilbe is a very handsome plant which complements Solomon's seal and hosta in a shady, formal garden. Plant the taller varieties toward the middle of the bed — once the flowers have faded, you will want that lovely mound of leaves where you can see them. Shorter varieties are ideal for edging a shady bed.

Common name: BACHELOR BUTTON, MOUNTAIN BLUET, PERENNIAL CORNFLOWER

Latin name: *Centaurea montana*

Blooming period: heaviest in June, light blooming throughout July and August if you consistently deadhead

Height and spread: height, about 24 in./60 cm; spread, an unruly 24 in./60 cm or more

Description: a rather sprawly plant with very attractive blue flowers which look like soft, ferny thistles

Wild or tidy: wild gardens only; too sprawly for tidy gardens

Sun: full, but worth trying in part shade

Soil: not picky, will grow in poor and dry soils

Moisture: evenly moist

Cut flowers: will not make a very satisfactory show by itself, but can be used as an attractive blue accent

Staking: In spring set fairly stout twigs in among the emerging stalks, or place a peony ring (a 24 in./60 cm diameter stiff wire ring on three wire legs) over each plant, before the plant leafs out fully. It is also all right to let it sprawl without support.

Pruning: deadhead spent blossoms

Division: early spring or autumn, only when its base is very crowded

Comments: This plant spreads nicely to fill the space around it, but never becomes invasive. It is very hardy and easy to grow. We could do without its tendency to sprawl, but good, long-flowering blues are hard to find. In mid-summer, cut back the long arms that have been flowering till now and are looking tired and scraggly and might also be slug-infested. Leave the central cluster of new-this-month leaves.

Common name: BLACK-EYED SUSAN, CONEFLOWER

Latin name: *Rudbeckia fulgida* 'Goldsturm' is the most obliging. *R. hirta* looks very much the same although it has fewer flowers.

Blooming period: July through to late October

Height and spread: height, 30 in./75 cm; spread, 36 in./90 cm

Description: The classic black-eyed Susan is the one your granny grew — a bright yellow daisy with a black eye

Wild or tidy: a little too coarse for a tidy garden

Sun: full

Soil: not too picky, but enjoys a little compost now and then

Moisture: this plant is one of the first to wilt in dry weather. It springs back, however, after a good watering — a useful reminder that it is time to water the whole garden.

Cut flowers: yes

Staking: no

Pruning: deadhead only

Division: divide it in spring or autumn about every five years, but if it is blooming nicely and the center is green and growing, leave it be.

Comments: good color for August when a perennial border sometimes lacks excitement. A happy, eager-to-please plant. Try planting its strong yellow-ochre flowers next to the equally strong brick red ones of the Maltese cross for a brilliant display.

Common name: BLEEDING HEART, DUTCHMAN'S BRITCHES

Latin name: *Dicentra spectabilis*

Blooming period: spring

Height and spread: height, about 30 in./75 cm, if happy; spread, 36 in./90 cm or more.

Description: pale to medium green, deeply cut leaves grow along graceful arching branches. Little pink and white (sometimes just white) hearts dangle all along the underside of the branches.

Wild or tidy: either

Sun: shade or part shade

Soil: not picky

Moisture: average

Cut flowers: awkward to make them sit tidily in a vase

Staking: no

Pruning: the only thing wrong with the bleeding heart is that its foliage completely disappears in August. Early in the month the foliage will start to yellow, and by mid to late August it will be quite dead. The roots will be fine — the plant just retreats into early dormancy. Clip it at ground level after the leaves yellow. The resulting large bare spot can be handled in one of two ways: put a planter of annuals in the spot (impatiens are ideal) or plant a late-blooming perennial such as a chrysanthemum next to it or in front of it.

Division: in autumn, only if the amount of blossom has decreased from the year previous. Can be left undisturbed for years.

Comments: This plant is a delight in the spring, especially as a backdrop to flowering bulbs.

Common name: CHYRSANTHEMUM, GARDEN MUM (as opposed to the kitchen mum or car-pool mum)

Latin name: *Chrysanthemum*. Be sure to buy the winter-hardy ones, not the ones available year-round at the flower shop in a pot which you give to your dinner hostess.

Blooming period: late summer until hard frost

Height and spread: height, 24-36 in./60 - 90 cm; one plant will soon clump up and cover a yard (a meter) or more of the garden.

Description: daisy-like (single), or pompom (multi-petaled) flowers in whites, pinks, purples, yellows, bronzes. Bushy plants with attractive grayish leaves.

Wild or tidy: newly purchased mums are compact and tidy, but by the next year they have become too sprawly for formal gardens

Sun: full sun, maybe a little shade

Soil: rich, so add lots of compost and/or manure

Moisture: evenly moist; do not forget to water during a dry autumn

Cut flowers: excellent, long-lasting

Staking: yes — stout twigs will work well as stakes

Pruning: during June and early July, pinch out the growing tips (the topmost pair of teeny little leaves at the end of each branch), to keep the plant short, compact and branchy. If left unpinched, it will flop and sprawl most irritatingly.

Division: in spring, when its green shoots are 2 in./5 cm tall.

Comments: This is the classic garden "mum," sold in pots at garden centers beginning in late August. Buy plants with a few open flowers (to check the color), but with large numbers of unopened buds. Plant as you would any perennial. Give them a layer of straw for winter insulation, just to be safe. The florist mum is not winter-hardy, and cannot be planted outside when it finishes flowering.

Common name: CORAL BELLS, HEUCHERA

Latin name: *Heuchera sanguinea*

Blooming period: all through June, July and August, if you consistently remove the dead flower stalks

Height and spread: its leafy mound grows about 12 in./30 cm tall and a little wider across. The flowers are held another 12 in./30 cm above the leaves.

Description: pretty scalloped leaves make a tidy mound. Airy clusters of small, hot pink bells are held well above the foliage on stiff, thin stems.

Wild or tidy: excellent in either kind of garden

Sun: full sun, maybe a little shade

Soil: rich, but worth trying in less-than-perfect soil

Moisture: evenly moist

Cut flowers: excellent; the hot pink bells make surprisingly good accents in mixed bouquets

Staking: never

Pruning: continually pick off faded flowers

Division: every two or three years, in spring or autumn, when the center becomes crowded, or when you want plants for a new location.

Comments: We highly recommend coral bells for the Reluctant Gardener. It makes an ideal edging plant, is excellent in rock gardens, and it is also said to attract hummingbirds. As with most perennials, a group of three or more looks better than a single plant by itself. This is one of the most pleasing, obliging, rewarding plants we know. Note: when its leaves collapse in autumn, leave them there, do not trim them off. The dead leaves will still be there in spring — resist the urge to tidy them away. They will disintegrate before long.

Common name: DAY LILY

Latin name: *Hemerocallis fulva, H. flava*

Blooming period: some early, some mid, some late season, so check the tag.

Height and spread: some as short as 15 in./40 cm, some as tall as 48 in./120 cm. Will spread between 24 in./ 60 cm and 48 in./ 120 cm across. Check the tag.

Description: a thick-growing mass of strappy, narrow leaves with flowers carried well above the leaves on stiff, non-branching stems. Flowers are rather course trumpets colored in many shades of yellow, orange, pink, russet or red. Some are fragrant.

Wild or tidy: wild

Sun: yes, but will take some shade

Soil: does not mind poor soil, but you will get more and better flowers is you work in some compost

Moisture: can tolerate dry periods

Cut flowers: no, the individual flowers usually last only one day

Staking: no

Pruning: deadhead faded blossoms

Division: maybe every four or five years in autumn, but can be left alone for years and years

Comments: Remember the orange lilies growing in ditches beside country highways in mid-summer? That is *H. fulva*. We had quite a little tussle over whether or not to include it. One of your authors loves it, the other hates it. The day lily does have an untidy habit of growth but it is incredibly hardy and trouble-free. It is an ideal choice if you have a large area to fill in a hurry. If the look of a low hedge is needed in a spot where heavy snow accumulation would damage a permanent shrub hedge, then this is the plant. Keep it deadheaded, though. The faded flowers can cling for days to the tips of the tall stems, although plant breeders are working on this problem. Try not to put it next to valuable plants, as it can be rather invasive, and could crowd out its less aggressive neighbors. Day lilies are resistant to most bugs and diseases.

Common name: DIANTHUS, PINK, GARDEN PINK, MAIDEN PINK, COTTAGE PINK, GARDEN CARNATION, GRASS PINK

Latin name: *Dianthus deltoides*. There are various species of dianthus available, but we like *D. deltoides*.

Blooming period: June

Height and spread: this is a low-growing plant, its foliage no taller than 3 in./7 cm. A small pot from the nursery will, in two years, expand into a dense mat about 18 in./45 cm across.

Description: forms a tight mat that defeats many weeds except grass. Small carnation-like single flowers are held above the mat on thin 6 in./15 cm stems. White, pinks and reds are available.

Wild or tidy: either

Sun: full sun

Soil: average, worth trying in hot, dry areas

Moisture: evenly moist, but can stand to be a little dry

Cut flowers: not really suitable, because of its short stems

Staking: no

Pruning: To induce a longer blooming season, shear off the flowers as they begin to fade.

Division: in early spring or autumn, when the center of the clump begins to look brown and is no longer flowering.

Comments: Not to be confused with creeping phlox (*Phlox subulata*, moss pinks). *D. deltoides* makes a much tighter, more weed-resistant mat than *P. subulata*. Excellent in rock gardens and in the front of the border.

Common name: EVENING PRIMROSE

Latin name: *Oenothera tetragona*

Blooming period: May and June

Height and spread: height, 18 in./ 45 cm; but can expand into as wide a clump as you permit.

Description: three or four, yellow, single flowers, like large, flattened-out buttercups, bloom at the tip of the single stalk. In spring, it is identifiable as a reddish-leaved rosette growing close to the earth. Foliage turns green as it grows up and looks good all summer.

Wild or tidy: good in either type of garden

Sun: full sun, will take a little shade

Soil: average, worth trying in poor soil

Moisture: evenly moist

Cut flowers: not really suitable, because of its habit of growth

Staking: no, the masses of stems hold each other up

Bugs and diseases: little trouble with either

Pruning: Although in late August, the current year's foliage will be brown and tired-looking, fresh rosettes will have formed underneath, close to the ground. Clip and compost the tall brown growth without cutting the attractive red-green rosettes.

Division: can be done when the clumps are crowded and fail to blossom. Divide in early spring when rosettes are forming, or autumn when only the rosettes remain. Spreads by underground runners, so when dividing, clip the root linking one plant to another. They are very tough, so do not be frightened of damaging them when dividing.

Comments: Evening primroses must be planted in clumps, in an area at least the size of a bathmat — a few plants together look floppy and useless. However, a couple of plants will spread very readily and clump up in two years.

Common name: FORGET-ME-NOT

Latin name: *Myosotis*

Blooming period: spring and early summer

Height and spread: height, under 12 in./30 cm; spread, less than 6 in./15 cm, but they grow together in a continuous mass.

Description: a dense-growing mounded plant with many tiny blue flowers on thin stems covered in small, pointed green leaves.

Wild or tidy: good for either kind of garden

Sun: yes, but some shade is all right

Soil: not picky

Moisture: average

Cut flowers: not suitable, except for use in small vases

Staking: no

Pruning: after blooming the whole plant will turn dry and gray. At this point, shake the plant to make it drop its seeds, then pull it up. As the seeds germinate and begin to grow through the summer, be sure not to weed them up — these new plants will bear next spring's flowers.

Division: no, because brand new plants grow every year where the seed has dropped

Comments: Many different small, blue spring-flowering plants are sold under the forget-me-not name. They could be annual, biennial, or perennial; they could be *Myosotis alpestris*, *M. sylvatica* or *M. rupicola*. They could even be a Cynoglossom (annual, biennial or perennial) or Anchusa (annual or perennial), although these last two tend to be taller than what is traditionally though of as a forget-me-not. They look wonderful planted among spring-flowering bulbs: imagine white tulips poking through a wash of blue forget-me-nots.

Common name: GLOBE THISTLE

Latin name: *Echinops ritro*

Blooming period: August, September

Height and spread: height, 36-60 in./90-150 cm; spread, 24-30 in./60-75 cm

Description: a dramatic, unusual plant — tall with very prickly leaves. The flower is an attractive ball of steel-blue prickles.

Wild or tidy: kind of wild, but disciplined enough to give it a try in a somewhat formal garden.

Sun: full sun

Soil: okay to try in poor soil

Moisture: dry to average

Cut flowers: yes. Excellent for air-drying, but pick it when it is just barely open; if picked too late, it will fall apart.

Staking: usually not, but if it gets a little too much water it may become a bit floppy and need to be tied to a thin stake.

Pruning: no

Division: can be left in one place for many years, which is just as well, considering how prickly it is. Divide in spring if it becomes really crowded.

Comments: This impressive plant is a great contrast to pretty-pretty flowers. It will give your garden an air of daring and sophistication that will wow the neighbors. You do not have to tell them how easy it is to grow. However, do buy the biggest plant you can get your hands on, because it can take two or three years to grow to full height. *E. ritro* is the most readily available. 'Taplow Blue' is 60 in./150 cm tall, and the flower is more blue than gray. 'Nivalis' is 48 in./120 cm tall, and sports white flowers.

Common name: HOSTA, PLANTAIN LILY, FUNKIA

Latin name: *Hosta undulata, H. glauca, H. plantaginea,* and others. These all look very much the same, and differ only in the shape and color of the leaves.

Blooming period: June, July

Height and spread: some varieties grow 24 in./60 cm tall, other 36 in./90 cm. They spread a little more than their height.

Description: grown for its lovely, vigorous fountains of leaves, some narrow, some heart-shaped, some solid colored, some variegated, some flat, some rippled, some yellowish, some bluish. The flowers are unexciting — tall stems skimpily covered in bells, white or feeble mauve, are held a couple of feet above the mound of leaves. *Hosta plantaginea* is nicely scented.

Wild or tidy: excellent in tidy gardens; fine for informal too

Sun: shade or part shade. Can take a fair bit of sun if you keep it well watered. If the leaves turn brown and the plant looks generally depressed, it is probably getting too much sun and should be moved.

Soil: rich, so add compost and peat moss

Moisture: likes to be on the moist side, but well-drained

Cut flowers: not really, as the plant's flowers are not very attractive

Staking: never

Pruning: let it flower and see if you like the flowers, if you do not, trim them off next year when the flower stems first appear.

Division: every three or four years in early spring or early autumn, if the clumps look crowded or if you want new plants. Can be left alone for several years.

Comments: This lovely plant is especially nice in a row alongside a shady walkway. New plants will take a couple of years to bush out, so be patient. It is one of the last plants up out of the ground in spring, so do not despair if everything but the hostas are up. In fact, take advantage of this: when you plant a hosta, try planting small spring bulbs (crocus, scilla) all around it. The growing hosta leaves will cover the ripening bulb foliage. Unfortunately, slugs enjoy munching holes in the leaves.

Common name: LILY

Latin name: *Lilium.* Going any further into the Latin names for lilies is unbelievably complicated. All you need to know is that we do not mean the African lily, or the Amazon lily, or the day lily, or the water lily, or the calla lily, or lily-of-the-valley. The one we are talking about here is the one that is called just plain lily. A familiar lily is the tiger lily, which has black-spotted orange petals.

Blooming period: June, July, August, depending on which one you choose

Height and spread: height will range from 24-60 in./60-150 cm, depending on which one you buy (check the tag). Each bulb sends up a single, non-branching stem. The bulbs soon reproduce themselves. Three bulbs planted 12 in./30 cm apart will, in three or four years, grow into a clump that can occupy at least a square yard (square meter) of the garden.

Description: a tall stem covered with many long, narrow leaves. Flowers are Turk's caps (petals curve right back to touch the stem with their tips) or trumpets, which may point up, out or down. Stamens are long, dramatic, velvety and will spread brown pollen all over you if you bump them. Color range includes many different whites, reds, pinks, yellows and oranges. Some, such as the classic tiger lily, are speckled.

Wild or tidy: either

Sun: full sun or maybe a little shade, but not too much

Soil: average, but would really like to be planted in a couple of feet of rich, compost-enhanced soil

Moisture: evenly moist

Cut flowers: excellent for long-lasting and elegant arrangements. A few stems alone in a tall, heavy vase look very chic.

Staking: yes, for the taller ones. Early in the summer they will stand up straight unassisted, but when the heavy flower buds are beginning to form, they will need some support. What works best for us is to jam some stout, branchy sticks into the soil when growth begins to appear in spring. No tying is necessary. The sticks can be removed when the flowering finishes.

Pruning: deadhead. When all the flowers on a stalk are dead, cut the top off the stalk, leaving about 75% of its original height to feed the bulb for next year's flowering.

Division: divide an over-crowded clump in mid-autumn, every four years or so. The bulbs will be nearly 12 in./ 30 cm down.

Comments: These classy, spectacular lilies are worth the trouble of staking, for they are hardy and long lived — one lily bulb can live forty years. They vary in so many interesting colors and heights that you can have several different kinds here and there in the garden. The earliest lilies to bloom in June and July are the Asiatic hybrids. Unfortunately they are scentless, but bloom in an amazing array of colors. Trumpet lilies, or Aurelian hybrids, are the most fragrant and are characterized by large, outward-facing flowers, usually blooming in July. One of the easiest to grow and the easiest to find is the Regale, a magnificent gold-throated, white lily. The Oriental hybrid lily group also contains many fragrant bloomers. They bloom usually in August, but can bloom anywhere from late July to early September. Flower shapes include trumpet, flat, recurved or bowl-shaped. "Imperial Gold," which has 6-8 in./15-20 cm flowers, is easy to find. The white flowers are marked with gold strips and maroon spots.

The Reluctant Gardener should not buy the specie lilies — the ones usually listed only by their long Latin names. Not only are they more difficult to grow than hybrid lilies, they are not as disease-resistant. As well, the bulbs are brittle and must be handled with extreme care.

Lily bulbs can take *forever* to sprout, so be patient. Try to buy them already growing in pots, although the selection of bulbs packaged in plastic bags filled with wood shavings is much wider. Because the bagged bulbs are quite tough, we will, this one time, allow you to buy a non-potted plant. Choose firm white or pale green bulbs with a few live roots showing, and a small (not much more than 1 in./2 cm) white sprout on the other end.

Plant small ones (golfball size) deep enough so that 4 in./10 cm of earth covers the top of the bulb. Larger ones (baseball size) should have a 6 in./15 cm covering of earth.

Plant them 12 in./30 cm apart, because they will clump up amazingly fast. Each bulb doubles itself every year if it is at all happy.

Some lilies produce bulbils, shiny little brown balls which nestle at the base of each leaf where it meets the stem. They drop to the earth and soon send up a single leaf, which will, within two years, be a flowering plant. You can transplant these elsewhere to start new colonies.

The only problem with lilies is that they are sometimes plagued by a red-orange beetle half the size of your thumbnail. It resists all but the most toxic sprays, so be brave and squish it, before it eats all your lily leaves and buds.

Note: fancy lily varieties can cost an unbelievable amount of money, so do not buy them until you know that lilies will grow for you.

Common name: MALTESE CROSS

Latin name: *Lychnis chalcedonica*

Blooming period: June, July, August

Height and spread: height, 30 in./75 cm; spread, 12 in./30 cm

Description: a rather coarse-leaved plant which may sprawl; grown for its showy clusters of brick-red flowers.

Wild or tidy: wild only

Sun: full sun, but some shade is OK

Soil: rich soil, so give it some compost

Moisture: evenly moist

Cut flowers: nice as an accent in an informal bouquet

Staking: yes. Position some stout twigs around it in spring, before it begins growing.

Pruning: deadhead only

Division: in spring or autumn, only if it looks crowded

Comments: The Maltese cross spreads by self-seeding. Keep it
deadheaded to prolong the blossoming period. It will take a couple of
years to clump-up and look its best, so suffer patiently through this
period. The taller ones are more vigorous and better colored than the
shorter. Very intense color — looks horrible next to pink, but lovely
next to black-eyed Susans.

Common name: MONARDA, BEE BALM, BERGAMOT, OSWEGO TEA

Latin name: *Monarda didyma*

Blooming period: July, August

Height and spread: range from 24 in./60 cm tall to 60 in./150 cm. Each
plant covers an area about 12 in./30 cm across. However, it soon
clumps up and covers as much as a yard (approximately a meter) of the
garden. Keep it weeded back to control spread.

Description: a big, bushy, rather sprawly, plant with whorl-shaped
flowers. The blossoms, which have green pincushion centers, are
usually pink, but are occasionally available in mauve or red. They
are supposed to come in white, too, but your authors have never
seen any.

Wild or tidy: definitely wild, unless you get the shorter varieties and keep the
clump weeded back to a civilized mound. The taller ones want lots of
space. This is a good plant if you have a large area to fill in a hurry.

Sun: full sun, or maybe a little shade — but not too much

Soil: average, but would really appreciate some compost

Moisture: evenly moist

Cut flowers: well, you can make a big unruly bouquet that will drop pink
fluff and little black pollen grains all over the table.

Staking: tall ones, yes. Prop up the toppling stems with a stout twig.

Pruning: deadhead if you have the energy — otherwise never mind, it will do fine without

Division: it will rapidly become big and clumpy, so divide every three years, in the autumn or early spring

Comments: This plant really does attract bees, so if you react badly to stings, do not plant it. The leaves are aromatic and scent the air nearby with a nice spicey smell. In fact, monarda leaves give Earl Grey tea its distinctive flavor. They are said to attract hummingbirds. Provide reasonable air circulation so that mildew does not become a problem. If mildew does strike, treat it with an organic fungicide. This is a hardy, vigorous plant that spreads rapidly but not invasively.

Common name: OBEDIENT PLANT, FALSE DRAGONHEAD

Latin name: *Physostegia virginiana*

Blooming period: late July into September

Height and spread: height, 36 in./90 cm; spread, 24 in./60 cm

Description: tall spikes of small white or pink flowers on a nice branchy, usually gray-leaved plant

Wild or tidy: wild

Sun: full sun or part shade

Soil: not picky about soil

Moisture: evenly moist, does not mind being a little dry

Cut flowers: all right for white or pink accents in an informal arrangement

Staking: usually not, but if needed, use a few stout, branchy twigs

Pruning: deadhead

Division: only if it looks crowded, or is failing to flower — perhaps every three years, spring or autumn

Comments: This is a rather humble plant, however, a pale gray-foliaged mass every here and there in the garden gives the eye a rest from flashier things. Physostegia is very hardy and vigorous, and spreads readily yet is easy to weed back. It is called obedient plant because the little flowers will stay where you put them if you shove them around with your fingers. We do not really recommend that you tell your children this interesting fact, because they will pester the poor plant half to death.

Similar to obedient plant, although more dramatic-looking, are *Lysimachia clethroides* (goose-neck flower) and *Cimicifuga racemosa* (black snakeroot). Don't you love these names? Unfortunately, they are both very difficult to find in gardening centers.

Common name: PEONY

Latin name: *Paeonia lactiflora, P. officinalis*

Blooming period: late May, into June

Height and spread: both measurements will be approximately 36-48 in./90-120 cm

Description: many large, usually double, white, pink or reddish flowers (no true reds available at this writing) on bushy plants. Good-looking leaves are deeply cut and dark green all summer long.

Wild or tidy: either

Sun: full sun or a little shade

Soil: the richer the better, so add several shovels of compost or well-rotted manure when you plant a new one, and topdress older ones every year.

Moisture: evenly moist

Cut flowers: excellent

Staking: in spring, when the new sprouts are only a few inches tall, set a peony ring (a 24 in./60 cm diameter stiff wire ring on three wire legs — *not* a tomato cage) over the emerging plant. As it grows, guide the stems inside the ring, which is soon completely hidden by the leaves. This must be done, otherwise the flowers will drag in the dirt when heavy with rain. You can leave the ring in place forever.

Pruning: deadhead spent blossoms

Division: only if it is very crowded. Peonies are best left alone, for they will live happily for years and years if undisturbed. If a clump needs to be divided, wait until mid-August, but not much later. Peonies have large fleshy roots which need the extra time after transplanting to grow and multiply before winter sets in. When you have divided the clump, check to be sure that each division has a set of pinkish buds where the roots and stem join. These buds should not be planted more than 3 in./8 cm below ground level or the plant will not flower for years.

Comments: Probably the most highly recommended plant in this listing, the peony is spectacular when blooming, and handsome the rest of the year. Some (the pale pink 'Sarah Bernhardt' and the white 'Festiva Maxima' — both readily available) are pleasingly scented. Buy a container-grown plant and be careful to keep the soil level the same when you plant it. This soil level business is very important for peonies — if their eyes (the pinkish buds at the top of their roots) are planted at the wrong depth, they will not flower. A young plant will take a good two or three years to enlarge, so be patient. Contrary to what you might hear, ants do not help the flowers open, they are after the sweet bud-coating, but do no harm to the plant itself.

Common name: PHLOX

Latin name: *Phlox paniculata*

Blooming period: July, August

Height and spread: height, 40 in./100 cm; spread, 24 in./60 cm

Description: *P. paniculata* is the old-fashioned tall phlox, a traditional mainstay of perennial flowerbeds. Big, fat flower clusters are composed of many little flowers, called florets. You have probably seen it in mauve, but there are lovely pinks and whites now available. Delicately scented.

Wild or tidy: wild, but tidy if properly staked

Sun: full, but might do all right in just a little shade

Soil: rich, so give it lots of compost

Moisture: evenly moist

Cut flowers: not really suitable, because a big cluster will tend to have unopened flowers, fully opened flowers and dead flowers all on the same cluster

Staking: maybe. Propping it up as needed with stout, branchy twigs of an appropriate length will probably suffice. Many varieties do not need any staking.

Pruning: deadhead, but this can be an irritating job, for the reasons noted in Cut flowers, above. Do what you can.

Division: divide in spring or autumn if it looks crowded, maybe every three years or so

Comments: *P. paniculata* does not enjoy being planted too close together, or too close to other plants — it needs good air circulation to discourage mildew. In fact, it is susceptible to mildew in late July and August, especially in sheltered gardens with poor air circulation, but prompt and persistent use of an organic fungicidal spray should control the mildew. Self-seedings are unlikely to look anything like the parent, so weed them up. The pale pink variety 'Mother of Pearl' is nicely scented. *Phlox divaricata* is 15 in./40 cm tall, has bluish flowers, and enjoys growing in the shade. *Phlox subulata*, a 3 in./8 cm high ground cover, flowers in mid-spring. It tends to look patchy the rest of the year, so instead try *Dianthus deltoides* or the shorter sedums. If you *must* have *P. subulata*, buy it with a flower or two open, since it seems to suffer more than most from, shall we say, optimistic labeling: many a pink-labeled plant turns out to be mauve.

Common name: PURPLE CONEFLOWER

Latin name: *Echinacea purpurea, or Rudbeckia purpurea*

Blooming period: mid-July into September

Height and spread: height, 36-48 in./90-120 cm; spread, 18 in./45 cm

Description: flowers are big rosy-pinky-purpley daisies whose high-mounded black eyes have yellow highlights; the leaves are attractively shaped like an elongated heart.

Wild or tidy: the plant makes a not-too-untidy mound, but would look best in a wilder garden. The color, quite eye-catching, might not strike the right note in a restrained garden.

Sun: full

Soil: average

Moisture: evenly moist

Cut flowers: all by itself it makes an attractive semi-formal arrangement. Try using Oasis (flower-arranger's foam) in a low bowl, and positioning the flowers in a mound. The arrangement will last almost a week. The stems are very coarse, so be careful not to scratch yourself.

Staking: no

Pruning: deadhead

Division: early spring, or in autumn, maybe every three years, if it looks crowded

Comments: This is a highly recommended reliable perennial that will add life to the late-summer garden and flower vase.

Common name: SHOWY STONECROP

Latin name: *Sedum spectabile*

Blooming period: late August, September

Height and spread: height, 18-24 in./45-60 cm; spread, the same

Description: There are many, many types of sedum. However, this one is a fleshy leaved, stocky mid-size plant. It develops unopened flowers (which look like broccoli heads) during July and August. These flower heads bloom pink as autumn approaches.

Wild or tidy: either, this is a tidy-growing plant that does not sprawl

Sun: full sun, or just a little shade

Soil: average, but would appreciate some manure or compost

Moisture: does not mind hot, dry conditions

Cut flowers: no

Staking: no

Pruning: nothing needed beyond cutting it down to 3 in./8 cm stalks when it turns brown in autumn

Division: maybe every three or four years, spring or late autumn

Comments: *S. spectabile* is a great boon to the garden from spring to autumn, and pleases us with its tidy habit of growth and its pink to deep pink, smoothly-shaped flowerheads. A flowerbed of any size would benefit greatly from having two or three good sized clumps.

There are many other types of sedum, including a large number of ground-hugging, 3 in./ 8 cm ones, usually blooming in pink or yellow. They are all trouble-free plants, invaluable where low growers are needed.

———————————————

Common name: SOLOMON'S SEAL

Latin name: *Polygonatum biflorum, P. commutatum* (synonymous with *P. giganteum*)

Blooming period: June

Height and spread: *P. biflorum*, 18-36 in./45-90 cm, *P. commutatum*, 36-48 in./90-120 cm. Spread: after a few years one root clumps up to about 24 in./60 m across.

Description: tall, gracefully arching stems with attractively paired leaves all along it; small white bell-like flowers dangle from beneath. Grown mostly for foliage.

Wild or tidy: good in a wild garden, but is ideal in a formal, tidy garden

Sun: full shade or partly shady

Soil: rich, does not mind clay

Moisture: evenly moist

Cut flowers: not suitable, because you would have to cut the entire (non-branching) stem at ground level

Staking: no

Pruning: no

Division: only if it gets very crowded. You can divide the plant in very early spring when its shoots are barely showing, but autumn division, when the foliage has turned brown, is better.

Comments: A vigorous, low-care plant for a shady area. It starts out with a couple of stems, and will increase steadily every year until it has formed a clump, but will not become invasive. Looks very smart and sophisticated against a modern house. A shady corner could not ask for more than a tall clump of Solomon's seal with some shorter hostas in front and an edging of white impatiens. Cool and lovely. It is one of the last perennials to sprout in spring, so do not panic if it still has not appeared when everything else is up.

Common name: VERONICA, SPEEDWELL, HUNGARIAN SPEEDWELL

Latin name: *Veronica*

Blooming period: June into July

Height and spread: comprises many different species which grow from 6 in./15 cm to 48 in./120 cm tall. Spread is hard to predict, because they like to topple over and sprawl — so give veronica lots of room.

Description: blue-flowered spikes composed of many teensy little flowers; leaves are feathery, many are gray-green. Shorter species will often mound nicely.

Wild or tidy: better in a wild garden

Sun: full sun, maybe a little shade

Soil: rich — add compost

Moisture: good drainage

Cut flowers: flower form is not really suitable for cutting

Staking: can be sprawly, but it is not a heavy-headed plant, so stick appropriately-sized twigs into the ground around it, and let it grow up into the twigs.

Pruning: deadhead to extend blooming period

Division: in autumn, only when it is failing to flower

Comments: Veronica is best grown in clumps, rather than one or two plants at a time. Pink and white are available as well as the more common blues. It looks very attractive growing next to coral bells or peonies. It may host mildew later in summer, so spray with organic fungicide to control this from the moment the gray-white patches appear, until they are gone.

Common name: VIOLET, WOOD VIOLET, SWEET VIOLET

Latin name: *Viola odorata*

Blooming period: early spring

Height and spread: height, 8-12 in./20-30 cm. Each plant will spread over the same range, until you end up with an uninterrupted carpet of violets.

Description: a low, compact plant with attractive all-summer-long heart-shaped leaves; flowers are very small, scented, deep blue-purple or white

Wild or tidy: suitable for either wild or tidy gardens. Violets spread readily to form a good ground cover but are easily confined by weeding or mowing.

Sun: shade or mixed sun and shade; will take quite a bit of sun if kept watered

Soil: will thrive in any soil, even poor soil

Moisture: do not let it dry out, although it will bounce back from a not-too-lengthy drought.

Cut flowers: you will need several dozen to make a small, very pretty potful that will last a day or two. The edible flowers, if they have not been sprayed with chemicals, make a beautiful garnish on cheesecake or vichyssoise.

Staking: never

Pruning: no, but if mown over in late July a crop of fresh leaves will appear in two weeks

Division: can be dug up and pulled apart any time it is not flowering; settles in again without any fuss. Only needs to be divided if you want new plants to put elsewhere, otherwise it can be left alone for years.

Comments: This is a hardy plant that is willing to grow almost anywhere. Because it is shallow rooting, it can be used around other plants that tend to be sparsely branched at their bases, like purpleleaf sand cherry shrubs. One violet plant will turn itself into a substantial, dividable clump in a year or two; it also propagates by self-seeding. It is good for rock gardens and edgings, and seems not to interest most bugs and diseases. Mow over it in late July — in two weeks you will have a nice crop of fresh leaves.

Common name: YARROW, MILFOIL, ACHILLEA

Latin name: *Achillea filipendulina*

Blooming period: June, July, August, September

Height and spread: height, 18-60 in./45-150 cm, depending on which one you buy — check the tag. Each plant covers a diameter of about half its height, but it can spread like mad to fill up all available space.

Description: grown for its flat heads of clustered flowers of white, yellow or pink. Nice feathery foliage, often gray.

Wild or tidy: Shorter varieties okay in a not-too-formal garden. Tall ones look quite wild.

Sun: full

Soil: not fussy; perfectly happy in poor soil

Moisture: does not mind at all being hot and dry

Cut flowers: yes. Good for drying, too — just hang a flower by its stalk someplace cool and well ventilated until it is dry and stiff.

Staking: yes, especially taller varieties

Pruning: deadhead if you like

Division: only when if becomes too crowded. Can usually be left alone for years.

Comments: Closely related to its wildflower ancestors, this is a tough, vigorous plant that will return year after year after year. Be aware that some people consider it too aggressive for a perennial bed, although it can be controlled with determined (but not terribly arduous) weeding. 'Coronation Gold,' 36 in./90 cm high, is a good garden variety that stays yellow when dried. It spreads readily, but is easily weeded back. 'Cerise Queen,' 'The Pearl' and 'Fire King' are very invasive, and only for use when you have a big area to fill in a hurry. 'Gold Plate' will grow to 60 in./150 cm in a sunny corner.

Common name: YELLOW LOOSETRIFE

Latin name: *Lysimachia punctata*

Blooming period: June, early July

Height and spread: height, 24 in./60 cm; spread, 18-24 in./45-60 cm

Description: a nice, dense fountain of non-branching stems with paired leaves. Bright yellow bells grow up and down the stems. Quite different from purple loosestrife — it is not the same genus, so do not worry about damaging the wetlands if you grow this plant.

Wild or tidy: wild, but fine in a not-too-formal garden

Sun: full sun, or maybe a little shade

Soil: average, but would not mind a little compost

Moisture: evenly moist

Cut flowers: useful as an accent in an informal arrangement if you do not mind it dropping its little yellow bells everywhere

Staking: no, but if you are a real neat freak, but a peony ring over it in early spring

Pruning: deadhead

Division: can be left alone for years, but if it looks tangled and intergrown, divide in autumn or early spring

Comments: A very obliging, hardy plant that will become a mainstay of your June border. The rest of the summer it acts as a well-behaved fountain of green. We are told by an old-time gardener that it was named after the pioneers' practise of feeding it to restless barn-confined cows and horses during the winter to calm them down. It looks surprisingly good next to coral bells.

PERENNIALS BY SEASON

To help you plan a perennial border, we have listed the plants from the YES! List in the order of when, during the summer, they blossom. Each subsection lists the shorter plants first and then the taller ones, which should also help planning the layout of the perennial bed.

EARLY SPRING FLOWERING:

Tulips, daffodils, crocus, grape hyacinth and other spring-flowering bulbs

MID-SPRING FLOWERING:

violet, forget-me-not, bleeding heart, peony, Solomon's seal

LATE SPRING, EARLY SUMMER FLOWERING:

dianthus, veronica (various heights, some bloom in July), coral bells (all summer, heaviest in early summer), evening primrose, bachelor button (all summer), astilbe (into mid-summer), day lily (different varieties flower at different times, so a well-chosen mixture will give flowers all summer long)

MID-SUMMER FLOWERING:

short sedums (into late summer), hosta, black-eyed Susan (into autumn), obedient plant, Maltese cross, yarrow, phlox (into late summer, maybe autumn), globe thistle (into late summer), purple coneflower (into late summer), monarda

LATE SUMMER, AUTUMN FLOWERING:

showy stone crop, chrysanthemum

Hardy As Hell List

These perennials have survived even the worst winters in our -40°F/ -40°C area.

black-eyed Susan (try *Rudbeckia hirta,* which looks a lot like *R. fulgida,* but is a little hardier)
bleeding heart
chrysanthemum
coral bells
day lily
dianthus
forget-me-not
lily
Maltese cross
obedient plant
peony
phlox
showy stonecrop (most sedums do well in cold regions)
sweet violet
veronica
yarrow
yellow loosestrife (completely different plant from the outlawed purple loosestrife)

Here I Am, Here I Stay

Many people cannot, for whatever reason, do the bending, digging and lifting involved in plant division. The following, therefore, are perennials (chosen from our Yes! List) that can be planted and left in place for many years if enough room has been provided. The real homebodies are marked with an asterisk.

* astilbe
  bachelor button
* black-eyed Susan
* bleeding heart
* day lily

evening primrose
* forget-me-not
* globe thistle
  hosta
  Maltese cross
  obedient plant
* peony
  purple coneflower
* Solomon's seal
* violet
  yarrow
* yellow loosestrife

The MAYBE List: Troublesome Plants That Require Extra Effort

The following are eighteen widely grown (well, widely attempted, anyhow) but persnickety perennials and biennials that you might not want to try until you are a more experienced gardener. When you are learning to knit, do you tackle a ten-color Fair Isle pattern first? Of course not. Same thing with gardening.

These plants tend to pine and pout if they do not get *exactly* what they need from soil, sun, moisture and fertilizer. If your absolute favorites are on this list, go ahead and give them a try — they might decide they like you. (Another basic rule of gardening is: you just never know.) The eighteen are commonly available in garden centers. But you have been warned — they are not easy to grow.

We should also point out that biennials are difficult to manage. A biennial is a plant that works like this: Year 1, you buy it in spring and plant it. It may or may not flower. Year 2, if it flowered last year, it will not this year. It will only grow foliage. If it did not flower last year, it will flower this year. Year 3, it is gone forever, unless it happened to seed itself, in which case you will get foliage one year, flowers the next, alternating every year. The whole cycle can drive you crazy.

Aster (*Aster, many species*): although they are quite hardy, asters tend to be very floppy and sprawly. Too many feeble gray-mauves out there are all labeled as pink or blue, however some deep rosy pinks are attractive.

Carnations (*Dianthus caryophyllus*): if you can find a non-sprawling variety, fine, but most of them get into an awful tangle. Flowers, often too heavy for their stems, are liable to drag in the mud. They are also preyed upon by a bug that eats all the petals out of an unopened bud.

Chinese lantern (*Physalis*): these produce the orange lantern-shaped seed pods you see for sale in farmers' markets in autumn. *Never, never, never* plant them at home, unless you plant them all alone in the middle of a huge field. They are unbelievably invasive, and send out vigorous underground roots that push up new plants a yard/meter away from the original plant.

Columbine (*Aquilegia*): not bad for shady corners, but very sprawly, and subject to disfiguring attacks by leaf miner.

Dahlia (*Dahlia*): the roots *must* be dug up in autumn and kept in a cool, dry basement all winter. In these days of central heating, who has a cool, dry basement anymore? Also, it is subject to too many diseases for the Reluctant Gardener: the leaves turn brown and curl up, flower petals turn a nasty brown, and buds do not open properly. Phooey.

Delphinium (*Delphinium*): we lust after these tall, gorgeous blue spikes, but they defy anyone who does not dance to their demanding tune. They are, however, very hardy in the north, even to -50°F/-45°C.

Foxglove (*Digitalis*): one of the more unfortunate gardening rules-of-thumb is that the taller a perennial is, the harder it is to grow. This is true of the biennial foxglove, which is lively, but very difficult to manage. Even if you get it to come up the next year, the flowerhead is often thin and disappointing. Plant nice, tall annual cleome instead.

Geum (*Avens chiloense*): just too unwilling to thrive. This short plant with its attractive leaves and red-orange flowers will take up space for years — never dying but never putting on much of a floral show either.

Gladiolus (*Gladiolus*): lovely for cutting, but must be staked, and must be lifted in the autumn and wintered indoors. Too much like work. It is also prone to minute insects known as thrips, which damage the leaves and flowers.

Hollyhock (*Althea rosea*): a tall biennial we would all like to grow because our grannies grew it. However, all too often hollyhocks succumb to rust, a disease which disfigures the leaves with ugly red-brown markings. It is difficult to eradicate this disease. It will reappear year after year. If you must have them, try the annual varieties (see Annuals, Chapter 6) which are said to resist rust.

Lupin (*Lupinus*): so lovely, but so persnickety about soil, sun, water, you name it.

Poppy (*Papaver orientale*): it is good-looking in spring, but horrible, dry and weedy looking all the rest of the year.

Pyrethrum, Painted daisy (*Pyrethrum roseum* or *Chrysanthemum coccineum*): an attractive plant, but just not as hardy as you might be led to believe. Might survive +14°F/-10°C.

Red-hot poker (*Tritoma, Kniphofia*): same problem as pyrethrum — it just cannot be trusted to survive a snow-bound winter.

Silver dollar plant, honesty, lunaria, money plant (*Lunaria annua*): a biennial grown for the shiny, silvery, papery disks popular in dried flower arrangements. The plant puts out a mediocre rosy-mauve flower spike in spring. After setting big round seed pods, it looks like a dead weed for the rest of the summer. You have to leave it there looking like a weed, because the silvery disks are busy ripening inside those nasty-looking casings. When the seed casings turn brown, pick them off to reveal the disk inside. You might want to grow this plant for two or three years, then pull it up completely when you have enough to use in dried arrangements.

Spiderwort (*Tradescantia*): a lovely indigo or rosy flower on a very ugly — messy and tangled — plant.

Trillium *(Trillium):* so pretty and welcome in spring, and so difficult to establish. *Never* dig up wild ones please, because they are becoming extinct in the wild and furthermore, their woodland environment is very difficult to duplicate in the home garden.

CHAPTER 8

The Shivering Rose — Cold Climate Cultivation

Who has not been seduced by pictures of vibrant, glossy-leaved, flower-laden rose bushes or the smothering mass of rose climbers on an English cottage or close-ups of rose flowers, with droplets of dew artistically placed on each velvety petal? Who has not then responded with a small acquisitive voice chanting, "I want, I want."

When we read that the queen of flowers was lovingly cultivated as along ago as 3,000 years before Christ, we want to get in on the act. Never mind the fact that growing roses is tricky, and really not for the Reluctant Gardener. Despite all warnings, we often head to the nearest nursery. The dark underside of rose-growing is far, far from our thoughts as we stroll, shivering with desire, through the rose section.

Roses are the stars of the garden, but you pay for the show they put on. They are expensive, high-maintenance plants, susceptible to bugs, diseases and severe winters. You will need the temperament of a gambler and the discipline of a soldier to enjoy growing roses in a cold climate.

Realizing that even Reluctant Gardeners are probably going to give roses a try, instructions follow for those difficult hybrid teas and their slightly more obliging cousins, the grandifloras and floribundas, and for other types of roses that are easier for the beginner. Luckily the local garden center makes selection relatively simple for you, since stock is usually limited to roses that will survive winters in your area, given reasonable care. Avoid mail-ordering roses until you better understand rose-growing.

What There Is to Choose From

A rose is not a rose is not a rose. Roses are divided into several types, such as hybrid tea and rugosa, each with a slightly different form and use. Each type is further subdivided. For example, the hybrid tea rose has hundreds and hundreds of different varieties, including the famous 'Peace,' 'Tropicana' and 'Mr. Lincoln.' The rugosa rose, another major group, is also made up of many varieties, such as 'Therese Bugnet' and 'Crimson Showers.' It makes the brain reel as you try to decide which one would thrive in your garden. As well, you have to choose between single, semi-double and double flowers. "Single" means a single-layer frill of petals around the center of the flower, like a wild rose. "Double" means what you see on a hybrid tea rose — dozens and dozens of petals which nearly obscure the flower's center. "Semi-double" is in between the two.

Let us begin our search by describing the different classifications of roses. To do so fully would fill a whole chapter all by itself, so we have compiled a short list of what you can reasonably expect to find at your neighborhood garden center.

HYBRID TEA is the most popular rose. This is the one people think of first whenever roses are mentioned, the one you get a dozen of on your birthday, the one Rudolph Valentino wanna–be's clench in their teeth. These elegant shrubs, first commercially cultivated around the turn of the century, carry long narrow buds which develop into delicate-looking, many-petaled flowers. Growing between 3-5 ft./1-1.5 m tall, some varieties produce flowers throughout the season. Their fragrance varies from the unscented to the wonderfully aromatic. Colors range from purest white to deepest red, in fact everything except blue and black. Breeders are constantly trying for a true blue, but so far they have produced only mauves and lavenders. Out of the hybridists' attempts to create black flowers have come some amazingly dark reds.

The 'Peace' rose is a vigorous favorite tea rose and has enhanced many gardens since World War II. Its flowers — fragrant, pale yellow tinged with pink — are offset by glossy green leaves. 'Chrysler Imperial' is another cold climate tea rose favorite, renowned for its strong, rich, spicy fragrance and its deep crimson color. The following widely-available hybrid teas are particularly noted for their fragrance: 'Mr. Lincoln' (dark red), 'Double Delight' (pink and red together on one blossom), 'Fragrant Cloud' (coral), 'Ivory Tower' (white), 'Prima Ballerina' (pink) and 'Sutter's Gold' (yellow).

FLORIBUNDAS are fairly disease-resistant, all-purpose roses. The plant itself looks like a hybrid tea shrub but has more flowers. These flowers, smaller than the classic tea rose blooms, mainly grow in clusters containing single, semi-double or double, often fragrant, flowers. They are less finicky than the hybrid teas, requiring less of everything: fertilizer, pruning and watering. These shrubs, which some gardeners use as they would perennials, grow between 2-4 ft./.5-1 m tall. They are striking when planted in large groups against a wall, in a bed bordering a driveway, or even as medium-depth plants in a flower border.

The group called polyantha is similar to the floribunda class.

GRANDIFLORAS are large shrubs, recommended as background plants. They look a lot like hybrid teas or floribundas, but grow as tall as 10 ft./3 m in protected sites. Rose enthusiasts, who care about these things, classify grandifloras as an intermediate type between its parents: the hybrid tea and the floribunda. Grandifloras, introduced into home gardens a little over thirty years ago, produce great clusters of delicately shaped, often double, flowers. Because the flowers are carried on long stems, they are suitable for cutting. Many varieties are fragrant. Grandifloras are disease-resistant, vigorous plants — their only negative feature is their vigorous growth which needs to be regularly controlled by pruning.

At the garden center you will often see hybrid teas, floribundas and grandifloras displayed together. The only way you can easily distinguish between them is by reading the little HT, FL or GR on the individual tags.

Still with us? Good. What we have described above are the most common *tender* roses. That means that their chances of surviving -4°F/-20°C winters are only so-so, although heavy-duty winter protection (described later in this chapter) will improve their chances.

The shrub roses described below are all hardy, which means they have a very good chance of coming through a -40°F/-40°C winter alive without protection.

SHRUB ROSES include shrub roses, rugosas, Explorers and climbers. Except for certain climbers, which are discussed below, these roses can be relied on to survive the worst winters. Many shrub roses have been cultivated for hundreds of years. Tough, disease-resistant, and low-maintenance, they make excellent hedges and screens. Pruning is minimal — just cut out the dead wood in the spring. The single or multi-petaled flowers are usually produced once in spring or early summer, although some varieties bloom throughout the season. After the flowers fade, many shrub roses develop colorful rose hips (the swollen base of the flower) which give life to the late fall garden.

One of the most popular groups of shrub roses grown in severe climate zones are the *Rosa rugosas*. Many people use the terms shrub and rugosa interchangeably. They are so hardy that winter protection is only needed in the coldest (-50°F/-45°C) areas, and so tough that they are favorite plantings on roads and freeways — they easily withstand winter salt spray from passing cars. Rugosas sport crinkly, dark green leaves and, in the autumn, bright red or orange-red hips. *Rosa rugosas* can reach 5-8 ft./1.5-2 m, but usually grow to only 3 ft./ 1 m. The single-petaled flowers (often fragrant) are produced once a season, usually in June, but some varieties have recurrent bloom. *Rosa rugosa* 'Thérèse Bugnet' and 'Hansa' are hardy and attractive.

A new group of rugosa roses has been developed in Canada which does not require winter protection. The group is called Explorer roses and is available through many commercial garden centers. These Explorer roses (named after early explorers of Canada) range in color, maintenance needs and growth patterns. 'Martin Frobisher,' for example, is a vigorous, disease-resistant shrub which carries clusters of fragrant pink flowers throughout the summer. It grows to 6 1/2 ft./2 m. 'Champlain' is a low-growing Explorer bearing velvety, deep red, single flowers.

'William Baffin' (pink flowers) and 'John Cabot' (medium red flowers) are Explorer roses classified as **climbers**. Unlike most climbing roses, they need no winter protection beyond tying their canes firmly to their trellis to prevent damage from forceful, drying winter winds. We have been growing various Explorer roses in the harsh Ottawa climate since 1985, and have had very good success with them. In addition to their winter hardiness, they decline the offer of potentially fatal diseases such as blackspot and mildew extended to them by their hybrid tea neighbors.

The classification *climbing* is almost a misnomer when applied to roses. They are not true climbers because their canes (branches) do not twine themselves cooperatively around a trellis. Each cane must be tied onto a support — a wall, pillar, pergola or trellis. Left untrained, a climbing rose could revert to a sprawling, untidy shrub. Canes usually grow between 8-15 ft./2.5-4.5 m. Flowers are borne in clusters, usually in early summer and sometimes again in August.

Many of us harbor a secret yearning for a rose-covered cottage, but bear in mind that most climbers require quite a bit of maintenance and much winter protection. We recommend that people living in areas experiencing -4°F/-20°C and colder plant only the Explorers if they want climbers. The non-Explorer varieties 'Blaze' and 'New Dawn' might be worth a try at such temperatures. Every autumn in colder areas the canes of non-Explorer climbers must be detached from their support, tied in a bundle, bent over to the ground and completely buried in earth. Far too much trouble for the Reluctant Gardener. Stick to Explorer climbers which can be left on their support all winter.

A note about planting and maintaining climbers: when fastening a cane to its trellis, try to run the cane as horizontal as possible. This promotes many more flowers than vertical-growing canes.

Attaching Climbers to Their Support

– growth is directed horizontally wherever possible
– tip of each cane is attached, plus one ot two other points along its length
– canes are attached only to the trellis, never to each other
– ties are soft, thick yarn, or strips of old sheets, or strips of nylon stocking. They are not
   tied too tightly — you should be able to slip the tip of your forefinger in easily.

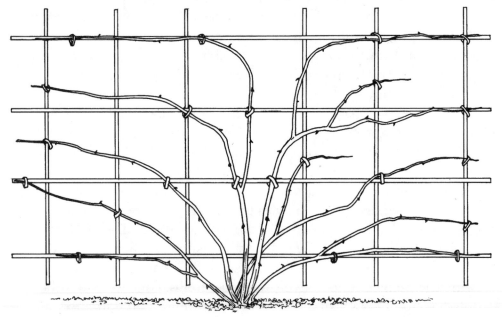

MINIATURE ROSES, which include representatives from all rose groups, are the latest fad in rose-growing circles. They usually grow less than 12 in./30 cm high, and thus are useful as ground cover, low border plants or as container-grown novelties. Miniatures need the same winter protection as hybrid teas, floribundas and grandifloras. Container-grown plants, however, must be sunk in the earth over winter so their roots are not killed by the freeze-thaw cycle. Miniatures are the only roses commonly grown in containers in cold-winter areas.

Be warned, miniature rose hybridists often have a tendency to use cutesy names. You may not want to admit to your garden visitors that you grow anything named 'Cuddles' or 'Little Buckaroo.'

We recommend that you not grow *tree roses*, which are actually three different kinds of roses grafted together to form one plant. A hardy rootstock is attached to a tall, skinny trunk (or standard) of another rose species, then topping this is a flowering, non-hardy variety from yet another rose. Tree roses must be dug up each autumn and the entire plant buried in a long, deep trench or it will not survive the winter. Unless you are dedicated to growing roses on top of sticks, tree roses are not worth the bother — and they cost a fortune.

Sometimes you will see a date (1943, 1982, 1751) on a rose label. This is the year that particular variety was introduced. The 'Peace' rose was introduced in 1942, for instance. If given the choice, you should buy roses introduced at least five years ago (ten is better). Plant breeding is big business, and new varieties are introduced every year, but only a few survive to be sold in succeeding years — just like car models. They fall by the wayside because of susceptibility to disease, general weakness, unwillingness to thrive, or simply because no one thinks they are attractive. So, just as sensible people never buy a car model during its first year of release, smart rose buyers will buy roses that have proven themselves by lasting a few years.

Deciding Where to Plant Your Roses

Before rushing out to the garden center, you should first decide how you want to use roses in your garden. For example, you might want to create a bed only for roses — a traditional, highly formal treatment. Rose beds are geometrically shaped, often rectangular, and isolated from the rest of the garden. Too stiff for you? Then why not mingle a few bushes into a mixed flower border. As well, larger specimens can be grown as shrubs, poked into a corner, or grown as a hedge. If space is tight, consider training a climbing rose up the side of your house or along a boundary fence.

Next choose the best site. Roses need at least six hours of sunlight a day, or they become spindly, fewer flowers are produced, and they become even more susceptible to rust and mildew. Roses are happier in sheltered positions, where strong winds will not shatter the blooms, nor dry out the plants. Sheltered roses also fare better in severe cold. Having said that, we must also say that they dislike broiling in the sun. So do not plant them in full sun in front of a brick or aluminum-sided wall.

Roses are a bit claustrophobic — they do not enjoy crowding in with their neighbors. Hybrid teas, grandifloras and floribundas should be planted a good 24-30 in./60-75 cm apart and the same distance out from any kind of wall or solid fence. Other roses should be planted far enough apart to ensure some air circulation when they are fully grown. Give them 6 in./15 cm of air between the tips of their branches and those of their nearest neighbor. The exception, of course, will be the planting of rose hedges. These shrubs will be planted a little closer together so that their tips intermingle. Rose hedges always, in consequence, have problems with diseases.

See what we mean about finicky?

The good news is that they will grow in almost any soil, as long as it is well drained. Roses are susceptible to root rot caused by constant sogginess around the roots. As well, locate your plantings well away from large trees or shrubs, as roses often lose the competition with other large plants for water and nutrients.

At the Garden Center

There are two ways to buy rose bushes: bare-rooted, and potted. Although bare-rooted plants are cheaper, potted (container-grown) roses are more dependable and easier to establish. Please note, however, do not attempt to plant roses in autumn — spring or early summer are the best planting times, because the plant then goes into winter with an extensive root system, which will greatly improve its chances of survival.

We recommend that you not buy bare-root stock (roses with little plastic bags full of soil around their roots also count as bare-root). They are often temptingly displayed in department stores and grocery stores as well as garden centers. The canes are usually coated with green wax to prevent the wood from drying out during their time in storage, a dormant period. These packages are not always properly stored, especially if sold in the hot, dry conditions of a retail store. Often the stems have begun to leaf out — that is, sprout a lot of pale shoots. You might think "oh, goody, it's healthy and growing," when in fact this premature growth takes the moisture from the plant, weakening it badly and making the rose difficult to establish. If these packages feel light, it is a sure sign that both rose and packing material have dried up. All in all, far too risky for the Reluctant Gardener.

The better buy is potted roses, even though they are more expensive and fewer varieties can be found than the bare-rooted ones. What you pay extra for is the well-established root system that has been actively growing in the soil-filled pot. The mature root system means greater ease of planting and less transplant shock.

When you are suddenly knee-deep in leafy little rose bushes growing in lumpy brown *papier-mâché* pots or black plastic pots, do not panic. Remember you have already decided which roses are right for your

Buying a Potted Rose

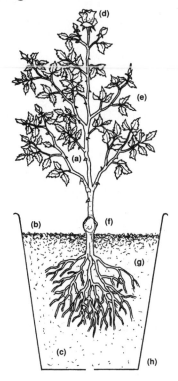

a) no twiggy growth in center; canes do not cross or touch; has the right number of canes for its type

b) no weeds

c) pot is heavy because soil is moist

d) one blossom is open, so you know exactly what you are getting

e) lots of nice, unmarred green leaves

f) graft union is usually exposed, but not always. Will wind up 2" (5cm) below ground when planted

g) you know there are lots of roots because the plant is steady and firm in the pot when you jiggle it

h) always remove the pot before planting — yes, even a peat pot

garden. Let us suppose you want one hardy climber and three hybrid teas. Now you have to decide on the varieties.

Flower color is probably your first consideration. Knowing this, most nurseries sometimes hang a little tag on each rose. On the tag is a color photograph of the blossom. Be aware that this photograph was reproduced very cheaply, and probably has been damaged by rain and sun, so it may bear little resemblance to the rose's actual hue. Occasionally all the color indication the customer gets is a plastic streamer — bright red, yellow or pink — attached to the stem of the rose bush. Never forget that plants are sometimes mislabeled even at the fanciest nurseries. This brings us to another advantage of buying roses in pots: they are often in bloom, so you can see exactly what you are buying.

You can sniff it, too. Fragrance is another important consideration in buying a rose. The perfumes range from fruity to spicy, from light to heavy, but consider that one person's delight is another person's olfactory horror. One of your authors sniffs heliotrope and smells cherry pie. The other sniffs the very same plant and smells licorice.

Many books will tell you to buy plants without buds or blossoms on the excellent principle that non-blossoming plants will transplant easier. This is true, but we believe that this is far outweighed by the advantage of getting exactly the flower you want. Flowers are, after all, the focus of the garden.

All right. You are doing very well here in the nursery. You have looked and sniffed your way into deciding on a 'John Cabot' (Explorer) climber, and three hybrid teas: a white, highly scented 'Ivory Tower,' a fragrant, pale-pink 'Sweet Afton,' and a deep pink 'Elizabeth Taylor' — not much scent but the blossoms are gorgeous.

How do you tell which plant is the healthiest? First check that the plant has three or four thick canes which do not cross or touch each other — a growth pattern which can cause health problems later on. The shrub should not have funny-colored leaves, deadwood or large amounts of twiggy growth. Any of these could indicate that it has been in the container for longer than a year. The plant could be pot-bound, suffering from deficiencies caused by a tangled, overgrown root system, struggling in an insufficient amount of soil. This all adds up to a weakened, poorly fed plant. After looking, feel the plant — give it a gentle wiggle. If it moves within the pot, it has been newly planted and has not developed a proper root system — you do not buy it (also see the plant buying guide in Chapter 5).

Back Home Again

The Reluctant Gardener exerts some willpower and does not purchase anything until the weather is warm enough to plant out — about the second or third week of May in cold-winter areas. Until you plant them out, set the bushes in dappled shade, sheltered from wind and extreme heat. Watch them to make sure that the pot soil does not get dry. If you must buy before warm weather, put your potted roses outdoors whenever

Planting Roses

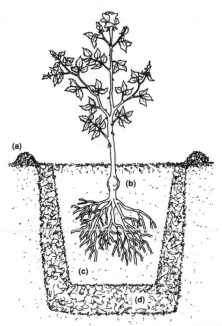

a) wall of moat rings new planting

b) graft union is 2″ (5 cm) below surface, measuring from top of graft's bulge

c) pot soil

d) new soil, including manure and compost

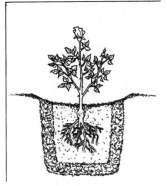

Alternate method: saucer-like depression, lower than surrounding soil level, to hold water.

the temperature is sure to stay three or four degrees above freezing, and indoors (the garage is usually fine) when it is not. When in doubt about the temperature, keep them inside.

Putting the Bush into the Ground

For some enthusiasts, rose growing is a religion with specified rites and practices. With the purchase of your first rose bush, you enter a cult whose initiation is the rite of planting, followed by the doctrines of maintenance. The Reluctant Gardener, however, need not feel faint upon hearing such a statement, because the rose is a more forgiving deity than is generally supposed.

Anyway, you have bought your rose and now it is time to commit yourself to it. First communion, if you like. You might feel anxious as you glance down at the following instructions. Fear not. We have described each step of planting and maintenance in minute detail because we want you to feel confident. Ready? Good. Here we go.

Water the potted rose thoroughly until the water runs out of the drain holes in the bottom. Plant on an overcast day rather than on a hot sunny one, but do not get too sweaty about this. Rosarians (rose enthusiasts, in common parlance), who do not agree on every detail, do agree that the soil that is to receive the rose should be well prepared. You may come across all sorts of intimidating instructions about five parts of this to four parts of that. These instructions are fine for fanatical gardeners, but you can give your roses a perfectly good start in life if you simply mix in *plenty of compost or well-rotted manure.* Lots and lots. It is impossible to add too much. Dig it in to a depth of 18 in./45 cm.

If you have clay soil, this may prove strenuous. In fact, those cursed with clay soil might want to reconsider their decision to grow roses — these shrubs really prefer an organically rich, well-drained soil. Those who have clay soil but are bound and determined to grow roses should dig out the entire bed, to a depth of 24 in./60 cm. Then these determined gardeners should fill it in with good new soil. A mixture of half topsoil and half compost or well rotted manure is best.

Once the soil is prepared, it is time to dig the holes for your plants. Hybrid teas, grandifloras and floribundas should be planted between 24-30 in./60-75 cm apart. The distance is measured from the trunk of one rose to the trunk of the next, or from the middle of one hole to the middle of the next. Shrub roses, depending if they are vigorous growers or not (the tag should tell you how wide the plant is likely to grow), should be planted between 3-6 ft./1-2 m apart. Climbers and ramblers do best if they have 5-8 ft./1.5-2.5 m between them. Miniature roses are safely planted about 10 in./25 cm apart.

Take your potted rose and measure the vertical height from the bottom of the pot to 2 in./5 cm above the lumpy bulge of the trunk, just below where the canes begin. That's how deep to dig your hole. Then measure the diameter of the pot. Add about 3-4 in./8-10 cm all around, and *voilà*, you have the width of the hole. Next dig the hole and fill it with water.

While the water is draining away, remove the rose from its pot. Do not do this until now. Exposing the bare rootball to sunlight will burn (and therefore kill) all the teeny root hairs on the outside surface. Also, do not take the advice of those who say you can plant a container-grown rose without removing its brown peat pot. It takes ages for the fiber pots to break down, and while they are intact they restrict root development. So, take your hand clippers, cut down the side of the pot as far as you can, then tear off the rest. Infuriating work, but necessary. Mangle the rootball as little as possible — remember those root hairs — but do not be afraid of it.

Put the root ball in the hole — remember to *never* hold *any* plant by its stem — by holding the rootball with both hands. Fill in a little soil (or, better yet, compost or well-rotted manure) and firm it, add a little more soil and firm, a couple of inches at a time, until the hole is full. The lump of the graft union will be 2 in./5 cm below the soil. This will greatly improve the rose's chance of surviving the winter. Once in awhile, you might buy a potted rose with the graft already covered. Plant such a rose so that the existing soil level is maintained.

Some books advise pruning the canes back heavily at this point, and to mound soil around the trunk of the newly planted rose — all to promote the development of a root system and protect new growth. This is not necessary for container-grown roses because vigorous growth is already underway. It is useful, however, to create a moat of soil around the plant, using the outer edge of the hole as your guide. The moat holds the water in, and ensures a proper root soaking while the plant establishes itself. Try not to get the leaves wet — wet leaves promote disease. Unless it has been very rainy, you will want to water a newly-planted rose every day for the next week.

Those with very firm willpower will now, with their fingernails, nip off all the buds and flowers (you can impress your friends by referring to this as disbudding) so the plant will direct its energy into producing roots. The other 99% of us will guiltily (but enormously) enjoy those first blossoms, and the plant will not keel over and die because it was not disbudded.

Roses prefer to be left in the same place year after year, but if you must transplant an established rose, be sure to thoroughly soak the soil around the bush the night before you intend to dig it up. This operation is best done in spring. For ease of handling, prune large bushes back by nearly a half. This also reduces the amount of energy the bush needs to feed itself — energy which now will be redirected into the root system. The next day dig the plant up with as much soil around it as possible to minimize root disturbance. Plant as a new rose — alternately filling the hole with soil and water, tamping firmly as you go. Keep it well watered until new growth begins.

Maintenance

On-going rose care consists of five things: watering, feeding, pruning, protection from bugs and diseases, and winter protection. If you are conscientious, your rose will develop into a healthy plant, whose strong, vigorous growth will bear more flowers and will protect it from winter and pest damage. The sportier types among you, who believe in "no pain, no gain," will probably enjoy the rigors of rose maintenance.

Watering Roses

Roses need a lot of water, but their roots cannot tolerate standing in water for long periods. It is difficult to give a precise watering schedule, since the amount of water required depends on the variables of soil type, temperature and weather.

When watering, be sure the soil absorbs the moisture deeply. Never water your roses just a little each day. Shallow watering encourages roots to form just below the soil surface, where they are liable to burn up and die on hot, sunny days. Also, surface roots are inadequate anchors in windy weather.

To consistently direct water to the roots, some gardeners never destroy the encircling wall of earth built when the roses were first planted. Others use soaker hoses or sprinklers with a rain gauge to estimate how much water has penetrated. If you are using an overhead sprinkler, water in the morning so that the leaves can dry off before evening.

You will, with time, develop a sense of when to water and how much. Remember, the type of soil you have will determine your watering schedule: sandy soils will absorb plenty of water, clay soils not so much. A good rule of thumb is to keep the soil as moist as a wrung-out sponge.

Feeding Roses

Like babies, roses want to be fed on a regular schedule, however rose growers disagree on the amount and frequency of fertilizing. Here is our advice: most garden centers sell fertilizers mixed especially for roses, but we think you will do fine with the same 10-10-10 or 15-30-15 all-purpose fertilizer, either granular or water soluble, that you use on the rest of your garden. Follow the directions for quantity on the package, but lean to the stingy side. (overfertilizing does as much harm as under, both to the plant and to the environment).

How often to fertilize roses? The Reluctant Gardener will do fine to fertilize the roses about once every three or four weeks. If you have sandy soil, try for every three weeks. If your soil is heavy or mostly clay, try for every four weeks.

If you wanted to be very virtuous about fertilizing, you could apply a half-strength application every two weeks — frequent light feedings are better than infrequent heavy feedings. In cold weather areas (most of Canada and the northern U.S.) it is best to stop feeding six weeks before frost is anticipated. Late feeding promotes new growth, which will not withstand winter temperatures.

Spreading compost or well-rotted manure ankle-deep over your rose beds every spring and autumn counts as both fertilizing and soil improvement. Your roses will thank you with stunning floral displays. Also, there is increasing evidence that a layer of compost over the soil surface helps keep diseases at bay.

 ————————————————————————

BRINGING CUT ROSES INDOORS — One of the rewards of rose growing is bringing the blooms indoors. Imagine the compliments you will receive from dinner guests oohing and aahing over your rose centerpiece. When you demurely say, "Why, thank you, I grew them myself," we guarantee more compliments will immediately follow.

To insure the best bouquets, cut roses in early morning or late afternoon when the flower's food supply is high. Choose flowers that have not opened completely. Sometimes you will be told to cut a flower when the tightly-furled but is just barely showing color, bud we have found that such buds frequently refuse to open. Infuriating.

Roses wilt easily, so carry a water-filled container with you as you cut. Cut each flower stem at the favoured 45° angle, just above a five-leaflet leaf. This is where new growth sprouts. During the first few years of a rose bush's life, do not cut long stems: the plant needs that extra foliage to feed itself. Also, when cutting late-season roses for the house, cut them with short rather than long stems. This way new growth, that will be too soft to survive the winter, will not be stimulated to grow. Cutting for the house counts as pruning, remember.

Back indoors: if you have cut a green stem, give it a fast, clean, new cut about 1/2 in./1 cm above the old cut. Making the cut underwater prolongs the flower's vase-life. If the rose stem is brown and woody, use a traditional English method — give the cut end a sharp whack with a hammer, which has the added benefit of being good for your frustrations. Remove all thorns and leaves which will be below water level — this prevents rot.

As you work, immediately put each rose in a container of warm water, so that the rose is never out of water for more than a few seconds. Place the entire container in the refrigerator or a cool place for a couple of hours — this will completely revive the flowers and straighten any bent necks.

Some florists say that a dash of a clear soft drink will prolong the flower's life. This seems to be due to the sugar content, since diet drinks do not work. Other people put a teaspoon of sugar in the vase for the same reason. Copper pennies in the vase water are also said to prolong cut flower life.

If you want to fiddle a little more with the arrangement after taking it out of the refrigerator, trim another half inch off the stems. Some people slit the end of the stem a quarter inch.

Display the finished bouquet in a cool place, away from the sun to promote a longer vase life. Keep enough fresh water, up to 2/3 the length of the flower stems, in the vase. Continue to cut the stems and change the water — every day, if you are up to it — and your flowers will last longer.

Pruning Roses

Pruning is an annual maintenance chore. Do not, however, prune until after the threat of spring frost is over. When properly done, it promotes vigorous growth, which in turn stimulates a goodly amount of bloom. You will need a sharp pair of pruning shears, and perhaps a small saw or long-handled loppers. We prefer loppers, which do not rock the plant, and therefore the root system, back and forth so much. This rocking can rip off feeder roots. Beware: roses

Pruning Roses

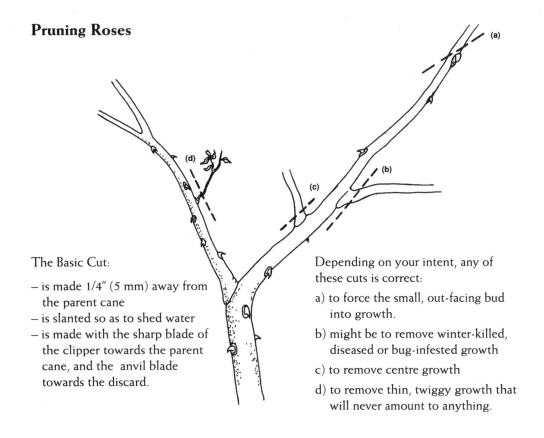

The Basic Cut:

– is made 1/4" (5 mm) away from the parent cane
– is slanted so as to shed water
– is made with the sharp blade of the clipper towards the parent cane, and the anvil blade towards the discard.

Depending on your intent, any of these cuts is correct:

a) to force the small, out-facing bud into growth.

b) might be to remove winter-killed, diseased or bug-infested growth

c) to remove centre growth

d) to remove thin, twiggy growth that will never amount to anything.

fight back when being tied up or pruned. Wear tough canvas gloves and tight woven fabrics (denim is ideal) when handling these thorny treasures.

Actually, most of us living in harsh winter climates will not have to think much about pruning — winter conditions often make our pruning decisions for us. We usually have the unambiguous choice of cutting out the winter-killed wood. This dead wood is easy to spot — it is usually brown and often shriveled. Cut these canes down to the outermost, healthy bud. If you cannot tell where exactly the dead stuff ends, cut off an inch of branch at a time, working from the tip down toward the trunk. When the wood inside is white instead of nasty brown, you have hit good wood. Go a little farther, so that your last cut is made just a little above a bud, preferably one that faces outward.

Do some additional pruning at the same time: trim any canes which cross one another, or rub together. The point where they rub together can become diseased or a doorway for insects to enter. Then cut off any weak, spindly canes, especially the ones in the center of the bush. *Clean out the center* is a cardinal rule when pruning anything. This opens up the bush, giving it a better form and letting in light and air, which in turn discourages bugs and diseases.

When pruning a cane, always cut at a 45° angle 1/4 in./.5 cm above an outward-facing bud. The angle of the cut should slope away from the bud to ensure better healing as water drains away from the bud. For sprawling varieties, you may want to prune some of the canes down to a few *inward-facing* buds to control size. Very virtuous gardeners will daub a wound sealer (or pruning paint) on the cut surface to reduce moisture loss and repel insect borers.

You should also remove all suckers, i.e., twigs which originate on the rootstock below the bud union, that is, graft union. Suckers are easy to identify because of their distinctive foliage. The seven-leaflet leaves are often dull green, heavily toothed, and borne on stems covered with a multitude of thin thorns. The suckers sprout from below the stubby lump low down on the rose trunk. Sometimes they grow sideways underground, emerging a foot or two away. Dig down to where they originate on the stem and clip them off. If clipped at soil level, suckers will continue to sprout. Planting the bush with the join exposed will not eliminate the sucker problem, they will still appear. For more information on grafts, see Chapter 15, Old Savvy.

All right, those were general pruning rules. Here are the details for each rose group:

Prune each *hybrid tea* cane so it has four or five buds along its length — if that many have survived the winter. Limit the number of canes to four strong branches. Ideally, the pruned shape should be open and vase shaped.

Floribundas are usually low growing with a tendency to produce lots of twigs growing towards the center. Prune the canes until six to eight remain, keeping the interior open.

Grandifloras are pruned like hybrid teas, but can often support up to eight canes.

Prune young *shrub (rugosa) roses* to the shape you desire. These bushes are much hardier, so less winter kill usually occurs. Flowers are often produced on last year's wood, so do not trim until flowering is over. A good rule of thumb for any flowering, woody plant is to prune when it has finished flowering for the year.

Some *climbers* bloom on the current season's wood, some on old wood, so prune after they have flowered just to be safe. First-year growth, easy to identify, is a lighter green than the older stems. Thin out enough of the old canes to prevent the shrub from becoming too thick. In the autumn it is sometimes necessary to cut back overly long canes which could be damaged by strong winds. Climbers can take two good seasons to become established, so pruning is not recommended during this time except to remove dead wood in spring.

Miniatures are pruned as you would the larger varieties. You want to create a pleasing bushy form.

Insects and Diseases

The most prevalent rose pests are aphids — minute, sap-sucking insects. They usually cluster on young growth, flower buds and under leaves. A sure sign of aphids is the sticky substance, called honeydew, that they leave behind. As well, affected parts of the plant become stunted or deformed. You can easily knock aphids off the plant with a stiff stream of water, or you can spray them with a non-detergent soap and water solution — one part soap to forty parts water.

Various beetles (rose chafers, Japanese beetles) eat all parts of the rose plant. Their larvae gnaw away at the roots. Pick the beetles off by hand and drop them into a mixture of soap and water, squash them, or drop them into a bucket of hot tap water, then dump on the compost heap. Be sure they are dead, before throwing them into the compost. As well, caterpillars, slugs, midges, spider mites, thrips and leafhoppers either eat holes in the leaves and flowers or suck the sap out of the plant. Try hand picking (with gloves on for the squeamish types) or spraying with a soap solution.

Insects are the visible enemy. However, roses are also plagued by the invisible-to-the-naked-eye world of plant diseases: fungi, bacteria and viruses. Many of these diseases have unpronounceable seven syllable Latin names known only to plant pathologists. The average rose grower will usually only meet the more common diseases such as mildew and black spot.

Mildew (a white powdery spore mass on leaves, shoots and buds) is promoted by moist, warm weather and poor air circulation, and spread by wind — remember how we told you to plant bushes apart from each other? Treat mildew with an organic fungicidal spray, being sure to zap it *the moment you see it*. Keep spraying faithfully every day until it is gone, because if mildew gets away from you, you are stuck with it for the rest of the summer. It seldom kills a plant, but it is very disfiguring. Also contagious.

Blackspot, another common rose disease, is a fungus spread by rain or by watering. You will recognize this disease when you see characteristic circular black spots with a fringed margin form on the leaves. Eventually the leaf turns yellow and drops off. You can try an organic fungicidal spray, but the best deterrent is good sanitation — trim off and dispose of dead or diseased foliage the moment you see it. Never leave these materials lying around near the plants all winter, it only leads to trouble later on. Diseased, or even suspect, plant material should never be composted — put it in the garbage and let the garbage man take it away.

Compost tea is worth a try against fungal diseases. Soak a shovelful of compost in a bucket of water for a week, strain and spray infected plants. When in doubt about pests, phone the garden center for help, but be aware that they usually recommend nasty chemical sprays. It is best to cut off the infected parts, rather than resort to environmentally questionable products. Mixing ground-up tomato leaves, 5 pints/about 2.5 L of water and 1 tbl/15 mL cornstarch, according to Louise Riotte in *Secrets of Companion Planting for Successful Gardening*, makes an effective spray against black spot.

If you are interested in organic methods of insect and disease prevention, you might want to experiment with companion planting. In theory, planting parsley, onions and geraniums around your roses repels a number of insect pests. Some rose growers swear that garlic interplanted among the roses enhances their perfume.

Rose hybridists have not only concentrated on developing the clearest yellow or the spiciest smelling rose, they have also produced a number of disease-resistant roses. To learn the names of resistant varieties, borrow some rose books from the library. Often the most commonly sold roses, which repeat year after year at your garden center, have some disease resistance bred into them.

Winter's Coming

We are sure that even Reluctant Gardeners do not want to treat their rose bushes as expensive, troublesome annuals. So, to insure that you will not be digging up dead roses next spring, give them proper winter protection. If your roses have been cared for all summer and into early fall, they will overwinter with greater ease.

Winter injury often occurs during spells of freezing and thawing. Warm weather in, say, January, can initiate new growth. When temperatures drop again, as they surely will, that new growth will die. This process weakens the plant enormously. Winter plant protection consists of insulating — just like a house — against these conditions. In this case, you want to keep the plant frozen solid, therefore dormant, all winter long. Snow is good insulation, but an adequate cover cannot always be counted upon, so you will have to give Mother Nature a hand.

The first step for winter protection of *hybrid teas, floribundas* and *grandifloras* is to mound new, clean, dry soil or peat moss around the plants to a height of at least 10-12 in./25-30 cm — this is winter mulching. Remove any remaining summer mulch and any leaves still clinging to the plant, or lying on the ground, before applying this new material. Some people trim the canes down to the top of the heap of soil, some people leave them. Your choice.

Apply the peat moss or soil after the first really hard frost, +23°F/-5°C or worse, or after the ground freezes. Make sure the mulch is spread sideways to a radius of about 18 in./45 cm to insulate the full root spread. A layer of straw can be added at this point, if you like. Cover the resulting mound with burlap to stop it blowing away. Weight the burlap down with rocks or bits of firewood to keep *it* from blowing away. *Never* use plastic sheeting for winter protection on any plants — it cooks them on sunny winter days.

You can add evergreen boughs to the above protection, if you can find such material. You can also buy rose covers — they look rather like Styrofoam picnic coolers — which fit over the rose bushes. These covers are cute, but we find them rather skimpy. You may need to prune the plant down to fit it in. These covers can be filled with additional insulating materials such as leaves, straw or other mulch. Be cautious when using leaves for mulch or protection: if they get wet at any time they will pack down and harbor amazing quantities of bugs and diseases. We avoid using leaves for anything other than compost.

Rugosa shrub roses and all the *Explorer roses* are very hardy, most will need protection only in the far north (-50°F/-45°C). In other areas, simply leave the roses alone except for the climbers. Tie the long canes firmly to the trellis to prevent them from thrashing around and breaking in strong winter winds.

Winter Protection for Tender Roses in Cold Winter Areas

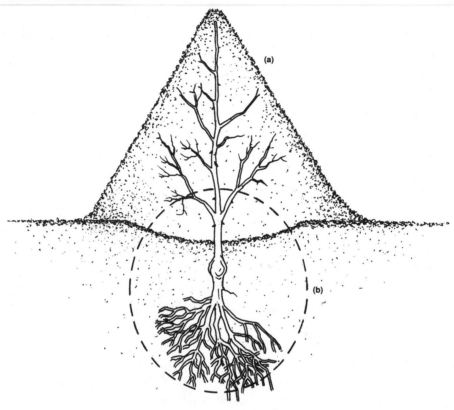

a) pyramid of clean soil or peat moss, about knee height

b) this is the area you are most interested in protecting. If all the branches die but this area survives, the plant will survive. If this area dies, you are out of business.

Non-Explorer *climbing roses* present huge problems. You must untie the canes from their supports, then tie them together and bend them gently to the ground — and good luck to you not to snap half of them off. You then secure this bundle to the earth by pounding long stakes into the ground on either side, at an angle so they cross above the bundle. Now cover the entire plant with a layer of peat, soil or straw, then with burlap. See why we recommend only the Explorer climbers?

Miniatures can simply be covered with peat or soil and burlap.

In the spring, when it comes time to undo all this protection, go slowly. If you have had warm weather, and the snow is pretty much gone, clear away some of the mulch. Has new growth started at the base of the plant? If so, you will want light and air to get at it. However, watch it carefully and push that mulch back in place if below-freezing temperatures threaten. The cleared-away mulch (peat or soil) can be spread over the bed — do not dig it in at the base of the rose bush, or you might harm the roots. A useful rule-of-thumb is that the removal of winter protection can begin when the native trees begin to leaf out.

Do Not Despair

Well, now you have the bare essentials of rose growing in northern climates. We realize your head may be spinning a little by now if this is your first introduction to rose growing. Do not lose heart — remember you can try walking before flying. Start with some nice tough rugosas or a couple of indestructible Explorer roses. Then, after successfully growing these hardy shrubs, you can soar into the realm of royalty, the hybrid teas, floribundas and grandifloras . . . 'Dream Time,' 'Garden Party,' 'Casanova,' 'Red Mercedes' . . . yum.

CHAPTER 9

Hedging Your Bets: Trees and Shrubs

Lots of emotion is wrapped up into a tree or even a shrub — those stalwart, solid members of the garden. Trees and shrubs usually have history and memories attached to them. Remember the first tree you ever climbed? Did you hide behind a favorite shrub when the dishes needed to be dried? Call us sentimental, call us environmental, or call us traditional, but we like to see shrubs or trees or both in the home garden.

Granted, planting a tree or a large shrub does give one pause. Annuals and perennials seem absolutely flighty compared to these solid garden elements. We can have a brief, intense affair with a new variety of delphinium, move it at whim, discard it without guilt if it does not please. However, planting a tree or shrub is not a one-night stand. It is better to have honorable, long-term intentions toward trees and shrubs, because you will wake up every morning for years and there it will be — looming over your landscape.

But we do not want to scare you away from what could become a meaningful relationship. We just want you to be careful about what you plant and where you plant it.

 ———————————————

TREES AND THE ENVIRONMENT — Planting a tree or shrub demonstrates a gardener's commitment to the health of the environment. These large, woody ornamentals are immensely important in soil stabilization and erosion control. Their spreading root systems hold water in the soil, and act as pumps, raising ground water levels. They are

air "conditioners" in that, like all plants, their leaves give off oxygen and "breath in"
carbon dioxide. Human respiration is just the opposite, so obviously we were made for
each other. They also remove some impurities from the air, cool the air, and send water
back into the cycle of evaporation and condensation. Along with grass and other plants,
they reduce the level of reflected city heat by throwing shade out over steel, concrete and
asphalt, which sponge up heat and throw it back into the air. Tree-shaded houses,
noticeably cooler than unshaded ones, need less mechanical air conditioning. As well,
trees and shrubs beautify residential and public properties, softening a harsh streetscape
of concrete and steel while giving an air of permanence to a transitory scene.

Uses on the Home Landscape

Trees and shrubs are versatile, fit into almost any design and can be used for many purposes. Trees are usually divided into deciduous (those that drop their leaves in the fall), and coniferous or evergreen (those that keep their leaves all year round).

Perhaps a living screen is just the thing to shelter your house from a busy street. A row of densely-growing shrubs would keep the traffic from view. Does a corner of your backyard patio need shade? — plant a tree. Perhaps your yard suffers from exposure to wind — plant a windbreak of trees or shrubs. An evergreen windbreak between your house and the prevailing winds, planted on the south or west side of the house, can measurably reduce winter heating bills. In the summer, a shady tree blocks much of the sun reducing heat build-up in the house.

Is your house foundation unattractive? Hide it with foundation plantings — trees, shrubs, vines, flowers. Foundation plantings, useful design elements, unite garden to house. Maybe your property is problem-free and you want to plant a tree or shrub just for ornament. Whatever the reason, the Reluctant Gardener can usually find a tree or shrub to suit each purpose. Our YES! list at the end of the chapter will help you make your choice.

No matter how you decide to use your trees and shrubs, there are a few considerations to bear in mind. Firstly, it is wise to check with your municipal government for a list of trees prohibited on city property. For example, in Ottawa, where we live, a homeowner is not allowed to plant poplar, willow, Manitoba maple or silver maple trees on the city-owned portion of the property for a variety of reasons (too brittle, too tall, invasive roots). Check your official lot boundaries, too — you may be surprised to see how much of your front yard belongs to the city.

Next consider the size of your lot. If your front yard is the proverbial postage stamp, you may want to rule out trees or large shrubs in favor of planters, lawn or a small flowerbed. The size of your house will help to determine your tree choice. Is it a bungalow or a three-storied mansion? Obviously a towering oak would be out of scale planted in front of a one-storey bungalow. Also consider your neighbors and how your shrub or tree placement might affect them. For example, will the mature tree or shrub spread to overshadow a neighbor's vegetable garden, will its roots draw away nutrients from neighbor's beloved rose bed, or will a fruit tree drop things into their pool? In the interest of peace and harmony, why not discuss major plantings with your neighbors?

If you plant a tree near your neighbor's property, you can be held legally responsible for any damage done by encroaching roots and overhanging branches. Imagine the uproar if one of your tree branches fell on their car. Trees planted too close to houses can crack foundations by the action of their roots. Some maple tree roots have been known to raise sidewalks. You can usually estimate that a tree's roots will spread to a distance equal to the tree's mature height, and sometimes farther.

Placement depends greatly on the mature height and spread of the tree or shrub. Look these statistics up before you buy — remember a tree will be the dominant horticultural element on your landscape. You must project into the future — do not practice denial in your horticultural life. The spindly specimen you find in a nursery is only a pale reflection of what its mature size will be. Do remember that the final height of a shrub or tree will also depend on the soil, temperature and rain in the location where it is planted. All these factors, too much or too little, can affect the height, spread, growth rate and life span of a shrub or tree.

Give some thought as well to the appearance of the tree or shrub. Do you like a multi-stemmed or single trunk plant? Is the bark attractive? Does the foliage color clash with your house color? Do you want flowers or fruit? If the tree or shrub has any unusual beauty of form, foliage or flowers, you might want to plant it as a specimen planting — that is, a tree or shrub that is placed well away from other plants, usually in the middle of the lawn. (Fruit-bearing trees and shrubs sometimes mean extra work raking up rotting fruit before it attracts wasps, raccoons and other pesky critters. And some fruiting varieties can become pest-ridden if not sprayed regularly.)

If you think you want to plant evergreens, ask yourself if their formality and denseness is right for your garden. Some evergreens, such as spruce, form dense growth down to ground level unless their bottom branches are cut off — you cannot walk under it, sit under it or see through it. Evergreens do have interesting outlines and form effective backgrounds for deciduous shrubs and perennial borders. Some gardeners enjoy the stark picture evergreens make against the snow. They are, however, best used sparingly on small city lots.

Decide also it you want a tree that casts a dense shade or a light shade. Maples, for example, cast a heavy shade, which can present problems if you want to grow grass underneath. It may be better to plant a small-leaved tree, such as honey locust, which casts a lighter shade. Shrubs, of course, grow low to the ground. Some, however, are higher branching than others, such as the purple-leaf sand cherry. To avoid ugly, bare, or weed-choked earth, plant a shade-loving ground cover such as ajuga or vinca under high-branching shrubs.

Think of the future. Plan replacement trees. If an existing, mature tree is beginning to look old and creaky, it is time to think about what-and-where to replace it. Plant the new tree then, so that when your old friend has to be cut down, a replacement is there to reduce the trauma of its loss.

Do realize that trees and shrubs are often planted too close to a house wall, their branches are jammed against the house. They struggle to survive in the hot, dry soil and poor air circulation usually present right next to house walls. These badly planted specimens look pathetic as they huddle unnaturally next to the house. They can also make house painting and repair a nightmare. To prevent damage to house and plant, constant pruning will be necessary. This nuisance can be avoided by planting shrubs and trees about one-third to one-half the diameter of the mature spread away from walls and fences. During the first couple of years, the immature specimens look a bit scrawny and forlorn, but they will soon spread and hold their own on the landscape.

Hedge planting also presents a number of decisions. First you must decide whether you want an evergreen or deciduous hedge. Evergreen hedges remain green all winter, a plus on a bleak, snowy landscape, but they are more easily damaged by ice and heavy snowfall than a deciduous hedge. After this decision, you then have to choose among the three styles of hedges: the formal, semi-formal and informal. Formal and semi-

Placing Shrubs Near Walls

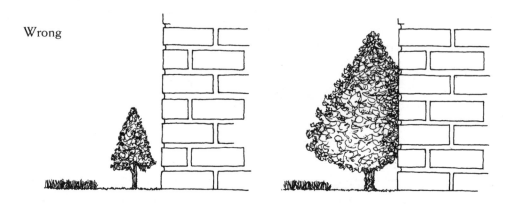

Wrong

Too-close placement looks fine when your shrub is still a baby, but when it grows up, half its branches will be crammed up against the wall. This provides a happy home for bugs and diseases.

Right

Correct placement looks silly when your shrub is small, but when it is bigger there will be lots of room for air circulation in behind. This discourages bugs and diseases.

formal hedges require at least one annual pruning. If fussing around shrubs is your thing, sharpen your pruning shears, and go for it. Formal hedges are stiff and geometric, and need an intense amount of pruning to retain their shape. The semi-formal hedge is occasionally pruned. The informal hedge, recommended for the Reluctant Gardener, needs only sporadic, maintenance pruning. These shrubs are allowed to assume a natural unclipped shape, which can be quite attractive, especially when flowering varieties are used. Evergreen hedges can be grown this way as well. The informal-style hedge, however, needs more space than the rigidly clipped, formal one.

After deciding what style of hedge suits your personality, decide how tall your hedge should grow. Remember that a shrub that can grow to 8 ft./ 2.4 m can be kept to, say, 6 ft./2 m by pruning. A larger lot is more comfortable-looking bordered by a tall hedge than a smaller lot would be. A hedge grown for privacy should reach a height of at least 60-80 in./150-200 cm. Smaller lots will not feel as closed in if the foliage color of the hedge is dark or mid-green. Brighter colors, such as golds, grays or purples, can make a small lot feel claustrophobic, but if you really like the idea of a colored-foliage hedge, plant low growers, or just clip away at the higher growers. We are charmed by the idea of a "tapestry hedge," which is a hedge composed of several (or many) different shrubs chosen for their foliage color.

How to Buy

Once you decide where and what to plant, you are ready to select your plants at the garden center. First of all, check that the chosen tree or shrub is not damaged — no broken branches, discolored leaves or gashes in the bark. Make sure the roots are wrapped either in burlap or plastic, or in a pot, and that they are well watered. The Reluctant Gardener is wise to buy container-grown shrubs, even though they are more expensive.

Young trees can be sold bare rooted or, more often, with their roots surrounded by soil and wrapped in burlap. We do not recommended buying bare-rooted trees — the burlap-wrapped ones are more reliable. Soil is heavy, however, and the larger the tree, the heavier and larger the rootball. A tree over 10 ft./3 m high is very heavy — you probably will not be able to lift it. This adds to the expense, for you will need to have it delivered by the nursery. If the rootball is over 3 ft./1 m in diameter, you might consider the services of a professional who has heavy-duty tree-planting equipment. A tree whose trunk is so skinny and scrawny that it must be supported by a tall stake has been poorly grown and is a bad investment.

Trees are quite expensive, so if you are not too fussy about tree choice and placement, take advantage of municipal street tree-planting programs which provide trees to homeowners for free or at a reduced price. Homeowners are given a choice of trees, and the tree is planted on the city-owned portion of your lawn. This means the front, near the curb — but the crew will let you specify left, right or center. It is a program well worth supporting and promotes the greening of your neighborhood.

When buying material for a hedge, smaller plants, even though we are impatient for results, are preferable to larger ones. Smaller plants establish themselves faster. We are not suggesting you buy seedling-sized plants. Try to buy deciduous plants which are at least two years old and evergreens which are at least four years old. Ask the nursery worker for assistance — often trees and shrubs are grouped by size and age. Bushes which have begun branching near the soil line are best. Never buy tall, spindly deciduous plants, they need severe pruning to make them branch and are not worth the money or the effort.

Planting Trees and Shrubs

Reluctant Gardeners have more success planting trees and shrubs in the spring, rather than in early fall. Early planting gives the plant time to establish itself before the onset of cold weather. If planting the shrubs or trees yourself, be sure to prepare the planting hole before you bring the plant home. (Measure the rootball at the nursery, or get an approximate size over the phone from a nursery staff person.)

First remove the sod from the area where you are going to plant. Compost the sod or put it aside to re-cover the bare earth around the plant. If you are planting a hedge, replace the sod, leaving a 12 in./30 cm bare space between shrubs and grass or walks. The branches will cover the bare area within a few years. Creating a space between your tree or shrub and the lawn will prevent damage to the plant when mowing. If you do not want to have grass around the base of your tree or shrub, plant ground cover or spread bark chips.

Back to the planting hole. After the sod has been removed and the rootball's height and width measured, dig the planting hole. Make the hole deep and wide enough to comfortably insert the rootball. Most plants are happy in holes 6-12 in./15-30 cm larger than the rootball or pot. For root balls larger than 3 ft./1 meter, dig the holes about 12 in./30 cm larger all round. Be sure to remove rocks and other debris. Mix well-rotted manure or compost into the soil removed from the hole. Before inserting the plant, loosen the soil at the bottom of the hole with a fork to allow easier root penetration. Mix some organic matter into the bottom of the hole.

When you return from the garden center with your tree or shrub, keep it well watered before planting. If the shrub is growing in a container, cut the container off the rootball, rather than trying to knock it off. Usually these rootballs are too heavy for you to simply hold the plant upside down and pull the container off. It is easier and safer to cut the peat, plastic, or, heaven help us, metal (wear gloves) pot away from the rootball. Take a good pair of shears, heavy-duty tin snips if necessary, and make three cuts from top to bottom equidistantly around the pot. Peel the strips off to expose the rootball and discard the massacred pot.

When planting a burlap-wrapped rootball, cut the wires off the bundle, but leave the burlap on so the soil around the roots is not disturbed. The burlap will eventually disintegrate in the soil. If you decide to plant a bare-rooted tree, examine the roots and prune off any damaged ones.

After you dig the hole but before you plant, drive a stake into the hole about 12 in./30 cm from where you judge the tree stem will be. Make sure it is vertical. The stake is driven in *before* planting, so that the roots are not damaged. The tree will be tied to this stake, so choose a sturdy one. If you are planting an evergreen tree, drive in two stakes, one on each side of the rootball.

A helper is needed to hold the tree straight and at the correct planting level while you madly shovel in the soil. As you fill in the hole, work the soil between the roots if the plant is bare rooted. If wrapped in burlap, make sure the soil is pushed under the ball where necessary. Remember not to bury the trunk of the shrub or tree below the level it was originally planted. Firm and tamp down the soil at intervals to ensure that air pockets do not form. If the circumference is large enough, tamp the soil down with your feet by walking around, not on, the rootball. Your partner-in-planting can be dismissed, or given a beer to toast the tree, at this point. Mound soil into a small earthen ring around the tree as far back from the trunk as the perimeter of the rootball. This will hold in the water until it has sunk into the soil around the rootball rather than letting it flow away into the grass. Water thoroughly.

Now all that remains to be done is to tie the tree to the stake, but remember that the stake is there to steady the tree, not to substitute for a weak, spindly trunk. A newly-planted tree needs extra support until a strong, spreading root system has formed. The extra support ensures that strong winds do not uproot it, or that newly-developing feeder roots are not ripped off by the tree rocking in the wind. Nor will staked trees grow at a slant, which can be caused by people pulling on the tree, the soil settling or the force of the wind.

Measure a length of heavy wire or strong cord long enough to encircle tree and stake, plus the amount needed to tie the ends together. Twist the wire or lead the cord around tree and stake in a figure-eight configuration. The cross-over of the figure-eight should be between the tree and the stake. Tie the cord or twist the wire against the stake, not the tree, keeping it taut, but not tight (you should be able to slip a finger in between). Be sure to cushion wire by wrapping a heavy cloth around it. Or, before tying, thread a piece of old hosing onto the wire. The cushion will prevent the rubbing wire from damaging the tree bark.

Evergreen stakes should be treated differently. Attach a cross strut to the two supports and tie the tree, again using the figure-eight method, to the cross strut. Trees over 10 ft./3 m high are best supported by three evenly spaced guy wires. Remember to cushion the wires wherever they touch the tree.

Planting Hedges

Hedge planting requires some special procedures. If you are planting on a lot line, for example, and it is a joint planting project between neighbors, plant the hedge right on the lot line. However, if you are the only one planting the hedge, be sure to plant it at least 30-40 in./75-100 cm, depending on the mature spread, inside the line so that the hedge does not encroach on your neighbor's property. Many cities and towns have bylaws governing where hedges can be planted on corner lots. In our city, corner lot owners cannot plant a hedge that would grow over 30 in./75 cm tall — a higher hedge would block a driver's line of vision. Check with city hall before planting in such a location.

In spring, before buying your hedge material, dig a trench at least 15-20 in./40-50 cm deep and 20-24 in./50-60 cm wide along the planned length of the hedge. Enrich the soil removed from the trench with well-rotted manure or compost. Dig some into the soil at the bottom of the trench as well. String a line, slightly off-center, down the length of the trench to guide the planting. This prevents planting a drunken hedge. A hedge planted along a straight line will be easier to train, that is the branches will mesh together neatly. Some experts suggest planting hedges in a staggered row, but this method requires more plants, uses more space, and creates more difficulty in trimming than the straight row method.

The planting distance between each shrub depends on the variety chosen. A general rule of thumb for hedge spacing, however, is to place each plant

How to Plant Trees

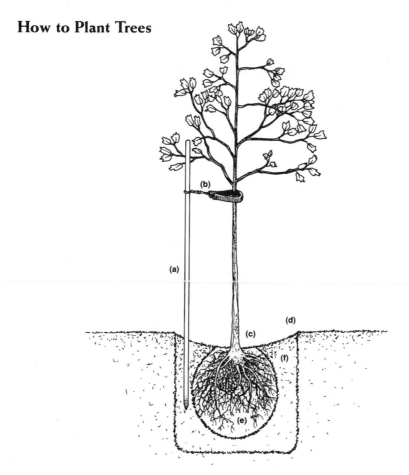

a) stake does not pierce rootball
b) tie is not too tight, and is padded with an old hose length
c) soil level on trunk is unchanged
d) saucer-shaped depression to direct water to roots
e) rootball the plant arrived with
f) enriched soil you have added. You firmed it down (with a hose or your foot) every few inches as you filled it in.

about half the distance of their eventual spread from one another. If the shrub grows vertically rather than bushy, plant closer together.

Bare-rooted material is cheaper to buy if you have a long hedge to plant. If your space is limited, buy container plants. If you have bought bare-rooted plants, be sure to prepare the trench, soil and planting line before bringing the plants home. Keep the bare-rooted plants in a pail of water so they do not dry out. Be sure to plant them within two days at most. Plant one at a time, working enough soil between the roots to force out any air pockets.

Placing Shrubs to Make a Hedge

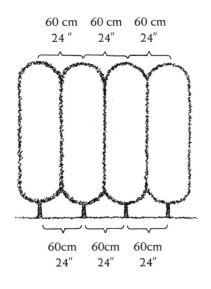

Suppose you want to make a hedge of densely-growing shrubs that will be 24" (60 cm) wide at maturity. Plant on 24" (60 cm) centers, ie., middle of 1st trunk is 24" (60 cm) away from middle of 2nd trunk. For a more solid hedge, use 20" (50 cm) centers.

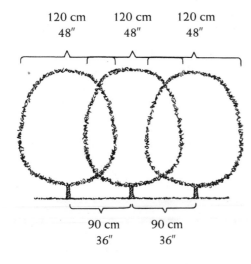

Shrubs with an open habit of growth should be planted a little closer together, so the tips of their branches mingle. For example, 48" (120 cm) diameter shrubs are planted on 36" (90 cm) centers.

Set the plants against the planting line to ensure that they will be in a straight line. Fill the trench in up to 3 in./8 cm below the soil line. Tamp down the earth, then with the hose fill the trench with water. When this water has completely soaked in, fill the trench in to about an inch from the top with the remaining soil, and water thoroughly again. During the first growing season be sure to keep the soil moist all season long.

After the shrubs and trees are planted, prune bare-rooted deciduous shrubs down about a fourth of their top growth. Do not prune the main leader (the main stem) especially on evergreens. If the main leader is pruned, the tree never properly grows vertically. However, light pruning on other parts of evergreens is permitted.

Maintenance

Most trees and shrubs, once the crucial first season has passed, require little care. During extremely dry weather you might want to thoroughly water young trees and shrubs. As well, an occasional pruning may be necessary for shrubs and sometimes younger trees. The "Three D's" are the most reliable guide to pruning: the dead, the diseased and the damaged. As well, prune out any branch which crosses over another and rubs against the bark. Ultimately, the rubbing can damage the bark and cause a wound to form where disease and insects can enter. You might, if you have an aesthetic eye, cut out any branches which distort the natural shape of the tree or shrub. Also cut off water shoots — soft, vertical, rapidly growing shoots similar to suckers — at soil level or below. These pale green, soft-feeling shoots do nothing to enhance the appearance of the plant and only use up nutrients needed by the tree. Water shoots are often found on crabapple trees.

Trees are best pruned in late winter (February/March) before the sap starts to flow. In spring the sap flow from a new wound could seriously weaken a tree. Winter wounds have usually healed by the time spring growth begins. Maples, which have a large sap flow, should be pruned in autumn after the leaves have fallen. However, dead and diseased limbs on any tree or shrub should be cut off as soon as you notice them. Depending on the size of the branch to be cut, you may need to use a saw. Whenever you prune and whatever you prune, be sure your tools are sharp and clean — you do not want to spread disease from an unclean tool. Dull tools cause ragged cuts, ripped bark and fissures where insects and disease can cause mischief. If you are pruning a small branch, cut back to just above the nearest bud, cutting at a 45° angle. Always prune to outfacing buds or branches, that is, the growth point should be pointing away from the center of the plant. New shoots emerging from these buds will grow away from the plant, and thus the center will be clear so that light and air can easily penetrate. If you prune to inside-facing buds, the shoots will grow through the center, cross and rub one another — a messy sight.

Where to Cut When Pruning

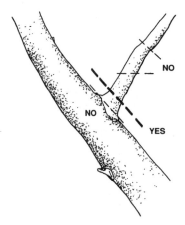

Make the cut 1/4" to 1/2" (5-10 mm) out from the parent branch, and slant the surface so water will be shed.

Be sure to cut tree limbs as close to the trunk as possible and large shrub branches close to the stem or branch. If you leave ragged stubs, rot from the wound easily travels into the tree. Always treat any wounds over 1 in./2.5 cm with a commercial wound dressing. It will protect the tree from disease. The wound will gradually disappear as the bark advances, covering the scar.

Early-flowering shrubs or ones that flower on the previous season's shoots, such as mock orange and spirea, can be pruned after their spring flowers have faded. "Previous season's shoots" are the non-flowering branches which develop in one growing season and produce flowers in the next. If you are pruning just for shape, cut back to where a new non-flowering shoot is sprouting.

The shrubs which flower on the current season's shoots, that is, the shoots which grow and produce flowers in the same growing season, are pruned in early spring. A good example are the hydrangeas. The harder these plants are pruned, the more vigorously they grow and bloom. A safe, general rule to follow is prune all flowering shrubs *after* they bloom.

If you have adventurously decided to create a formal hedge, sharpen up your pruning tools and limber up your muscles, you will use a lot of both. Careful pruning must be practiced to create a healthy, pleasant-looking hedge, rather than one that looks as if it had been gnawed by rats. First of all, it is important to prune the hedge so that the top is gently pointed or rounded — the base broader than the top. The snow load will fall off rounded hedges. In most cold-winter areas the accumulation of snow and ice will eventually break the branches of flat-topped hedges. As well, by pruning hedges so that the top is narrower than the bottom, sufficient light will penetrate both sides of the hedge. This is especially necessary for very tall hedges. The lower foliage will grow happily, because it will not be shaded by the top foliage. Resist the temptation to turn your shrubs into ice cream cones.

Shaping a Shrub

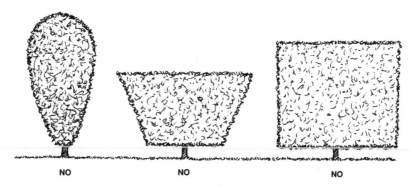

NO NO NO

All three shrubs above have broad tops that will load up with snow, which will break twigs and branches, especially if they are evergreens. The first two are wider at the top than at the bottom, which will starve lower branches of sun, rendering them weak and leafless.

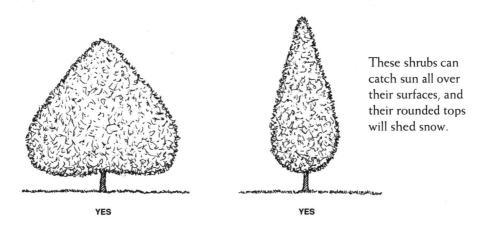

YES YES

These shrubs can catch sun all over their surfaces, and their rounded tops will shed snow.

At first, prune the previous season's top growth on a formal hedge by one-half every year to encourage bushy growth. Once the mature height has been reached, prune the hedge at least once a year, if not more, snipping off ends of branches close to the base of the current season's growth, but not into the woody, leaf-free section of the branches. This restricts the hedge's height. If you have neglected pruning, and then prune drastically and too far in, the hedge will look gnawed. The pruned ends will be woody rather than leafy.

Formal hedges are a lot of work. If you do not feel that you have the eye, the stamina or the interest, not only in the pruning, but also in the cleaning up afterward, which is a pain in the neck, choose hedge material which works well as an informal hedge. If this does not appeal to you, then build a fence, which takes less maintenance. You can always plant shrubs and flowers to soften its architectural hardness. If you have inherited a hedge, and, for good reason, do not want to tear it out, remember there are many professionals out there eager, for a fee of course, to trim hedges.

Thinning

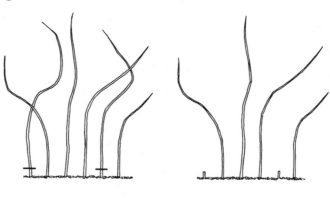

Cutting Back

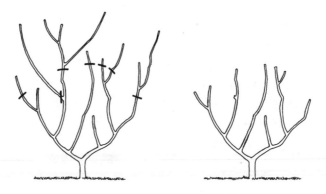

Before reading our YES! list of trees and shrubs, there are a few other maintenance tips to bear in mind. It takes about three years for a tree to become established and two for shrubs. After that you will notice that the larger material will grow faster because the root system has spread and can support a larger top. Occasionally you might want to work some organic material into the soil surrounding trees and shrubs. This will help smaller plants growing close to trees and shrubs, which sometimes lose the competition for soil nutrients and water. Tips on fighting tree-destroying bugs and diseases are found in Chapter 14.

Some winter protection may be needed for young trees and shrubs in exposed locations. Sun scald, caused by the sun's reflected rays off snow, can cause harm. The reflected rays may be so powerful they burn bark, kill dormant shoots or scorch evergreen leaves. Threatened material can be protected by wrapping burlap *loosely* around them. Trunks of deciduous trees can be wrapped with burlap or special trunk protection paper. Smaller shrubs can be protected by wrapping them in burlap or, if you are really handy, with a home-made A-frame — two hinged boards placed over the plants. These boards are especially protective for shrubs planted next to the house. Masses of snow or sheets of ice sliding off the roof will break apart on the boards rather than on the plants — an event that usually leaves unprotected shrubs with broken branches. If road salt spray is a problem, burlap is also useful. Even a rope wound around and up the shrub to hold the branches against the trunk is better than nothing. Otherwise, snow and ice will spoil the line of the branches, if not snap them right off.

AUTUMN LEAVES — *Cleaning up leaves shed by deciduous trees and shrubs become one of the year's most tiresome chores. They should not be left on the grass, because this will promote infestations of bugs and diseases. Depending on what help your local public works department offers, you have several options:*

- *Rake and bag them and leave them out for the garbage collectors. Increasingly frowned upon as landfill sites fill up.*
- *Rake and bag them and leave them for community leaf collection. Better, but uses lots of plastic.*
- *Rake and compost them in your own compost box. An excellent option, except that they will need to be stockpiled, as you wait for space in the box to become available.*
- *Run them over with the mower to reduce their mass, then compost them. This is, in our opinion, the best option.*

Useful Things to Know

- If you are looking for a narrow tree, look for one with the word *fastigiata* or *columnaris* in its name.
- If you are looking for a weeping tree, look for one with the word *pendula* in its name.
- Most maples, pines and oaks do well in dry areas.
- Most spruce and pine will tolerate salty air.
- Red maple does not mind wet soil.
- Think twice about buying a big tree — the size that is delivered by a specially-built truck with a pointed, peculiar scoop-cum-claw on the front. These mature-when-dug-up trees take literally years to get over their transplant shock, by which time a smaller (and much cheaper) balled-and-burlapped tree will be a long way toward catching up.
- Remember that the only way to grow what is called a specimen tree — one with an even, balanced shape, such as seen in tree catalogue photographs — is to plant it well away from any sources of shade. Shade from nearby buildings or other trees will slow growth on that side of your tree. It will still look very nice, but not like the pictures.

Now read through our YES! list and enjoy the diversity of these stalwart plants. Years of satisfaction will be yours without much work. Most of these plants are hardy to -30°F/-35°C, many are worth a try at -40°F/-40°C. Check at your local nursery.

The YES! List of Trees and Shrubs

Trees

Evergreens

Common name: CEDAR, EASTERN WHITE CEDAR, ARBORVITAE

Latin name: *Thuja occidentalis*

Height and spread: height, 20 ft./6 m; spread, 6 ft./2 m — these are approximate measurements, each species may be different.

Description: Commonly used in foundation plantings, cedars are dense and compact. Their scalelike, dark green leaves cover a multitude of divided branches.

Sun: full sun

Soil: likes moist soil

Moisture: water during extreme dry periods, especially when plant is young

Pruning: in early spring or late summer prune lightly to promote new growth.

Comments: Cedars are commonly grown shrubs and trees. Many cultivars have been created from *T. occidentalis*, a tough tree, native to North America. One of the most commonly sold is 'Fastigiata,' a tall, slender, columnar tree. The taller varieties are often used as screening hedges and should be planted 28 in./70 cm apart. This is a reliable, trouble-free tree, although a particularly bad winter may kill off its tips. These brown tips are usually shed during the next summer, and replaced by healthy green growth. Cedar grows at a medium rate.

Common name: PINE

Latin name: *Pinus*

Height and spread: grows at least 50 ft./15 m tall; spreads up to 20 ft./6 m

Description: Large trees with clusters of long, dark green needles. Branches are not symmetrically arranged, and have a rugged appearance.

Sun: full sun

Soil: average

Moisture: average

Pruning: rarely

Comments: Scot's Pine, *Pinus sylvestris*, is commonly found in most garden centers. It is a fast growing tree with bluish-green needles. However, it grows to 60 ft./18 m and spreads 20 ft./6 m. A dwarf form also exists which only grows to 7 ft./2 m. Lodgepole pine (*P. contorta latifolia*) will grow to 50 ft./15 m in -50°F/-45°C areas. Pines hardy to -40°F/-40°C also include Eastern white (80 ft./25 m), Ponderosa (125 ft./40 m) and Red (70 ft./20 m). Pines are subject to attack by a variety of insects.

Common name: SPRUCE

Latin name: *Picea*

Height and spread: some varieties of spruce grow at least 150 ft./45 m tall and spread up to 15 ft./4.5 m

Description: Most spruce are pyramidal, with long graceful, yet stiff branches, covered in short dark green needles. You probably know it from the Christmas tree lot.

Sun: sun

Soil: likes moist, sandy soil

Moisture: keep on the moist side

Pruning: rarely

Comments: Mainly used as specimen trees (that is, planted singly) on large lots. Hardy and relatively fast growing. Blue spruce (*P. pungens glauca*) is hardy -40°F/-40°C, grows to 70 ft./20 m and needs to be well away from any shade-casting neighbor to grow fat, straight and even, the way it looks in the pictures. It is relatively slow-growing. White spruce (*P. glauca*) is hardy to -50°F/-45°C and will grow to 80 ft./25 m. Spruces can host a variety of insects.

Common name: ROCKY MOUNTAIN FIR

Latin name: *Abies lasiocarpa 'Compacta'*

Height and spread: height, 30 ft./9 m; spread, 10 ft./3 m

Description: silver-blue needles, compact pyramidal form

Sun: full sun

Soil: average, but prefers moist soil

Moisture: average

Pruning: pruning only occasionally necessary

Comments: This slow-growing, adaptable tree is used as a specimen plant on small lots. Other fir trees are quite stately and look out of place on the small urban lot. They belong in the forest. However, if you have space, the Balsam fir (*A. balsamea*) will grow to 30-60 ft./9-18 m in -50°F/-45°C at a moderate rate of growth. It is bug and disease resistant, thick and beautiful. Often commercially grown for Christmas trees.

Common name: TAMARACK, EASTERN LARCH, AMERICAN LARCH

Latin name: *Larix laricina*

Height and spread: height, 30 ft./9 m; spread, 12 ft./3.5 m

Description: A tree native to North America, the tamarack has an upright, pyramidal form, and reddish bark when mature. The orange-brown branches are slender and covered by clusters of blue-green, 1 in./2.5 cm long, needles and small 1/2 in./12 mm wide cones.

Sun: full sun, intolerant of shade

Soil: well-drained, but is adaptable

Moisture: likes soil on the moist side

Pruning: no need to prune

Comments: The tamarack is an attractive tree on a large property, it can grow as tall as 90 ft./27 m. Unusual for a conifer, it sheds its needles, which first turn yellow, in fall. It does not cast a heavy shade. The tree's profile is rather diffuse as the nearly horizontal branches are not clustered together nor is the foliage dense. Hardy to -40°F/-40°C.

Deciduous

Common name: BLACK ASH

Latin name: *Fraxinus nigra*

Height and spread: height, 65 ft./20 m; spread, 45 ft./15 m

Description: Narrow, pyramidal form with large compound leaves composed of at least seven leaflets, each nearly 5 in./13 cm long.

Sun: does not mind light shade

Soil: will grow in moist soil

Moisture: average to moist

Pruning: no

Comments: A hardy (-40°F/-40°C) native ornamental tree. Some craftspeople use the wood to make baskets.

Common name: DOWNY SERVICEBERRY, SHADBLOW

Latin name: *Amelanchier canadensis*

Height and spread: height, 20-26 ft./6-8 m; spread the same

Description: a shrubby tree, it has been known to grow up to twelve attractive gray-barked trunks. The green leaves are fuzzy on both sides and turn yellow or orange in fall. Small white flowers bloom in early spring, followed by small red, edible berries in June.

Sun: full sun

Soil: average

Moisture: average

Pruning: to keep it shrubby, prune branch tips after flowering in spring

Comments: If you do not mind ripened berries falling on the lawn, this small tree is for you. Susceptible to a variety of insects. Hardy only to -22°F/-30°C.

Common name: FLOWERING CRABAPPLE

Latin name: *Malus*

Height and spread: height up to 25 ft./8 m; spread the same

Description: a flowering, small tree which may, or may not (according to variety) bear edible crabapples. Foliage can be green or purple and flowers can be white, pink, red or rose depending on the variety.

Sun: full sun

Soil: average

Moisture: average

Pruning: take out the dead, diseased, damaged

Comments: The flowering crabapple is a common spring sight. There are many, many varieties on sale in garden centers, but check that they are hardy in your area. Most crabapples grow at a medium rate. The only drawback is cleaning up the fallen fruit in the fall — rotting fruit can attract bees and wasps. You may want to buy non-fruiting varieties, if they are available. Some Reluctant Gardeners will not plant trees with fruit, but these are so pretty, they might be worth the work. They are susceptible to tent caterpillars.

Common name: GINKGO, MAIDENHAIR TREE

Latin name: *Ginkgo biloba*

Height and spread: height, 50 ft./15 m; spread 30 ft./10 m

Description: known for its distinctive lobed, fan-shaped leaves. Slow growing. Leaves turn yellow in fall.

Sun: full sun

Soil: average

Moisture: average

Pruning: no

Comments: This tree will appeal to the dinosaur-lovers in your house — it is one the few plant survivors from the dinosaur age. Do not plant the female of the species, the fruit smells terrible. Ginkgo are very resistant to bugs and diseases. An excellent tree, which survives in heavily air-polluted areas. This slow grower is hardy to -22°F/-30°C.

Common name: HAWTHORN

Latin name: *Crataegus*

Height and spread: height, up to 25 ft./8 m; spread is about the same

Description: compact growers, with small white or pink flowers amid bright green leaves. Unfortunately, most hawthorns have spines on their branches.

Sun: full sun

Soil: average

Moisture: average

Pruning: only when necessary

Comments: The small pretty fruit has to be cleaned up and the spine-covered branches dampen the spirit of even the most enthusiastic pruner. The Chinese hawthorn or *C. pinnatifida* is one of the better species. It only grows 15 ft./4.5 m and has few thorns. Abundant white flowers cover this slow–growing tree in early spring, followed in fall by large red fruit. The pink-flowering *C. mordenensis* 'Toba,' grows to 15 ft./4.5 m.

Common name: HORSE CHESTNUT, OHIO BUCKEYE

Latin name: *Aesculus glabra*

Height and spread: height, 25 ft./7.5 m; spread 18 ft./5.4 m

Description: shiny green leaves divided into five leaflets, each about 4 in./10 cm long, are shaped like large hands. Small greenish-yellow flowers appear on upright spikes on branch ends. Leaves turn a brilliant orange in fall. The mature tree has a rounded shape.

Sun: full sun

Soil: average

Moisture: average

Pruning: no

Comments: This slow-growing tree can be multi-trunked. The seeds are poisonous. Hardy to -40°F/-40°C.

Common name: LITTLELEAF LINDEN, BASSWOOD, SMALL-LEAVED LIME

Latin name: *Tilia cordata*

Height and spread: height, 40 ft./12 m; spread, 20 ft./6 m

Description: Densely branched, pyramidal form. Leathery, heart-shaped leaves are dark green above and pale green on undersides — pretty when the wind blows. Sweetly scented clusters of ivory-colored flowers appear in June.

Sun: sun

Soil: prefers an organically enriched soil

Moisture: likes moist soil and will not withstand hot dry periods

Pruning: only when necessary

Comments: 'Glenleven' and 'Greenspire' are varieties commonly found in garden centers. Do not plant near a road or sidewalk where the tree would be hit by winter salt spray. Their abundant flowers attract many bees. Borers, pests that tunnel into the wood, find them tasty. Hardy to -22°F/-30°C.

Common name: RED MAPLE

Latin name: *Acer rubrum*

Height and spread: height, 40 ft./12 m; spread a bit less than its height

Description: Its small flowers and leaf buds show red in early spring, but the leaves are green. In fall the leaf color varies from yellow to brilliant red.

Sun: full sun

Soil: organically enriched

Moisture: average

Pruning: only when necessary

Comments: There are many cultivars of this reliable tree. It grows at a medium rate. Some maples are too brittle, too susceptible to air pollution or too tall for city conditions.

Common name: RED OAK

Latin name: *Quercus rubra*

Height and spread: height, 40 ft./12 m; spread is a little less

Description: Broadly pyramidal, the red oak has green leaves which turn bright red in fall.

Sun: full sun

Soil: likes a soil that is a bit acid, so add peat moss

Moisture: average

Pruning: only when necessary for shape

Comments: The red oak is a fast grower, native to Canada. It is easy to transplant if done in spring. Oaks have long, main taproots, so be sure to prepare the soil deeply and well. White oak (*Q. alba*, grows to 75 ft./ 23 m, hardy to -22°F/-30°C) is a magnificent tree, but s-l-o-w growing.

Common name: SHADEMASTER LOCUST, HONEY LOCUST

Latin name: *Gleditsia triacanthos* 'Shademaster'

Height and spread: height, 45 ft./14 m; spread the same

Description: very fine foliage because each leaf is very finely divided into many leaflets. Branches haphazardly.

Sun: full sun

Soil: average, very adaptable

Moisture: average, will withstand short periods of drought

Pruning: no

Comments: The shademaster locust casts a light shade so grass grows well under it. Easy to transplant. Be sure to buy the thornless locust — some have very sharp 3 in./7.5 cm triple thorns which could injure not-looking-where-they're-running children.

Common name: TATARIAN MAPLE

Latin name: *Acer tataricum*

Height and spread: height, 25 ft./7.5 m; spread, 20 ft./5.4 m

Description: has a low-growing, rounded form. The leaves on this slow-growing tree turn yellow or bronzy red in fall.

Sun: sun

Soil: average

Moisture: average

Pruning: rarely

Comments: There are numerous hardy maples recommended for northern zones, but unlike the Tatarian maple their mature height is usually higher than the urban gardener would prefer. Hardy to -40°F/-40°C or worse.

Shrubs

Evergreen

Common name: CEDAR

Latin name: *Thuja occidentalis*

Height and spread: height up to 7 ft./2 m; spread 5 ft/1.5 m

Description: low-growing varieties with the standard cedar characteristics (see cedar trees above)

Sun: sun

Soil: average

Moisture: average to moist

Pruning: prune new growth in late summer for compact growth.

Comments: The low-growing types such as 'Goldtipped,' 'Little Champion,' 'Little Giant,' or 'Globe' are often used in foundation plantings. The 7 ft./2 m cedars make the most trouble-free hedge you could wish for. Hardy to -40°F/-40°C.

Common name: DWARF SPRUCE

Latin name: *Picea*

Height and spread: height up to 7 ft./2 m; spread is a bit less

Description: slow-growing, miniature spruce shrubs.

Sun: sun

Soil: average

Moisture: average

Pruning: no

Comments: Most dwarf spruce offered for sale are at least ten years old and can be expensive. *Picea abies* varieties such as Nest spruce, are hardy to -22°F/-30°C, *P. glauca* types such as Dwarf Alberta spruce, Dwarf Globe Alberta spruce (not quite so hardy), Hedgehog spruce and *P. omorica nana*, the Dwarf Siberian spruce, are useful where a small evergreen is needed in the design.

Common name: JUNIPER

Latin name: *Juniperus*

Height and spread: range of heights as short as 3 in./8 cm up to 10 ft./ 3 m; spread varies

Description: Leaves may be scale-like or needle-like depending on the age of the plant. Foliage can be silver, golden or green depending on the species. Because junipers are available in a range of heights, they are popular in graded foundation plantings.

Sun: full sun

Soil: average

Moisture: average

Pruning: only when necessary

Comments: There are many varieties of juniper shrubs which are not hardy to -40°F/-40°C or colder. It is safer in colder regions to buy the *Juniperus horizontalis* and *sabina* cultivars. However, *sabina* varieties are susceptible to spider mite infestations. The Golden Pfitzer, *Juniperus chinensis* 'Pfitzeriana Aurea,' is hardy to -40°F/-40°C and useful in a spot where you might want a fast growing-evergreen with golden tips on its branches in spring. The *J. virginiana* hybrids are hardy to -22°F/-30°C and include a number of the fast-growing, columnar shrubs, such as 'Skyrocket,' which are very attractive in a formal planting.

Common name: MUGO PINE

Latin name: *Pinus mugo mugo*

Height and spread: height, 5 ft./1.5 m; spread 7 ft/2 m

Description: spherical shrub covered in clusters of long needles

Sun: full sun

Soil: average

Moisture: average

Pruning: cut off new growth, called "candles," every spring to maintain a compact, attractive form

Comments: These slow-growing shrubs are effective foundation plantings. If you don't mind cutting the new growth off every year, plant mugo pine. But they are expensive and they also attract a variety of pests. Hardy to -50°F/-45°C.

Deciduous

Common name: ALPINE CURRANT

Latin name: *Ribes alpinum*

Height and spread: height 4 ft./1.2 m; spread, 6 ft./2 m

Description: a dense, bushy shrub with distinctive three-lobed dark green leaves

Sun: will tolerate shade, but grows denser in full sun

Soil: average

Moisture: average

Pruning: prune old wood out, down to nearly ground level to a point where live buds are sprouting. Do this occasionally for shape immediately after flowering

Comments: A hybrid, *R. aureum*, or flowering currant, is also hardy and bears fragrant yellow blossoms in early spring. Leaves turn deep red in fall. Alpine currant is particularly useful as a hedge plant, but needs an annual clipping to keep it in the right shape. Hardy to -40°F/-40°C.

Common name: AMUR TAMARISK

Latin name: *Tamarix pentandra*

Height and spread: height, 8 ft./2.5 m; spread, 6 ft./1.8 m

Description: very fine, feathery, bright green foliage. The leaves are scale-like, similar to the leaves of some junipers. Young growth is purple. Pendulous clusters of small rosy pink flowers are borne on the end of its shoots. These flowers are extremely small, but quite attractive.

Sun: sun

Soil: prefers a light, well-drained soil

Moisture: average

Pruning: prune in spring to promote flowers

Comments: Slow to establish itself, the amur tamarisk is a showy shrub. It is the hardiest member of this ornamental genus survives -40°F/-40°C and does not mind salt spray or pollution.

Common name: BURNING BUSH

Latin name: *Euonymus atropurpureus*

Height and spread: 8 ft./2.5 m

Description: dark green, finely toothed leaves turn a brilliant scarlet in fall. Flowers and fruit are dark purple.

Sun: will tolerate partial shade

Soil: average

Moisture: average

Pruning: as needed

Comments: Burning bush, a shrub native to North America, is hardy to -22°F/-30°C.

Common name: COMMON NINEBARK

Latin name: *Physocarpus opulifolius*

Height and spread: height, 8 ft./2.5 m; spread, 6 ft./2 m

Description: a coarse-textured shrub, bushy from the ground level up, with graceful, arching branches. Flowers are small, usually white. Crimson fruit follows in late June. The shaggy bark looks interesting.

Sun: full sun or a little shade

Soil: average

Moisture: average, but tolerates periods of dryness

Pruning: prune after bloom has faded

Comments: Common ninebark is hardy up to -40°F/-40°C. Mountain ninebark, *P. monogynus*, is also known as the "lazyman's hedge," because it is easy to care for and has a compact, neat appearance. It grows 5 ft./1.5 m tall and flowers in May and June. 'Luteus' is a cultivar of the common ninebark. A strong growing shrub, it grows nearly 7 ft./2 m tall and bears lime-green tinged golden foliage. It needs to be pruned drastically every two to three years to stimulate new growth.

Common name: DOGWOOD

Latin name: *Cornus*

Height and spread: many varieties grow up to 8 ft./2.5 m; and spread to 5 ft./1.5 m

Description: a very ornamental shrub for the home garden. Some varieties have attractive red or yellow branches. One type, *Cornus alba* 'Elegantissima,' has pretty green and white leaves. Small clusters of white flowers don't put on a show you'd pay to see.

Sun: tolerates light shade

Soil: average

Moisture: average

Pruning: prune to keep shape and promote new growth

Comments: Many northern cities have experienced a population explosion of dogwood shrubs, doubtless because the red twigs provide visual relief from winter snow cover. We may recommend them for the award of most popular landscaping shrub used by federal and municipal governments. They are hardy to -40°F/-40°C. The best varieties are *C. alba* 'Elegantissima,' *C. alba* 'Siberica,' *C. alba* 'Spaethi,' and *C. stolonifera* 'Flaviremea' or Yellowtwig. Keep an eye out for borers and canker disease.

Common name: DWARF EUONYMUS

Latin name: *Euonymus nanus*

Height and spread: height, 5 ft./1.5 m; spread, the same or a little less

Description: a compact bush with dark green leaves which turn purple in fall. The pretty fruit unfortunately is not abundant. Has attractively arched branches.

Sun: sun

Soil: average

Moisture: average

Pruning: as needed

Comments: Hardy to -40°F/-40°C.

Common name: DWARF EUROPEAN HIGHBUSH CRANBERRY

Latin name: *Viburnum opulus nanum*

Height and spread: height, 24 in./60 cm; spread 3 ft./1 m

Description: a dense grower with attractive three-lobed leaves. Produces few flowers and no fruit.

Sun: will tolerate light shade

Soil: average

Moisture: average

Pruning: an occasional light haircut — perhaps once a year.

Comments: Hardy to -40°F/-40°C, the dwarf European highbush cranberry is an excellent low hedge plant.

Common name: FLOWERING ALMOND

Latin name: *Prunus triloba multiplex*

Height and spread: height, 10 ft./3 m; spread, 10 ft./3 m

Description: has coarse, three-lobed, pale green leaves. Its large (1 1/2 in./4 cm) rose-pink double flowers appear in mid-May before the leaves, although -22°F/-30°C temperatures will probably kill the flowerbeds (the shrub itself will survive).

Sun: full sun, some shade

Soil: average

Moisture: average

Pruning: prune to retain shape

Comments: Flowering almond is a very strong grower and is not advised for foundation plantings. All shrubs in the Prunus group are plagued by bugs and diseases. They can be troublesome, so it is a good thing they are so pretty.

Common name: GOLDEN ELDER

Latin name: *Sambucus canadensis* 'Aurea'

Height and spread: height, 10 ft./3 m; spread, 8 ft/2.5 m

Description: a coarse-looking shrub with compound leaves composed of eleven yellow leaflets. It has a spreading, open appearance. Large heads of white flowers are followed by dark berries.

Sun: grow in full sun to maintain golden foliage color

Soil: average

Moisture: average

Pruning: prune after flowering when necessary for shape and size

Comments: Golden elder makes a good contrast shrub. It is fast growing and useful as a screen, but susceptible to insect borers.

Common name: HIGHBUSH CRANBERRY

Latin name: *Viburnum trilobum*

Height and spread: height, 8 ft./2.5 m; spread, 8 ft./2.5 m

Description: a large shrub with gray stems and maple tree-like leaves. Flower heads are composed of small white flowers. The red fruit is used in preserves.

Sun: will tolerate shade

Soil: average

Moisture: average

Pruning: only when necessary

Comments: The highbush cranberry makes a good hedge and grows well in partial shade. It is a very tough shrub. One of your authors has one that has sturdily survived the two highly informal transplants that resulted from her indecision about its location. Hardy to -40°F/-40°C.

Common name: HONEYSUCKLE

Latin name: *Lonicera*

Height and spread: depending on species, can grow between 3-10 ft./ 1-3 m and spreads between 3-8 ft./1-2.5 m

Description: coarse-textured, fast growing shrubs with dark green foliage. Flowers, small, sometimes fragrant, are available in white, yellow, pink or rose. The whites and yellow are rather dingy. Flowers are often followed by small, usually red, sometimes orange, inedible berries. Also available as a vine (see Chapter 10 on vines and ground covers).

Sun: sun

Soil: average

Moisture: average

Pruning: prune for shape after flowering. In late winter cut down some of the older wood to ground level to encourage strong young growth.

Comments: The Tatarian honeysuckle, *Lonicera tatarica*, is commonly found in the garden center. There are many varieties hybridized from this species, among which are the popular 'Arnold's Red,' 'Morden Orange,' and 'Hack's Red.' They are very vigorous, bushy shrubs. Unfortunately, you have to take the good with the bad, because they, and many other honeysuckles, are prone to aphid infestation. The aphids do not necessarily kill the shrubs, but can substantially weaken them. You can spray all you want, but they seem nearly impossible to eradicate. The little critters are everywhere and float on the wind to new homes. However, the above-mentioned shrubs are very hardy and make an effective screen or informal hedge.

Do not buy just anything labeled "honeysuckle." Make sure you check the hardiness of the species you are considering.

Common name: HYDRANGEA

Latin name: *Hydrangea*

Height and spread: depending on the variety, it grows between 3-6 ft./1-2 m and spreads about 3-6 ft./1-2 m

Description: coarse foliage; small white flowers form rounded clusters in late summer. The flashy blue one, *H. macrophylla*, is unfortunately only hardy to about freezing point.

Sun: sun or light shade

Soil: adaptable, but likes slightly acidic soil, so add in good amounts of peat moss when planting.

Moisture: moist soil

Pruning: prune for shape in early spring

Comments: This old-time favorite fills a niche in the flower border or shrub grouping for its blooms in mid-summer, late summer, and sometimes into fall according to variety. The most dependable varieties are: *Hydrangea arborescens* 'Annabelle', *H. paniculata* 'Floribunda', and *H. paniculata* 'Grandiflora' or Peegee hydrangea. The Peegee hydrangea is a low-growing, abundantly flower-covered shrub that obligingly blossoms in August, which can be a time of few flowers. Some Peegees have been know to grow into small trees in the right conditions.

Common name: LILAC

Latin name: *Syringa*

Height and spread: depending on the variety, lilacs can grow as high as 12 ft./3.5 m and spread to about the same

Description: Dark green, heart-shaped leaves cover multi-stemmed bushes. Small fragrant flowers are borne in long pyramidal clusters of lavender, rose, purple, white or pink. A yellow blooming variety is available, but we have not seen it yet.

Sun: full sun

Soil: organically enriched soil

Moisture: does not like to be dry

Pruning: cut off the faded flower clusters down to the next bud or where a new shoot is emerging in order to promote greater flowering the next year; but if you neglect to do this, the lilac will still put on a good show next year. (Freeway ramps in cold climates are planted with many untended lilacs which are laden with blossom year after year.) Cut out the thin, weak, vertical shoots that sprout along the branches and around the base of the shrub. These shoots (or suckers, as they are called) take forever to grow to blooming size. If the shrub has been grafted onto a hardier root, as most commercial lilacs are, then these shoots might not resemble the blooming lilac. The spindly shoots also give the lilac a messy look.

How to De-flower a Lilac

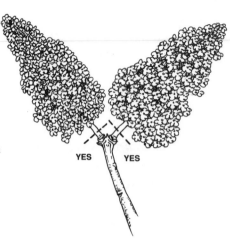

YES   YES

Dead-heading a lilac in this fashion
will promote more flowering the
following year.

Comments: Lilacs are available in many hybrids and flower colors. To be
sure to get the color you want, wait to buy a shrub until it blooms, in
mid to late May. Lilacs are hardy shrubs and can be grown at -50°F/
-45°C. Many are strong, expansive growers, so plant in an adequate
space. Some homeowners use lilacs as screening plants. Lilacs make
delightful cut flowers, and will scent the whole room. Bash the woody
stem-end with a hammer to promote longer vase-life.

Common name: MOCK ORANGE

Latin name: *Philadelphus*

Height and spread: depending on the variety, mock orange can grow
between 3-13 ft./1.4 m tall and spread about the same.

Description: very fragrant white flowers, either single, semi-double or
double, appear in June. The foliage is coarse-looking.

Sun: will tolerate light shade

Soil: average

Moisture: average

Pruning: to promote a bushier plant, thin the thicker stems down to a
point where strong new shoots are visible, after bloom has ended. Do
this every two or three years depending on the rate of growth. Mock
orange blooms on the last season's wood.

Comments: Mock orange is a wonderfully scented shrub. The double-flowered varieties tend to stay in bloom longer, but the single varieties are more fragrant — your choice. We have been quite pleased with a hybrid, 'Buckley's Quill,' originated at the Central Experimental Farm in Ottawa. Its double flowers are very fragrant and literally cover the bush in early June. It grows about 7 ft./2 m high and spreads slowly. The old favorite *Philadelphus virginalis* grows nearly 10 ft./3 m tall. Many of the *P. coronarius* hybrids are also quite hardy, if a little sparse. The 'Aureus' variety bears lime-green foliage, which, mixed into the right planting, is quite attractive.

Common name: NANNYBERRY

Latin name: *Viburnum lentago*

Height and spread: height, 20 ft./6 m; spread, 10 ft./3 m

Description: although sometimes listed as a tree, nannyberry is usually grown as a multi-stemmed shrub. Large, dark green, shiny pointed leaves turn purple-red in autumn. Small clusters of white flowers are followed by red oblong fruit which eventually turns black.

Sun: will tolerate light shade

Soil: average

Moisture: average

Pruning: only when necessary or to keep at a certain height

Comments: Plant this attractive specimen where adequate space is available. Watch for aphids. Hardy to -40°F/-40°C.

Common name: PEA SHRUB

Latin name: *Caragana*

Height and spread: depending on the species, caraganas can grow from 3-15 ft./1-4.5 m tall; and spreads between 6-12 ft./2-4 m.

Description: This well-known prairie shrub has a fine-textured look due to its compound leaves, which are often tipped by spines. Flowers, either yellow or orange, look like pea plant blossoms.

Sun: sun

Soil: average

Moisture: does well in drought conditions

Pruning: the common caragana, *Caragana arborescens*, needs to be cut back after flowering to control its tendency to become leggy

Comments: While they are extremely hardy (-50°F/-45°C) and effective windbreaks, they require a lot of room. The common caragana has a tendency to scatter seeds and pods in the fall. These seeds readily sprout wherever they touch ground. The pygmy caragana, *C. pygmaea*, grows only to 3 ft./1 m and has a much more compact shape than its larger cousin. Its bright yellow flowers appear in late May and early June.

Common name: PURPLE-LEAF SAND CHERRY

Latin name: *Prunus cistena*

Height and spread: height, 5 ft./1.5 m; spread, 5 ft./1.5 m

Description: a purple-barked shrub, with reddish-purple leaves, and sparse pinkish-white flowers

Sun: sun

Soil: average

Moisture: average

Pruning: prune to control shape. Pinching out the top shoots will force it to bush out its otherwise skimpy bottom half.

Comments: Very striking shrub and one of the first flowering shrubs to bloom in spring. Because of its color, it needs to be placed where it will not clash with its surroundings. It looks very smart against a blue-gray wall, but is invisible against red brick, and looks vile against yellow-toned brick. It is hardy to -40°F/-40°C. Unfortunately, tent caterpillars and scale like it.

Common name: RUSSIAN OLIVE

Latin name: *Elaeagnus angustifolia*

Height and spread: height, 6 ft./1.8 m and spreads the same

Description: the attractive leaves are long, narrow and silver. The mature bark is a dark, reddish brown. Clusters of small, fragrant yellow flowers appear in June.

Sun: sun, tolerates heat

Soil: average

Moisture: grows well in dry conditions

Pruning: prune to keep height down, but not too much a season for the sap bleeds out freely.

Comments: A beautiful shrub, quite hardy, which can grow into a 20 ft./ 6 m high tree if not pruned. It enjoys sheltered positions where shallow roots will get a good snow cover. Tolerates salt and is quite pest-resistant. Its branches tend to be a little weak though. Some gardeners, who enjoy pruning, use it as a hedge. However, we do not recommend undertaking so much work when there are other suitable hedging plants which do not require such vigorous pruning.

Common name: SPIREA

Latin name: *Spirea*

Height and spread: depending on the variety, 2-8 ft./.8-2.5 m; spread the same

Description: Spireas are characterized by a loose, open growth, and slender, arching branches. The small white flower clusters profusely cover these branches in late May and early June. However, some varieties have a more upright form and bear red or pink flower clusters. Leaves are usually small and green.

Sun: all white-blooming varieties should be grown in full sun; the red and pink bloomers can stand some shade

Soil: average

Moisture: average

Pruning: Spireas need to be pruned every few years to keep the flowers
coming and their legginess within bounds. The white varieties bloom
on second year wood (that is, branches that are at least two years old)
so prune these plants only after blooming. The red and pink blooming
plants can be pruned each spring before the leaves sprout. Cut about 6
in./15 cm off the top of each branch. Sometimes a second blooming
can be encouraged on the red bloomers by trimming off the spent
flower heads, but this can be a tedious job. Older shrubs need to be
rejuvenated because the plants become leggy, woody and rather
unattractive. Simply cut the old, thick grayish branches off at ground
level and let new shoots take over.

Comments: Spireas are the most commonly grown shrubs in Canada,
their arching sprays of small white flower clusters make a lovely sight
in early summer. Many varieties are hardy to -40°F/-40°C, but there are
a few that are less hardy. Spirea 'Van Houttei,' the Bridalwreath spirea,
is a profuse bloomer hardy to -22°F/-30°C. It is one of the most
popular shrubs sold in garden centers. The dependable *Spiraea trilobata*,
very hardy, is a twiggy shrub with a fan-like form. White flower clusters
are borne on the previous year's stems in June. It mixes well into a shrub
grouping and is an attractive foundation planting. Spirea 'Froebelii' is the
common red-flowered spirea found in garden centers. Hardy to -40°F/
-40°C, it grows 30 in./75 cm tall and spreads about double its height. The
long oval leaves are light green. It blooms during the month of June.
Cutting back the spent flower heads will stimulate a later crop of flowers.

Common name: SNOWBALL TREE

Latin name: *Viburnum opulus sterile*

Height and spread: height, 10 ft./3 m; spread, 8 ft./2.5 m

Description: Large shrub with gray stems bearing nearly 4 in./10 cm long
maple-like leaves. The dark green leaves are downy underneath. White
flowers appear on short side shoots in June, clustered into densely
packed, globe-shaped heads.

Sun: will tolerate light shade

Soil: average, but will grow best in moist, rich soils

Moisture: average

Pruning: only when necessary

Comments: One of the oldest recorded shrubs in cultivation, snowball tree is very showy, but unfortunately very susceptible to aphid attack. The best cultivar is 'Roseum.' Hardy to -40°F/-40°C.

Common name: SNOWBERRY

Latin name: *Symphoricarpos rivularis*

Height and spread: height, 5 ft./1.5 m; spread 7 ft./2 m

Description: a very compact, upright bush sporting small, dark green leaves, with small white inedible berries clustering on the top of the young shoots. The berries form on new wood.

Sun: tolerates partial shade

Soil: adapts to all soils

Moisture: average

Pruning: only for shape

Comments: Snowberry is a useful plant for a low dense hedge. Its cousin, *Symphoricarpos orbiculatus*, or Coralberry, bears red fruit and its leaves turn an attractive reddish-orange in fall. It suckers freely, but is a good shrub to cover slopes. Tolerates air pollution. If fungus attacks the berries, remove infected fruit and throw into the garbage. Snowberry and coralberry are hardy to -40°F/-40°C.

Common name: WAYFARING TREE

Latin name: *Viburnum lantana*

Height and spread: height, 8 ft./2.5 m; spread, 8 ft./2.5 m

Description: an open, branchy, coarse-textured shrub. Its twigs are downy and its leaves are large (up to 5 in./13 cm long and 3 in./8 cm wide), oval and light green. Large flattened clusters of small white flowers appear on the branch ends in late May. Flowers are followed by bright red inedible fruit which eventually turn black.

Sun: will tolerate partial shade

Soil: average

Moisture: average, but will withstand some dryness

Pruning: as needed, after bloom but it is best to let the shrub grow as it will

Comments: The Wayfaring tree needs lots of space. There are many viburnums, but not all are hardy in colder areas. Unfortunately, the fragrant varieties fall into this group. Hardy up to -40°F/-40°C.

Common name: WEIGELA

Latin name: *Weigela florida*

Height and spread: depending on variety, weigela have pointed green, purple or variegated leaves. Blooms are either white or pink and appear in May and June.

Sun: sun

Soil: average

Moisture: prefers dry conditions

Pruning: prune after flowers fade. May have to be pruned drastically every two or three years, cutting out thick older branches to keep it in good form and vigorous.

Comments: 'Dropmore Pink' and 'Variegata' are the most dependable varieties of weigela. Quite resistant to bugs and diseases. Needs to be sheltered from winter winds, or few blossoms will appear the next summer.

Common name: WINGED EUONYMUS

Latin name: *Euonymus alatus*

Height and spread: height, 6 ft./2 m, but can grow taller. Spread, 6-8 ft./2-2.5 m.

Description: Its dark green foliage turns bright red in fall. Red fruit. The bark is winged — which means that three long, brittle, thin strips of bark grow vertically along the main stems.

Sun: will tolerate light shade

Soil: average

Moisture: average

Pruning: as needed

Comments: There is also a dwarf variety, 'Compactus,' which is useful planted near the house or where its fall color will show to advantage. Susceptible to scale, aphids and mildew.

The MAYBE List

The following shrubs and trees are unsuitable, for a variety of reasons, for city or suburban lots:

Trees

Black walnut: its roots secrete a natural herbicide, which may kill nearby plantings.

Norway maple: nothing grows under its dense shade.

Silver maple: weak limbs.

Sugar maple: does not thrive in areas with a high degree of air pollution.

Willow: weak limbs; invasive roots; requires copious amounts of water.

Paper birch and silver birch: react badly to air pollution; invaded by birch-leaf miner.

Poplar: fast-growing, but weak and short-lived.

Shrubs

Forsythia: a pretty, hardy shrub unless you live in -4°F/-20°C or colder areas where the flower buds are often killed by low winter temperatures.

Potentilla: yellow flowers all summer, but some varieties do not shed their flowers; they linger on as dirty brown blobs.

Siberian or Chinese elm: too vigorous for hedging use — needs to be pruned at least three times a season.

Yew: foliage and red berries are poisonous, also not reliably hardy in most northern gardens.

Grumble, Grumble

By now you may be feeling confused and cranky — there are so many trees and shrubs to choose from out there. We advise you to just take your time. Most people plant far too many trees and shrubs for the size of their property anyway.

CHAPTER 10

Creep and Climb:
Vines and Ground Covers

Why, you ask yourself, would a Reluctant Gardener choose to grow vines or ground covers? Aren't they a lot of work? Aren't they fearsome treasures, limited to the gardens of keen green thumbs? No, not at all. We have put together a list of plants that will enable you to incorporate these pleasing alternatives to the usual annuals and perennials into your own low-maintenance yard. They are worth the little extra work they need, for they give the garden an extra dimension. Have some fun with vines and ground covers, give your horticultural imagination free rein. The use of either in the small or large garden give the whole design extra pizazz.

Some of these plants solve garden problems, others are simply enjoyed for their beauty on the landscape. There is such a diversity of ground covers and climbing plants to choose from that you will be able to find one to thrive in any problem area: a hot, dry spot shunned by most garden flowers (except portulaca), a steep slope (try creeping thyme). Perhaps there is a sight you would like to screen — your neighbor's plaster deer statue, for instance. A dense, permanent sprawl of honeysuckle vine might be the perfect choice.

What exactly are ground covers? Basically ground covers are low-growing, tough plants that spread to cover or blanket an area, preventing soil and water loss, as well as retarding the spread of weeds. Your lawn grass, for example, is a ground cover. However, if this ultimate ground cover does not thrive in a given area, another ground cover can be substituted for the grass.

Vines, or climbers, are plants which are genetically programmed to climb, either by twining, sprawling over upright supports, gripping or twisting their tendrils onto a support. Some need to be tied to their support.

Using Vines

Vines play a unifying role in the garden. Gardeners are always going on about planting vines to "anchor" the house to the ground, to unite garden to house. Vines, great concealers, can hide less-than-beautiful house walls or hideous boundary fences, including the disastrous do-it-yourself fence your inept neighbor erected. If you dislike the view that your neighbor's yard affords you (they sunbathe, but could use a stint at a health club), erect a trellis and cover it with vines — an instant, living screen (vigorous, large-leaved vines are best for creating dense screens). Is there an ugly stump in your garden that is too costly to remove or in an inaccessible spot? Train sprawling vines up and around it, place a pot of geraniums on it and the stump instantly becomes a horticultural asset. Bear in mind the vine's neighbors: if you plant a red-in-autumn Virginia creeper next to a purple-leaved sandcherry, the colors might shriek at each other.

When choosing a vine, you must decide not only where it will go, but also what it will climb on. A heavy, woody honeysuckle climber, for example, will rip apart a flimsy lattice trellis in no time flat. In addition, vines should be chosen by how they climb. If you have a stucco, stone, masonry or brick house, a vine such as Virginia creeper, which climbs by gripping the house surface, and clematis, which clings by use of tendrils, can safely be used on most surfaces. However, you should occasionally check that the vines are not damaging the house. If your house, garage or fence is made of wood, you would wisely avoid clinging vines. The amount of moisture they retain around their aerial roots and gripping pads is, in the long run, damaging to wood.

How to Plant Vines

Vines are planted like any other perennial or annual. Buy good stock, and, for perennials, plant in spring rather than autumn, so they will be well established by the time winter arrives. Vines need some special care, especially early in life. Before digging the planting hole, securely attach any trellises, wires or other forms of support where the vine is to be planted. Are you planting close to a house wall? The soil next to the foundation is often nutrient-starved and full of rubble. Before planting, it is even more necessary than usual to enrich such soil. As always, add lots of organic matter — compost is hard to beat. Plant as you would any other ornamental, making sure to leave a slight depression to retain water.

Then take a deep breath and cut the vine back by about a third of its above-ground height if the vine was bare rooted, or if the roots were damaged during planting. This helps the plant to establish itself quickly and strongly as it directs energy and nutrients into the root system. If roots are damaged in transplanting and reduced in number, they cannot adequately support the full top growth. After planting and pruning, tie the vine stems to the support, using soft twine, without binding the stem too tightly. If you use wire or tie the stem too tightly, you risk damaging the stem — wire especially can cut into a soft wooded stem. Space the stems evenly across the trellis or support. Water well for the first couple of weeks.

The next consideration is support. Most vines need some sort of support, such as a wooden or plastic trellis, found in most garden centers. Trellises can be bought in different heights and widths, so study the requirements of the vine before choosing the size, type and number of trellises. Inexpensive commercial trellises, available at garden centers and home renovation stores, can be rectangular or fan shaped. Do not waste money on cheap, flimsy trellises — too much time will be spent repairing them until, exasperated, you break them into kindling.

When buying a trellis, look for ones made of cedar, a durable wood that can be left unpainted — it weathers to an attractive gray. The laths should be thick enough not to bend in your hands and should be securely attached to one another. Plastic trellises are not usually attractive, except for the white fan-shaped ones. Use these trellises for lighter vines, not rampant growers.

There are alternatives to using a trellis. Wires can be anchored to house walls in a regular pattern through a system of screw eyes. This is a rather advanced project, so study a book on garden structures for details. If stout wire and anchors are used, this arrangement will support the heaviest of vines. Similarly, strips of wood lath can be screwed to the wall (use spacers to hold it a couple of inches out from the wall). Use more wood depending on the heaviness of your vine.

If you decide to use a trellis, it is, of course, necessary to attach it to a wall or fence. Nothing is more frustrating than a poorly-attached trellis which, under the strain of a vigorous vine, sways, twists, lists and needs constant adjustment. Angle brackets are useful attachments which hold the trellis a few inches out from wall or fence. This spacing allows the breeze to move behind the vine keeping it cooler in summer heat, and discourages bugs setting up homes in such sheltered places. Use screws rather than nails to attach the trellis, because screws can be backed out (and then screwed back in) if you ever need to detach the trellis — to paint or repair behind it, perhaps. The trellis, vine and all, can be laid carefully on the ground while work progresses.

Heavy vines need stout, permanent supports. A dead tree, or a thick post (well-anchored in the soil and wrapped with chicken wire) is suitable for a heavy, woody vine like honeysuckle. The large wooden posts of a well-built porch or a solid arbor of, say, 1 x 3 cedar will take a determined climber like Dutchman's pipe. Medium-heavy Virginia creeper will do well winding itself through a chain-link fence, in fact this makes a fine hedge substitute if something narrow is needed. However, do not ask chain-link to support a heavier climber: down the road from one of your authors is a chain-link fence that has been heaved clean out of the ground by an old honeysuckle vine.

Maintaining Vines

Check the vine every week during its first summer to ensure that the stems are growing in the direction you want them to go. This is the fun part of growing climbers — bending them this way and that as they grow, sending them in the right direction to create a dense screen a few years down the road. Once established, let Mother Nature take her course. Fertilize as you would the rest of the garden.

Be aware that some rampant growers will need to be restrained occasionally by pruning. If the vines are growing up house walls, they will not politely avoid windows, eavestroughs or any other spot where a vine is not wanted. Be prepared to take out the ladder when it becomes necessary to free your house from this leafy invasion. Simply snip off the growing tip whenever you see a branch headed for forbidden territory.

There are two schools of thought when it comes to cutting vines back in autumn, and the adherents of each thinks the adherents of the other are idiots. We are non-cutters. Our perennial vines are never cut back in autumn because winter-kill does plenty of cutting back for us, thank you very much. Any length of stalk that survives will put out new growth all along its length. Those gardeners who clip their vines back to the ground in autumn have to start from scratch every year.

Most perennial vines do not die back to the ground during winter, which means that in spring new growth sprouts all along the surviving branches. Because of this, it is important that in autumn you give nature a hand and make sure that each branch is firmly attached to the support at several points along its length. Do this for every branch, otherwise the loose branches will whip about in winter winds and risk damage or death.

Using Ground Covers

Traditionally, ground covers are planted around the base of deciduous trees where grass does not grow happily. A shade-loving ground cover, such as lily-of-the-valley, will provide an attractive ground-level setting for a tree. As well, ground cover creates a mowing buffer between lawn and tree trunk. Ground cover planted on steep slopes alleviates the need for mowing, which might be dangerous. As well, it prevents erosion on slopes. An annual ground cover, such as portulaca, can temporarily fill up a large, bare area while you make up your mind what to plant there permanently.

The use of ground cover is an excellent way to unify a garden design, bringing together diverse parts of the yard. For example, planting the same ground cover beneath every tree or around every shrub on your lot would give a feeling of visual unity, especially valuable in a small yard. Ground cover can enhance a design in other ways. For example, if your yard contains a dramatic contour, such as a dip or rise, ground cover could be planted in it or along it as a dramatic highlight. Ground cover can also be used to define or fill unloved spaces, such as the area between your garage and the neighbor's.

When choosing a ground cover, do not forget what it is paired with. You will want to consider whether or not it is in scale with nearby objects. For example, you might not want to plant a miniature ground cover around a massive oak. Think about color combinations. Would a red-tinted sedum planted at the base of a pink clematis be an attractive combination? Leaf characteristics are important too. Bergenia has coarse leaves which might not show to advantage under, say, a delicate-leaved birch tree.

How to Plant Ground Covers

Ground covers are often planted "on centre." That is, if the ground cover spreads 18 in./45 cm, place each plant so that its central stem is 18 in./45 cm away from the central stem of its neighbor. Thus, two plants placed side by side will brush tips when mature — 9 in./23 cm from stem to branch tips of one plus 9 in./23 cm from stem to branch tips of the other add up to 18 in./45 cm, so use 18 in./45 cm as your planting center, see? However, if you can afford it (ground covers can be a significant expense if a large area is to be covered), plant them more closely. Planting ground cover plants in staggered rows not only looks better in the first years, but this arrangement also covers the area more efficiently. Staggered row plantings on slopes helps retard soil erosion while the plants are establishing themselves.

Let us say you have an area between two garages which is difficult to mow. You have decided to plant bronze-leaved ajuga in this space which measures about 9 ft./3 m by 4 ft./ 1 meter. Ajuga can be planted on 12 in./30 cm centers. First, figure out the number of 12 in./30 cm sections in the length: in this case 9. Then, figure out the number of 12 in./30 cm sections in the width: 4. You would thus multiply 9 x 4 = 36, so you need 36 plants to fill the area. In other words, divide the spacing distance into the length, then into the width, then multiply the two together to calculate the number of plants needed to fill the space.

A major drawback of using ground cover is that for the first two or three years the area must be meticulously weeded. It takes this long for most ground covers to fill their given areas. If the cover must compete with weeds, it will take all the longer, or perhaps even give up completely. So, for the first two or three years, weed vigilantly. The job will gradually diminish and then vanish, because many ground covers carpet areas so densely that weeds are smothered. If you do not like looking at bare earth while the cover is spreading, interplant the newly planted ground cover with annuals, which has the extra advantage of helping prevent weed build-up.

Maintaining Ground Covers

Once established, ground cover is low-maintenance. Not no maintenance, however. Watering is important, because this concentrated planting will use a lot of water. If your ground cover needs a little help remaining dense and bushy, do an annual pruning. A very low ground cover (many sedums are under 6 in./15 cm) can be mown over — use the highest setting on the mower to give it a reviving brush cut. It will look alarmingly awful for a while, then will look remarkably better than it began. Hand pruning is adequate in small areas — use large loppers or hedge clippers. Woody ground covers, such as *Alyssum saxatilis*, should be hand-pruned.

How does the gardener know when to prune? Trim flowering plants after the flowers have faded. Also, check your ground cover to see if it has lost its "fresh" look. Are fewer flowers blooming, are more woody, leafless stems showing than you would like? For example, Snow-in-summer, left without an occasional pruning, can become very leggy, its pretty silver leaves sprouting only from the ends of long, creeping bare stems. To remedy such a case of the blahs, prune back about 25% of the branches. One function of pruning, remember, is to stimulate new growth.

BEWARE OF THINGS THAT CREEP IN THE NIGHT — We would like to warn you away from two particularly invasive ground covers. The first is Aegopodium podagraria 'Variegatum' or goutweed, a deciduous perennial bearing deceptively innocent-looking variegated green and white leaves. It spreads so rapidly by underground stems that it is quite difficult to eradicate once it is established. One of your authors, after three years hard weeding and digging, thought she had eradicated it from a corner of her yard where it had stealthily crept from under the neighbor's fence. She dug up the ground, traced each root and stem, thinking each year she had seen the last of it. But once again, it is panting at the fence, eager to retake its former territory. Goutweed will take over your entire yard, lawn and all, if not contained somehow. It is best not to plant it in the first place.

Another perennial ground cover with a bad attitude is Coronilla varia or crown vetch. It is an excellent erosion control plant because its deep roots and proliferating underground stems hold the soil fast on steep slopes. However, plant it only if you have a large area well away from more desirable plantings, where absolutely nothing else will grow. We knew people who planted it, thinking it would rapidly fill an ugly, clay-filled area. The vetch certainly fulfilled their hopes and more as it threw itself into the lawn and flowerbeds. Its legendary weed-choking abilities were practiced on every ornamental in sight. At least three years of steady digging was needed to rid that yard of the pest.

In general, the upkeep of our recommended vines and ground covers is minimal. These plants are all hardy to at least -22°F/-30°C (often to -40°F/-40°C) and do not need elaborate methods of winter protection. As well, we have chosen varieties that are not plagued by a host of insect pests or diseases.

The YES! List of Vines and Ground Covers
Vines

Common name: CLEMATIS

Latin name: *Clematis*

Height: Grows about 10-20 ft./3-6 m high

Description: a brittle-stemmed perennial with heart-shaped leaves. Climbs by means of twining leaf stalks. Grown for its beautiful flowers (white, lavender, purple, pink, red and yellow) which appear in early summer and thereafter sporadically until late summer.

Wild or tidy: tidy

Sun: full sun, but clematis likes its roots in the shade

Soil: average

Moisture: keep well watered during dry spells

Staking: needs good support

Pruning: cut back dead wood in spring, no other pruning will be necessary

Comments: Clematis likes a sunny head and cool, shady feet. Many gardeners plant the vine behind a perennial or a bush large enough to cast a shadow over the clematis roots. If this is not possible, place a large, flat rock over the root area. Do not plant annuals for this purpose, because the planting and removing could harm the clematis roots. Be careful not to break the brittle stems when training them onto the support. There are many large-flowering hybrids on the market. *Clematis jackmanii*, a deep purple-flowering variety, is especially hardy in gardens in -22°F/-30°C, although a little winter protection would do no harm. Do not be discouraged over its initial poor showing, as clematis takes a couple of seasons to establish itself.

Common name: DUTCHMAN'S PIPE

Latin name: *Aristolochia durior*

Height: climbs up to 35 ft./10 m

Description: perennial. Large heart-shaped leaves on vigorous twining stems. Inconspicuous brown flowers appear in late spring, early summer, hidden in the heavy foliage. The flowers look like tobacco pipes, hence its common name.

Wild or tidy: wild

Sun: full sun, but tolerates some shade

Soil: average

Moisture: can withstand short dry periods

Staking: needs a very strong support

Pruning: no

Comments: This twining vine is an old-fashioned favorite. Usually grown as a screen, its large leaves and prolific shoots guarantee coverage in a short time. Do not prune woody stems in spring because new growth sprouts from them. In the beginning you may have to train the stems in the direction you want them to grow, then step back and let nature take its course. Heavy wire, arranged in a fan-shape, attached from foundation to roof, works as an effective support. Bugs are not a problem on this vine. Hardy to -4°F/-20°C, or a sheltered spot in a colder area.

Common name: HONEYSUCKLE VINE

Latin name: *Lonicera*

Height: grows at least 10 ft./3 m

Description: woody perennial. Twining stalks support medium-sized, pointed, green leaves. Grown for the clusters of buff and pink tubular flowers which appear in early summer and sporadically during the rest of the season.

Wild or tidy: either

Sun: full sun

Soil: average

Moisture: will withstand drought

Staking: needs a strong support

Pruning: only the dead wood in spring

Comments: There are only two honeysuckle vines hardy to -22°F/-30°C: the Dropmore scarlet honeysuckle, bred for harsh prairie conditions, and 'Goldflame' honeysuckle. The Dropmore variety, also know as 'Dropmore Trumpet' and 'Scarlet Trumpet,' has bright red flowers and blooms mainly in midsummer, but will produce flowers until frost. Goldflame's flowers, slightly fragrant, are pink on the outside and golden yellow inside. The stems need to be trained, at first, around a support. Take care, as the stems are easily broken. Honeysuckle vines make a brilliant show against a strong wood fence or wall, once they are established — which can take up to three years. Unfortunately caterpillars and wooly aphids like to munch on this plant.

Common name: MORNING GLORY

Latin name: *Ipomoea purpurea*

Height: grows to at least 12 ft./4 m until frost kills it

Description: an annual vine that twines around its support. Fresh green-colored, heart-shaped leaves. Flowers range from a deep blue, to white, pink or lavender.

Wild or tidy: either

Sun: full sun

Soil: average

Moisture: keep well watered

Staking: needs a strong trellis

Pruning: frost kills it. Remove dead growth from support before snowfall.

Comments: Morning glories are strong growers and quickly cover a trellis, fence or strong strings attached to a house. They do not begin blooming until late summer, but then do not stop blooming until frost. The easy-to-grow seeds are slow to germinate. We soak them in warm water for a day until a root appears. Plant the seeds immediately where the plants are to grow. Sometimes morning glory falls victim to spider mites and aphids.

Common name: SCARLET RUNNER BEAN

Latin name: *Phaseolus coccineus*

Height: can grow over 16 ft./5 m

Description: an annual vine which twines around a support. Produces brilliant red flowers which look like typical bean flowers.

Wild or tidy: either

Sun: full sun

Soil: average

Moisture: keep well-watered

Staking: can be grown on strong strings

Pruning: frost will kill it

Comments: Scarlet runner bean vines are inexpensive, old-fashioned favorites used to screen a porch or cover an ugly fence. Easy to grow from seed, the vines are vigorous and prolific. You can eat the beans if they are picked when young and slender. If you let the beans mature, they become starchy and woody tasting. A good plant for kids, but do not let them handle the chemically-treated seed. As with all annual vines, pull it off its support in autumn, chop it up and compost it.

Common name: VIRGINIA CREEPER

Latin name: *Parthenocissus quinquefolia*

Height: can grow as high as 50 ft./15 m

Description: a rapidly growing perennial, it climbs by using its tendrils. The five-lobed, green leaves are long, serrated, and turn purple-red in autumn.

Wild or tidy: either

Sun: full sun

Soil: average

Moisture: water in times of drought

Staking: it will climb anything by clinging with tendrils and small disks. Becomes heavy when mature, so its support must be strong.

Pruning: only when it becomes invasive

Comments: Virginia creeper, an effective screen, is the most common vine used to cover house walls. It grows rapidly, establishing itself within a couple of growing seasons. *P. quinquefolia* has large leaflets and *P. quinquefolia engelmannii* (Engelmann's ivy) has smaller leaflets. Hardy to -40°F/-40°C.

Ground Covers

Common name: BERGENIA, SIBERIAN TEA

Latin name: *Bergenia crassifolia*

Height and spread: height, 18 in./45 cm; space new plants 18 in./45 cm apart.

Description: perennial. Plants form rosettes of bright green, finely-toothed, leaves about 6 in./15 long. Clusters of rose-colored flowers. Grows along a creeping rhizome — a sort of above-ground root.

Wild or tidy: either

Sun: prefers light shade

Soil: likes well-drained soil, but is generally not fussy

Moisture: average

Pruning: needs to be cut back when rhizome becomes leggy

Comments: Divide when clumps become crowded. Good for small spaces, especially near shrubs and around rocks. Bergenia combines well with hostas and ferns. Cannot be walked on. Hardy to -22°F/-30°C.

Common name: BUGLEWEED

Latin name: *Ajuga reptans*

Height and spread: height, 4-6 in./10-15 cm. Space new plants 6-10 in./15-25 cm apart.

Description: perennial. Low, fast-growing mats of brilliantly colored foliage. Spring-blooming, lavender-blue flower spikes. The oval, tightly clustered leaves are found in bronze, green, purple or green edged with pale yellow.

Wild or tidy: tidy

Sun: prefers light shade

Soil: needs a fast-draining, rich soil

Moisture: keep moist, but not soggy

Pruning: lightly mow on the highest setting after spring bloom to rejuvenate

Comments: Grown for its foliage. When area becomes too crowded simply divide the clump and transplant elsewhere. The creeping stems root wherever they touch soil. Good underplanting for shrubs, but be careful, it may spread into the lawn. Susceptible to various insect and disease attacks. You can walk on it. Hardy to -50°F/-45°C.

Common name: CHAMOMILE

Latin name: *Chamaemelum nobile*

Height and spread: height, 1-8 in./2.5-20 cm. Space plants about 6 in./15 cm apart

Description: Perennial. An evergreen herb which forms mats of finely cut green leaves. Small green or yellow flower heads surrounded by white petals are held on slender stems above the foliage.

Wild or tidy: either

Sun: full sun

Soil: average

Moisture: can withstand drought

Pruning: run the mower over it

Comments: Chamomile is a favorite European lawn substitute. You can walk on it without fear of harming the plant. In fact it gives off a pleasant odor when walked on. If you like herbal teas, cut off the flowerheads and steep in boiling water — very soothing. Hardy to -40°F/-40°C.

Common name: CREEPING JUNIPER

Latin name: *Juniperus horizontalis*

Height and spread: depends on the variety, of which there are many. Height, between 8-12 in./20-30 cm; spread, from 3-10 ft./1-3 m

Description: perennial shrub with flat evergreen, scale-like leaves growing along long prostrate branches. Depending on the variety, the shrub's foliage can be silver-blue, green, gray-green, variegated blue-green or light yellow.

Wild or tidy: tidy

Sun: full sun

Soil: needs a well-drained soil

Moisture: will tolerate drying out

Pruning: no

Comments: Creeping juniper is a hardy, low-maintenance ground cover. It grows slowly, but, once established, individual plants cover wide areas and form dense mats which effectively smother all weeds. Too prickly to walk on. A drawback is its high price tag. Most varieties are hardy to -50°F/-45°C.

Common name: DAY LILY (**see Chapter 7 on perennials**)

Common name: HEN AND CHICKENS, HOUSE LEEK

Latin name: *Sempervivum*

Height and spread: height, 2-4 in./5-10 cm. Plant rosettes about 6 in./15 cm apart.

Description: perennial. A large group of fleshy, succulent plants which hug the ground and usually grow in rosettes. Spreads by offsets (small baby replicas of the mother rosette) which form on the side of the mother plant. Wide range of color and leaf shape. Flowers usually form on the top of the tall (up to 12 in./30 cm) spikes it sends up later in the season. Green, red and bronze foliage can be found.

Wild or tidy: either

Sun: full sun

Soil: average

Moisture: will withstand drought

Pruning: cut off spent flower stalks at ground level

Comments: Slow-spreading, but fun. Break off the offsets from the mother plant and poke into the soil; they root very easily. Too brittle to walk on. Hardy to -22°F/-30°C.

Common name: HOSTA, PLANTAIN LILIES **(see Chapter 7 on perennials)**

Common name: JAPANESE SPURGE

Latin name: *Pachysandra terminalis*

Height and spread: height, 6-8 in./15-20 cm. Plant 12 in./30 cm apart.

Description: an evergreen perennial bearing green, shiny oval, lightly toothed leaves, which grow in clusters at the top of upright stems. Creamy white blooms appear in spring. Spurge spreads by underground stems.

Wild or tidy: tidy

Sun: will grow happily in filtered to dense shade

Soil: rich

Moisture: needs to be on the moist shade, but can withstand drought

Pruning: no

Comments: Slow to establish itself, Japanese spurge is a favored ground cover for shady spots where not much else will grow. Some gardeners report success when spurge has been planted in the dense shade of maple trees. Can be walked on once it is thickly established. Hardy to -40°F/-40°C.

Common name: MOSS PHLOX, MOSS PINK

Latin name: *Phlox subulata*

Height and spread: height, 4-6 in./10-15 cm; spread, 18 in./45 cm or wider. Plant 12-18 in./30-45 cm apart.

Description: this perennial forms dense mats of thin, green-leaved stems and masses of 1/2 in./1 cm star-shaped flowers which appear by mid-May. Varieties can be found in shades of pink and red, as well as white and lavender.

Wild or tidy: either

Sun: full sun

Soil: average, but tolerates some dryness

Moisture: needs good drainage

Pruning: lightly mow after flowering to promote new, compact growth

Comments: Pretty moss phlox blooms from late spring sporadically into mid-summer. After the flowers have faded, the fresh green–colored mats remain quite attractive. When the plants become crowded, simply divide them, planting the divisions elsewhere or give them away to a friend. Can be stepped on occasionally but not walked on. Hardy to -40°F/-40°C.

Common name: PERIWINKLE

Latin name: *Vinca minor*

Height and spread: height, 6-10 in./15-25 cm; spread 12-24 in./30-60 cm

Description: perennial. Low mats of long, trailing stems which root as they spread. The evergreen leaves are dark green and shiny. Spring flowers are usually blue or lavender, however white varieties can be found.

Wild or tidy: either

Sun: prefers light shade, but will take some sun

Soil: average

Moisture: average

Pruning: no

Comments: Periwinkle is very slow growing, but easy to care for and adaptable to many conditions. Root stem pieces or divide when area is crowded. Be careful not to confuse a pink-blooming annual variety with the perennial ones. Too tall to walk on. Hardy to -40°F/-40°C.

Common name: PORTULACA, MOSS ROSE (**see Chapter 6 on annuals**)

Comments: Too brittle to walk on.

Common name: ROCK CRESS

Latin name: *Arabis alpina*

Height and spread: height 5-10 in./12-25 cm; spread, 24 in./60 cm. Plant 10 in./25 cm apart.

Description: perennial. Forms mats of evergreen, smooth gray leaves covered by profuse white flowers in spring.

Wild or tidy: tidy

Sun: fine in a full sun, hot area, or maybe in just a little shade

Soil: average

Moisture: drought-resistant

Pruning: after flowering, lightly mow to cut back upright stems, and stimulate more horizontal growth.

Comments: Not suitable for a large area or for walking on, arabis works best in small, contained spaces. It is easily propagated by division and cuttings. Hardy to -22°F/-30°C.

Common name: SEDUM, STONECROP

Latin name: *Sedum*

Height and spread: Depending on the species and variety, sedums can be found growing between 1-24 in./2.5-60 cm high and spreading from 10-24 in./25-60 cm wide.

Description: perennial. There are over 300 species and hundreds of hybrids to choose from. Fleshy leaves and trailing, creeping growth characterize these succulent plants. The leaves vary from tiny, fat needle-shaped leaves to broad fleshy ones. Flowers are white, pink, red or yellow.

Wild or tidy: either

Sun: full sun

Soil: average

Moisture: can withstand drought

Pruning: remove flower stalk as soon as flowers fade

Comments: Sedums are easily grown and propagated. They root willingly from cuttings, but will also root wherever their stems touch ground. Most of the sedums are brittle, but the broken pieces can be stuck back into the soil, watered and left to happily root. Too brittle to walk on. Most are hardy to -40°F/-40°C.

Common name: SNOW-IN-SUMMER

Latin name: *Cerastium tomentosum*

Height and spread: height, 4-6 in./10-15 cm; plant 12-24 in./30-60 cm apart

Description: perennial. Dense mats of small, narrow, wooly gray leaves on slender creeping stems. Masses of small white flowers are held well above the foliage. Flowers appear in July.

Wild or tidy: tidy

Sun: full sun

Soil: needs well-drained, rich soil

Moisture: average

Pruning: after flowering, mow high to cut off dead flower stems

Comments: Good in areas where gray is wanted. It is a rapid grower, and easily self-seeds. Cut off the flower stems to maintain a neat appearance. Too fragile to be walked on. Hardy to -40°F/-40°C.

Common name: THYME, CREEPING THYME

Latin name: *Thymus*

Height and spread: height, 1-6 in./2.5-15 cm; spreads up to 24 in./60 cm. Plant about 6 in./15 cm apart.

Description: perennial. There are many species of thyme which form creeping mounds. The tiny aromatic leaves, depending on variety, can be green, gray, variegated or chartreuse. Nearly all are edible. Flowers are either white or purple — all are small.

Wild or tidy: either

Sun: likes sun, but can tolerate some light shade

Soil: average, but not too rich

Moisture: average

Pruning: lightly mow after bloom is spent

Comments: You can safely walk on a carpet of thyme. Thyme looks attractive planted between stepping stones, near rocks or on gentle slopes. Wooly thyme with its fuzzy gray leaves can be contrasted nicely with the green-leaved thymes. If you grow thyme in an area which does not get much foot or pet traffic, you can use the leaves in your cooking. Thyme is easily propagated by division.

Common name: VIOLET (see Chapter 7 on perennials)

Comments: Cannot be walked on.

The MAYBE List of Ground Covers

Basket-of-gold *(Alyssum saxatilis)*: This frequently used perennial rock garden plant can also be used as a ground cover. It grows about 12 in./30 cm high and spreads about the same. Its gray-green leaves are complemented by clusters of golden yellow flowers in spring. Alyssum likes full sun and well-drained average soils. Cut it back after flowering to encourage compact growth. Useful in small spaces, but has a tendency to become leggy.

Dusty miller (*Artemisia*): The perennial forms of this plant can be used as ground cover. The gray feathery foliage is attractive in the right spot. Artemisias favor hot, sunny locations. 'Silver Mound' forms 12 in./ 30 cm wide, 8 in./20 cm high mounds. Not reliably hardy in temperatures of -22°F/-30°C. Can look ragged by late summer. Some varieties bloom, but the flowers are small and insignificant.

Ferns: There are many, many varieties of ferns to choose from. They are excellent for moist, shaded, organically enriched areas. However, some varieties are so vigorous and tough, we have seen them poke through an asphalt driveway. We are particularly attached to *Adiantium pedatum*, the maidenhair fern. Its finely leaved stems do not exceed 24 in./60 cm in height. This fern is a slow spreader. It looks great in a cool, lightly shaded corner. However, ferns in general are not the best ground covers, for they cannot be walked on without breaking and some varieties can be quite invasive.

Lily-of-the-valley (*Convallaria majalis*): A sentimental favorite, lily-of-the-valley can be quite invasive. It spreads aggressively by underground stems and can be difficult to eradicate if allowed to grow into the perennial border. However, this hardy perennial thrives in shady spots and produces fragrant, small white bell-shaped flowers, which make good cut flowers. Unfortunately, the bright red berries which appear in the fall are poisonous and can be attractive to small children.

Ribbon grass (*Phalaris arundinacea 'picta'*): Ribbon grass is tough, tall and tolerant of poor growing conditions and low winter temperatures. Its attractive green and white variegated leaves flourish in spots where nothing else will grow. However, it is very invasive and spreads by vigorous underground runners. It can be difficult to eradicate. In late summer it produces plumes of buff-colored seed stalks.

CHAPTER 11

Magic in Small Packages: Bulbs

Your authors live in Ottawa, and so are spoiled rotten when it comes to spring bulbs, especially tulips. The people of Holland send us thousands of bulbs every year because the city gave asylum to their royal family during World War II. These bulbs, combined with what the city contributes, make our parks look like vast Persian carpets all during May. You can hardly move through the parks for the numbers of winter-weary Canadians drifting, dreamy little smiles on their faces, from one swath of color to another.

Certainly, those first spring flowers seem almost miraculous. However, when you meet them at the garden center, bulbs look like brown lumps heaped in unexciting piles. But remember that inside these dull exteriors lies the promise of spring. Bulbs are just waiting to burst into life the minute conditions are favorable. Their amazingly accurate inner clocks know exactly when to cue their leaves and flower spikes to poke themselves above ground. Their above-ground life is short and intense, for all spring bulb flowers and foliage are gone by late June, and have returned to their underground activities. But while they last, they are cheery additions to any garden.

What Is a Bulb?

Although we associate bulbs with spring, there are also summer and autumn-flowering ones — 3000 species world-wide. They range from the giant, globular-flowered allium to the tiny specie crocus. Luckily for the home gardener, many bulbs are quite adaptable and will grow almost anywhere, except for very damp spots. This eager adaptability is supported by the plant's efficient food storing mechanism. It is easy to get bulbs to bloom the first season, but after that the gardener must maintain bulbs in such a way that enough food is stored to bring them back for another year of bloom. Reluctant Gardeners will be happy to know that with minimum care many bulbs will bloom happily for a number of years.

Although bulbs are lumped together under one name, they are actually divided into five broad classes: true bulbs (for example, tulips and daffodils); corms (gladiolus and crocus); tubers (tuberous begonias); tuberous roots (dahlia); and rhizomes (iris). True bulbs enclose a nearly complete embryo of the mature plant. If you do not mind sacrificing a tulip or hyacinth bulb, cut it in half and you will see a profile of a miniature plant — layers of leaves surrounding a small, perfectly shaped flower bud on a miniature stem.

A corm, a solid mass of storage tissue, often looks like a slightly flattened ball — the bottom and top are somewhat indented. From the bottom indentation, or basal plate, roots emerge, and from the top — from eyes or buds — flowers and leaves originate. As the plant grows the corm shrivels away, and a new corm forms on top of, or next to, the old, original corm.

A tuber is also a solid mass of storage tissue, but does not have a discernible base plate. Tuberous roots are swollen, food-storing roots. To decide which end is up when planting, look for the bud eyes where flowering stalks will emerge.

A rhizome is defined as a thickened underground stem which grows horizontally just under the surface of the soil. Roots emerge from the bottom edge and flowers from the upper.

Despite the differences, all bulbs share the same general characteristic — they are highly developed food-storage systems which have adapted themselves to live underground.

How to Buy Bulbs

Let's start at the beginning, when the thought of tulips, daffodils, crocuses and lilies are just a gleam in your eye. Maybe you have skipped through the book to read our YES! bulb list, or maybe you have fallen under the spell of the bulb listings in a mail-order catalogue. Be careful: catalogue descriptions can weave their magic over the most hardened gardeners. Before you can break the trance, you have ordered more bulbs than you have the space or budget for. One of your authors succumbed to a tantalizingly described fragrant specie crocus and ordered two dozen. She planted them in large clumps in the small front yard flowerbed, eagerly anticipating the waves of perfume which would waft over her porch in spring. The trance was not broken until the next spring when she gazed down at the miniature, washed-out lavender blooms and realized — as she should have done earlier — that specie crocus grow only about 1 in./2.5 cm tall. Therefore, in order to fully enjoy their supposedly wonderful fragrance, she would have to lie flat on her stomach — nose in the clump and feet dangling over the street curb. Just call her gullible.

Although we recommend that beginning gardeners buy from local garden centers you can, if you really want something rare, order from bulb suppliers' catalogues. If the firm is reputable, you have some protection against bad material. A reputable firm is one that does *not* offer fifty tulip bulbs for $2.99, or load bulb descriptions with words like "fabulous" and "fantastic." While these deals may sound great, the bulbs you receive are not always the best quality and probably will not last long in the garden. While catalogues are the main source for hard-to-find colors and varieties, your local garden center usually carries an adequate general selection of bulbs. A good bulb catalogue, however, is a valuable planting guide. Often instructions for spacing, depth of planting, hardiness and location are noted.

We have had varying experiences ordering by mail. One of the main problems is the bulbs do not always arrive in the best condition: mail-order bulbs may be covered in aphids and mold. The packing material — sphagnum moss, sometimes sawdust — obviously provided optimum conditions for the eggs to hatch and the mold to grow. If you deal with a reputable firm, however, you are usually reimbursed for damaged bulbs. Until you want out-of-the-ordinary bulbs, it is best for the beginning gardener to shop at a garden center — where you are spared mail-order postage and handling charges.

Spring-blooming bulbs usually appear in garden centers in labeled boxes in late August. Autumn bloomers are available in mid-summer. Summer-blooming bulbs go on sale when garden centers open in the spring. The boxes are often identified not only by name, but also by a color picture of the bulb in bloom. Sometimes small reproductions of these pictures are offered to customers. The reproductions usually have planting information as well as height and spread measurements printed on the back. Handy little slips, indeed, to take home to remind you, if you do not write it down, what you have just bought.

Now, do not just grab the first bulbs your eager hands touch. Examine each bulb, choosing it as carefully as you would a tomato. You want firm, not spongy or shriveled, bulbs, ones without bruises, cuts, soft spots or obvious blemishes. As well, each bulb should feel heavy for its size — overly light-feeling bulbs may have dried out. Do not worry if the bulb has small nicks or if its papery covering is loose. If you have a choice, select large-sized bulbs — larger size can often mean more and larger flowers. Sometimes larger sized bulbs are more expensive. As well, newer hybrids are more expensive, just like the latest clothing styles.

We do not as a rule like to buy pre-packaged bulbs, because they prevent us from accurately judging their condition. We also do not buy bargain bulbs offered in non-gardening stores. These packaged bulbs are stored and displayed under less than optimum conditions. Not a bargain at all, since their performance and survival rate will probably be low.

Try to buy bulbs close to the time you plan to plant them. If planting is delayed, open the bags and store them in a cool, dry place. If they are stored in a damp place or in a closed container, the bulbs may turn moldy or rot.

Where to Plant

Given good drainage and enough sun, there is almost no limit to where bulbs can be planted. If flowers are already successfully growing in the locations you have chosen, bulbs will probably also thrive there. Remember that bulbs are allergic to soggy soils, because they will rot there.

Bulbs display well when mixed into the perennial border, in beds on their own, under trees or even in the lawn. Your choice. Wherever you choose, however, try to plant the bulbs where their dying foliage will be hidden by other plants. This is easy to do in the perennial border, but takes a bit of planning if you choose to display bulbs on their own. Some gardeners interplant bulbs with a tall ground cover to hide this withering foliage. Others plant forget-me-not, pansies or hardy primroses to provide extra spring color and a screen for dying foliage in the bulb bed.

Why this concern over dying foliage? Because you cannot cut the leaves away once the flowers stop blooming. Rather you must let the stem and foliage wither and die. Why, you ask? Through photosynthesis and other chemical processes, the leaves and stem manufacture the food necessary to support the bulb through its dormant period and into the next season's growth and bloom. If the leaves are trimmed off while they are still green, the bulb will come up blind, that is, flowerless, next year.

Therefore, after the flower has dropped its petals, prune off the seed case — nothing else.

If the sight of yellowing, wilting foliage is bothersome, try to tuck the offending leaves behind a nearby plant. Some gardeners tie the leaves together in a business-like clump or even braid them, but we do not recommend this because it reduces the amount of leaf surface exposed to the sun, and thus the bulbs cannot manufacture all the food they need. Once the leaves have turned yellow and have fully withered, you know the bulb has stored its food and you can carefully pull out or cut off the foliage and compost it.

In the perennial border, plant bulbs as you would other flowers — their planting positions governed by height and spread. Thus, small bulbs such as crocus and grape hyacinth should be planted at the front of the border, medium tall varieties, such as hyacinths, in the center and tall-growing bulbs such as lilies near the back of the border. Bulbs look best planted in clumps. Usually five tulips or six crocuses to a planting makes a good display. The smaller the bloom, the more bulbs should be planted together. If you plant them in rows or singly, their flowers are lost in the overall garden display or look a bit ridiculous — like stiff little soldiers standing on parade. This type of planting is best left to the city parks department.

Naturalized plantings, a favorite British technique, is often used in North American gardens. Essentially, naturalized bulbs are planted to look as if Mother Nature herself had plopped them into place. Bulbs are planted in lawns, under deciduous trees, in woodland settings, along shrub groupings — wherever a wilder look is wanted. Naturalized plantings are allowed to grow as they will, with little or no maintenance necessary. This does not mean that you can skimp on adequate soil preparation — on the contrary, good soil will ensure long bulb life.

Naturalized bulbs are usually planted in irregularly-shaped clumps or drifts. The largest concentration of bulbs should be planted in the center of the grouping, while dribbling out the bulbs around the edges. A more haphazard method is simply to walk to the area where you have decided to naturalize some bulbs and toss the bulbs here and there, planting them where they land. Or, stand with your back to the lawn and toss handfuls of bulbs over your shoulder. Who cares if the neighbors think you have gone mad?

Not all bulbs are happy to be treated this way — some want more respect. However, daffodils, grape hyacinth, crocus, scilla and glory-of-the-snow are especially suited to naturalizing in lawns, for they multiply easily and are very hardy. The only drawback in the urban garden is that you must wait for the foliage to wither down before cleaning up or mowing the area if you want the bulbs to multiply, let alone bloom the next year. As well, it is hazardous to walk on the naturalized area in early spring, because you might step on an emerging shoot.

When to Plant

Early autumn is the best time to plant spring-flowering bulbs. We like to plant our bulbs in mid- to late-September before the weather becomes too chilly. There have been years, however, when the pressures of work and family life delayed all good intentions. Both your authors have found themselves in winter coats and gloves digging madly in freezing garden soil as the first snow fell. This is not recommended for the Reluctant Gardener who might just say the heck with it and stay inside and read a good book.

Summer-blooming bulbs, such as lilies, are planted in the spring. And autumn blooming bulbs, such as the autumn crocus, are planted in August.

How to Plant Bulbs

Choose a warm, fresh autumn day. Before collecting your equipment, be sure you know exactly where you are going to plant. Gather up bulbs, shovel, trowel, bulb planter (if you have one), garden gloves and kneepads. It is usually more efficient to dig all the necessary holes before tossing in the bulbs. What you want to do is dig-dig-dig, toss-toss-toss, cover-cover-cover, rather than dig-toss-cover, dig-toss-cover. This procedure prevents disaster. If you are interrupted and cannot complete the bulb planting in one day, empty holes will signal where to start up the next time. (We used to dig a hole, plant the bulbs, cover them up, then move to the next area. However, once we had to stop in the middle of planting for some household emergency — it may have been the day the cat got her head stuck in the inner workings of a reclining chair. Anyway, by the time we got around to finishing off the bulbs, we had forgotten where what was planted. We soon regretted our memory lapse when the spade thunked into and split three tulip bulbs planted a few days before). Actually, it is not a bad idea each year to draw a crude map of the bulb plantings so that in the spring or fall you do not dig into these spaces. The next spring the map will help you determine what bulbs did not make it through the winter, which clumps should be replaced, etc.

The size of the holes depends on the bulb to be planted. Crocuses, for example, need to be planted about 4 in./10 cm deep, whereas tulips and daffodils should be planted about 12 in./30 cm deep. As well each bulb type has a preferred planting distance from its fellow bulbs. The area of the hole is easily determined given the type of bulb. Say you are planting a clump of six crocuses, the hole would need to be 4 in./10 cm deep and about 12 in./30 cm in diameter to fit the corms in comfortably. Planting them about 4 in./10 cm apart gives them room to multiply. If you are planting bulbs in their own bed, clear and dig out the entire area to the proper depth, which is measured from the *bottom* of the bulb. In a rush, you could rely on the old rule of thumb which says planting depth equals about four times their height.

If you dig the holes a little deeper than they should be, do not worry, since it is better to plant deeper than shallower. Deep planting delays the rate of bulb multiplication — bulbs get smaller as they multiply. This is a good thing, because as bulbs multiply the clumps become congested, and must be dug up, separated and replanted — extra work for the Reluctant Gardener. Deep planting also prevents frost damage and provides a greater challenge for the bulb-hungry squirrel. However, there is such a thing as planting too deeply. We do not recommend planting crocuses a foot deep — you would never see them again. (Proper planting depths and distances will be noted in the description of each bulb in our YES! list.)

Once the holes are dug, dribble in about a 1 tbl./15 mL of bone meal for large holes, say the ones which will hold five tulip bulbs, and 1 tsp./5 mL for the smaller holes. Scratch it in with the tip of your trowel. Bone meal provides phosphorus which stimulates good root formation and thus future food storage. For extra nourishment, it is also wise to scratch in some well–rotted manure or compost.

You are now ready to plop in the bulbs. We often plant our bulbs in circles for maximum effect, say, four tulips on the outside and one in the middle. Be sure to plant the bulbs root-side down. Generally, the messy-looking patch is where the roots grow from. If you cannot decide which end is up (some crocus corms keep their secrets too well), plant the bulbs on their sides.

Give each bulb a firm twist downward into the soil to ensure solid contact. Then fill the hole with the earth you neatly pushed to the side when digging the hole. Tamp it down with your hands every couple of inches, squeezing out any air pockets. Voilà, you have planted your first bulbs. Now move through the garden, planting each hole in the happy knowledge that spring will bring your just reward for a day spent planting. Do not water these plantings unless your garden is experiencing an unusual dry spell.

You might want to use a bulb planter. This handy tool has an open cylinder on its working end. You place a foot on top and push it into the ground. Pull or twist it out of the soil. Inside the cylinder will be a plug of lawn and soil. Plop the bulb into the hole and replace the plug.

If planting groups of bulbs close together in a lawn, it would be easier to remove the grass instead of digging individual holes. Some garden books advise you to cut the letter "H" into the lawn, using an edging tool or a spade, to the desired measurement of the bulb area needed. Grab the edge of the sod on one side of the "H's" mid-line. Fold it back, undercutting, that is slicing it with an old bread knife, at the root level, as you continue to fold the turf back. Do the same to the other half of the "H." Or if you do not like such a rigid shape, cut the outline of whatever shape you want into the lawn. Dig the uncovered soil to the required depth for the type of bulb you are planting. Enrich the soil with compost, plant the bulbs, fill in the hole, level, then replace the turf.

Some General Considerations

The following YES! list of bulbs only notes those which are hardy — that is the ones which are safely left in the soil winter after winter in areas reaching -30°F/-35°C. There are many tender bulbs, such as gladiolus, for the gardener who enjoys a lot of extra work — digging up the bulbs, storing them properly indoors all winter, planting them out again in spring — over and over again. However, we do not recommend these for the Reluctant Gardener.

Because the soil, sun, moisture, insects and cut flower information is similar for most bulbs, we have not listed these categories separately in the YES! list. Most bulbs will grow in average garden soils, although clay soil may be a problem. Not only is clay difficult to dig, it also retains more moisture than bulbs usually enjoy, which puts them in danger of rotting.

All bulbs need a great deal of sun to grow properly. A few, such as snowdrops and winter aconite, can be planted in light shade and will bloom nicely if they get great quantities of dappled sun. An advantage of planting bulbs in light shade is that they will bloom later than their neighbors, thereby extending the bloom season around the garden. Do not forget to water bulbs as you would any other garden plant during a dry spell.

As previously mentioned, bulbs need to be planted in areas of good drainage to prevent rot. You cannot plant bulbs in outdoor containers for this reason. Alternately freezing and thawing weather creates a very wet environment in an exposed container. Nor do outdoor pots and window boxes provide adequate protection from freezing temperatures. If you plant bulbs in outdoor containers, you have the choice of seeing them rot or turn into dead, frozen lumps, their potential totally destroyed.

When bulb clumps become overcrowded, it is time to divide them. This is usually signaled when the flowers one year appear smaller and the foliage a lighter green Dig up the entire clump after the foliage has begun to wither. Pull the clump apart with your hands, separating the bulbs from one another. Make new groupings and replant. Unfortunately hybrid tulips seldom increase in the colder areas of the country (-22°F/-30°C or colder). A gardener feels lucky to get four or five years of bloom from them. Spent tulips will put out leaves but not blossoms. Simply dig up the tired bulbs and throw them into the compost. Any tulips which do multiply should be planted in new areas to ward off viruses.

Although a number of different types of aphids, bulb fleas and nematodes can attack flowering bulbs, the incidence is fairly low in most gardens, except for gladiolus which attract thrips. Bulbs seem to die more from weakening due to splitting and from alternating winter thaws and freeze ups. There is also a significant mortality rate thanks to the squirrels who find most bulbs, except the awful-tasting daffodil, quite the autumn snack.

Some desperate gardeners bury tasty bulbs in metal mesh to thwart squirrels. Others bury mothballs with bulbs, or scatter cayenne pepper, bonemeal or bloodmeal over planting holes. All have equal success and failure rates depending on the tenacity of your neighborhood squirrels. They usually get what they want.

Most flowering bulbs make great cut flowers. Tulips have a disconcerting habit of following the sun, but what the hey, they still look beautiful even though the stems bend. We have heard that one should not put cut tulips in a vase with daffodils, because they secrete a sap poisonous to tulips. However, we have never tested this, because we cannot bear to sacrifice even a single flower — so precious it is after our long northern winter. Some short-stemmed blooms such as winter aconite or crocus are obviously not suitable for cut flowers. Miniature bouquets of grape hyacinth, forget-me-not and violets are one of our favorite combinations.

The YES! List of Nearly Foolproof Bulbs

Common name: AUTUMN CROCUS

Latin name: *Colchicum autumnale*

Description: large, crocus-like flowers, blooming in late August through September. Blooms can be found in shades of purple, pink and white.

Height: 8 in./20 cm. Plant them 3-4 in./8-10 cm deep, 6-9 in./15-25 cm apart.

Comments: a very striking flower for the late summer garden. Best planted where they will not have to be moved. These hardy bulbs do well in front of shrubs or among low-growing perennials where their coarse leaves, which take considerable time to wither away, are hidden. The flowers, contrary to the way most bulbs grow, appear first and are followed by leaves. Leaves appear again in spring, but no flowers until autumn. The bulbs could use a little winter protection in -40°F/-40°C.

Common name: CROCUS

Latin name: *Crocus*

Description: six-lobed, long-necked flowers which never open completely flat. Grass-like foliage. Crocuses bloom in shades of purple, yellow, white, pink, dark gold and lavender. Striped and bicolor flowers can also be found.

Height: various heights from 1-10 in./2.5-25 cm, depending on the variety. Plant about 2-4 in./5-10 cm deep, 2-6 in./5-15 cm apart in groups of at least six bulbs.

Comments: The crocus is usually the first harbinger of spring in the garden and on the potted flower shelves in grocery stores. The large flowering Dutch hybrid crocuses are the ones commonly on sale. However, we are seeing more specie and specie hybrids being offered. Smaller flowered, these corms are very hardy, free-flowering and, in some areas, bloom a week earlier than their Dutch cousins. One of our favorites is a yellow, bronze-striped specie crocus.

Common name: DAFFODIL: **See Narcissus, below.**

Common name: GLORY-OF-THE-SNOW

Latin name: *Chionodoxa sardensis*

Description: bright, rich blue, six-petaled flowers with white throats, 3/4 in./2 cm in diameter, clustering in sets of six on single stalks. They bloom in early spring shortly after the first crocus.

Height: 6 in./15 cm tall. Plant 3 in./8 cm deep and between 1-3 in./2.5-8 cm apart

Comments: These long-lived bulbs look quite lively planted under deciduous trees — clumps of at least six are effective. Once planted, they need no care. If they are happy, the flowers may self-seed and spread slowly throughout the garden.

Common name: GOLDEN GARLIC, LILY LEEK

Latin name: *Allium moly*

Description: thin leaves with clusters of bright yellow flowers 2-3 in./5-8 cm across, held on top of erect stems

Height: 12-18 in./30-45 cm. Plant about 4 in./10 cm deep and about 6 in./15 cm apart, in clusters of at least five bulbs.

Comments: Decorative relatives of the onion family, alliums come in a wide range of colors: purple, yellow, pink, white and lavender. *Allium moly* is one of the most common alliums sold in garden centers. It is a dependable bulb for the late spring garden and is excellent mixed with grape hyacinth — the combination of bright yellow and blue can be stunning. It multiplies readily. Because of their close relationship to onions, alliums are used by some gardeners to repel aphids as a companion planting among other spring bloomers. The bulbs themselves are very resistant to insect attack. When the leaves are crushed, they emit a faint garlic odor.

Common name: GRAPE HYACINTH

Latin name: *Muscari*

Description: small spikes of tiny blue, bell-shaped flowers clustered along thin stems. The leaves look like grass. Sometimes a white variety is sold.

Height: 6-9 in./15-23 cm. Plant in clusters of five bulbs, 3 in./8 cm deep, 3 in./8 cm apart.

Comments: These bulbs multiply like rabbits. They are very easy to grow, and their blue color is gorgeous. Blooming in May, grape hyacinth groups well with other spring bloomers, especially the creamy yellow daffodil. Grape hyacinth are quite adaptable to most soil and light conditions. It is best to divide and replant clumps in July. Do not be alarmed to see these bulbs throwing out new foliage in the fall. The leaves winter under the snow and perk up again in spring, so do not cut them down in the fall as you would perennials. Hardy to -50°F/-45°C.

Common name: HYACINTH

Latin name: *Hyacinthus orientalis*

Description: fat, fragrant, tight clusters of waxy-looking flowers on tall, thick stems. Blooms in shades of red, pink, white, blue, lavender, purple, rose and some sickly-looking yellows. Available in double and single flowers. Is it just us, or is the scent not as pleasant as when we were little?

Height: 6-12 in./15-30 cm depending on the variety. Plant 6 in./15 cm deep and 6 in./15 apart. Clusters of three bulbs are effective.

Comments: Hyacinths are classified as singles, doubles, miniatures, Roman and multiflora. We do not advise buying the tender Roman varieties for the open garden. Multifloras are recent arrivals on garden center shelves. Unlike the common hyacinth, the multiflora throws out several slender flower spikes instead of one large one. Flower spikes of the commonly sold *Hyacinthus orientalis* usually become smaller and less floriferous after the second year of bloom because the bulbs begin to split and divide. Hyacinths need to be replaced at least every three years. By the end, they dwindle down to one, sparsely flowered stalk. The single-flowered varieties are the hardiest.

Common name: LILY (see Chapter 7 on perennials)

Common name: NARCISSUS, DAFFODIL, JONQUIL

Latin name: *Narcissus*

Description: immense variation between the different types — there are 8,000 known varieties. They range from miniatures to tall, large trumpet-flowered species. Whites, yellows, almost-pinks, oranges and bicolors. Many are fragrant. Flowers range from the elongated trumpet to the flattened trumpet to frilled doubles. Some people call it the cup-and-saucer flower.

Height: ranges from 6-18 in./15-45 cm. Plant from 6-12 in./15-30 cm deep depending on the size of the bulb. A deeper planting depth, for all but the miniatures, in very cold zones gives better protection from the effects of severe winters. Clumps of at least five bulbs give a good show.

Comments: These hardy bulbs last for years. They are easy to naturalize, that is, to be left to grow and multiply as they will in the lawn, or under trees. The Narcissus family has many, many divisions, and most laid-back gardeners today use the division names interchangeably — thus daffodils, narcissus and jonquils have all come to be synonymous. Squirrels dislike the taste of daffodil bulbs, a definite plus for the urban gardener. Some gardeners plant a few daffodils near bulbs which squirrels consider a delicacy. An old, reliable favorite is the 'King Alfred' daffodil.

Common name: PUSCHKINIA, LEBANON SQUILL

Latin name: *Puschkinia scilloides*

Height: 4-6 in./10-15 cm. Plant 3 in./8 cm deep.

Description: clusters of light blue flowers with a darker blue stripe through the center of each petal.

Comments: Puschkinias blossom after crocuses. These bulbs are best left undisturbed. Hardy to -22°F/-30°C.

Common name: SIBERIAN SQUILL, SQUILL, SCILLA

Latin name: *Scilla sibirica*

Description: Star-shaped, intensely blue flowers on thin stems. Ribbon-like leaves.

Height: 4-6 in./10-15 cm. Plant in clusters of five or six bulbs 4 in./10 cm deep and 4 in./10 cm apart.

Comments: Scilla are perky additions to the late May flower border. They are very easy to grow, multiply rapidly, and naturalize readily in the lawn. One of your authors has an army of blue scilla advancing from her neighbor's yard, spreading across a large corner of lawn — delightful. Your other author, however, has for five years been trying to nurse her tiny patch into a big patch. Ah, well, gardening is like that.

Common name: STAR–OF–BETHLEHEM

Latin name: *Ornithogalum umbellatum*

Height: 9-12 in./23-30 cm. Plant them 3 in./8 cm deep..

Description: clusters of white, star-shaped flowers on short spikes appear from late spring to early summer.

Comments: Multiplies easily to the extent that you may be constantly dividing and replanting Star-of-Bethlehem. Hardy to -50°F/-45°C.

Common name: TULIP

Latin name: *Tulipa*

Description: immense variety can be found in this group due to hundreds of years of plant breeders' interest. Colors range from white, through the whole spectrum (except blue), to velvety black. As well, flamboyant Parrot tulips sport the most fantastic color combinations —

often the colors are etched in fiery patterns on the feathery petals. Flowers can be found shaped like peonies, the classic tulip "cup," lily tulips (long pointed petals that arch outward at the tips) and other forms in-between. Usually one bulb produces one flower. Bouquet tulips are a new introduction, with four or five flowers on a branching stem. Unfortunately they sometimes grow unhappily and look a bit tatty and feeble.

Height: miniatures or specie tulips grow between 8-20 in./20-50 cm tall, the other varieties between 18-30 in./45-75 cm. Plant in clusters of five, about 12 in./30 cm deep and about 5-7 in./13-18 cm apart for the larger varieties. Plant the larger varieties deeply so that they multiply less rapidly. As the bulbs multiply, the flowers become less abundant and smaller. Except for the specie tulips and some Darwin varieties, most tulips show less vigor the second year of bloom. Thus you may want to replace your tulips every second or third year for a strong showing.

Comments: Unlike some fussy customers, tulips never fail to bloom the first year after planting, unless they have been eaten by a squirrel. One of your authors dotes on clumps of a *Tulipa kaufmanniana*, a bright orange-red specie tulip, which have bloomed year after year for the last six years. The specie tulips (the ones with long Latin names) extend the tulip season by blooming before the other types. If you choose among early and late varieties of the various classes, your tulip season could extend well into early June. When you see tulip bulb displays in the garden center, the bulbs will be marked early, mid-season and late blooming. However, in our city where spring sometimes lasts only a few days before the summer heat begins, all but the earliest tulips simultaneously bloom and then begin to wither.

Common name: WINTER ACONITE

Latin name: *Eranthis*

Description: six-petaled, bright yellow flowers on short stems appear in very early spring. The flowers are set off by a ruff of thin green leaves.

Height: 2-4 in./5-10 cm high. Plant in clusters of four or five bulbs, 3-4 in./8-10 cm apart, 2-3 in./5-8 cm deep.

Comments: If left undisturbed, aconites spread to form honey-scented, golden carpets in the garden. They do not mind growing in light shade. Some gardeners soak the tubers in lukewarm water for a day before planting.

The MAYBE List of Bulbs

These bulbs are for the more adventuresome who do not mind spending money on bulbs which may or may not take a liking to their gardens.

Camassia: Actually regarded as a wildflower, these spiky star-shaped blue flowers bloom for several weeks in spring. Plant about 6 in./15 cm apart and 4 in./10 cm deep. Because of their nearly 3 ft./1 m height, camassias blend well into the perennial border, but, unhappily, do not survive -22°F/-30°C or colder for more than a couple of years.

Dahlia: Easily grown and come in a multitude of shapes, heights and colors. The tuberous roots are expensive. The main drawback for the Reluctant Gardener is that they are not hardy and must be dug out and stored in a cool, dry place all winter. The taller varieties need to be staked. Dahlias are also prone to fungal diseases.

Fritillaria: The one we have grown most often is *Fritillaria meleagris.* It is an intriguing-looking flower: bell-shaped blossoms, covered in an unusual maroon and white checkerboard pattern, are held on thin, wiry stems. Fritillaria prefers to be planted in light shade. Alas, the bulbs do not last long in our gardens.

Galanthus or Snowdrop: The common snowdrop is one of the first flowers to open in spring. The hanging, translucent white flowers look wonderful in spots where the snow melts early on. They prefer growing in light shade and being left undisturbed. We have tried a number of spots in our gardens without success. Either they never show up the spring after they were planted or one or two blooms straggle up and that is it. If they like you, the bulbs display well in informal plantings. They can take a few years to become established. Plant the bulbs immediately after purchase because they dry out quickly.

Gladiolus: Better to buy the cut flowers than try to grow them yourself. In the home garden they are all too often attacked by the gladiolus thrip. These sucking insects cause ugly brown streaks to form on both leaves and flowers. If you do decide to grow gladioli, do not buy the bagged corms in the hardware or dime store, they usually are not worth the money. The taller varieties need to be staked. Gladioli are not hardy and must be dug up each fall and stored until spring. Too much work for the Reluctant Gardener.

Tuberous begonias: Often sold already blooming in individual pots, tuberous begonias should be treated like annuals. They certainly brighten up a shady corner with their white, pink, yellow, orange or red camellia-like flowers, whether in the flower border or in containers on the porch. If grown in the flower border, their brittle stems need to be staked to prevent breakage in strong winds. Sometimes the gardener can successfully winter the tubers in a cool place. If they are left in their pots, do not overwater during the winter. In fact, stop watering after the foliage withers, then do not water until you see leaves sprouting.

Dinah's Foolproof Method of Forcing Bulbs Indoors in Winter

Before basements were heated, ambitious gardeners forced bulbs, that is, brought potted bulbs into bloom indoors in the winter to relieve the winter doldrums, by storing them in their cold basements. Bulbs need a cold period not only to grow sufficient roots, but also to properly set their biological clocks to bloom the next year. Today, you can provide bulbs with a cold period by putting them in the refrigerator.

Not all bulbs respond to this treatment. The ones that do will be indicated in the descriptions attached to bulb boxes at the garden center or noted in bulb catalogues. Usually hyacinths, crocuses, daffodils, (especially 'King Alfred,' 'Mount Hood,' 'Pink Glory,' and the multi-stemmed miniature 'Tête-à-Tête) are relatively easy to bring into bloom indoors. Tulips (Early Singles, Triumphs, some Darwin Hybrids and Parrots) can be forced, but they are less reliable. The popular Paperwhite narcissus are sold pre-chilled and thus do not require a cool period, but can be planted immediately after purchase in soil or in a layer of pebbles and put on the windowsill (although some people find their perfume unattractive and overwhelming).

1. Buy your bulbs at the regular time and begin planting them in pots from mid-September to mid-October for bloom in February and March. For a succession of bloom, plant and refrigerate a new potful

every week. Buy bulb pans, or plastic flower pots which are wider than they are deep. For tall-blooming bulbs such as tulips and daffodils, choose a pot about 6 in./15 cm deep. A better display is created if more than one bulb can be fitted into each pot.

2. Put an inch or two of pebbles or light, open soil in the pot (use purchased sterilized soil, not soil from the garden). Space the bulbs in the pot so that they do not quite touch each other. Dribble more pebbles or soil in around them, gently firming as you go. Fill the pots until the pebbles or soil cover about two-thirds of the bulb, leaving the top third exposed. If you are using soil, firm one last time, then water well and drain off any excess. If you are using pebbles, water until the water just tickles the bottom of the bulb. Using glass containers makes this easier, and allows you the pleasure of watching the roots grow.

3. Put the pots on the bottom shelf of the fridge. The bulbs need a period of darkness and cool but *never* freezing temperatures. Remember that you want the bulbs to think they are wintering underground — in Holland, not the North Pole. Your fridge's usual temperature setting will be fine. Check the pots once a week. If they are dry, water just enough to keep the soil as moist as a wrung-out sponge. For pebbled bulbs, keep the water just touching their bases. Never any more, never any less. If the pots are overwatered the bulbs may rot. You may see mold form on the soil surface — just gently wipe it off. Now starts the long wait — often from two to six months.

   Do not take the pots out of the fridge until the flowerbuds are showing — not just the tips, but the entire bud. If some bulbs show buds and some do not, wait until one-half to two-thirds are showing buds or if it seems obvious that no more buds are going to appear. Some bulbs never bloom, these are called blind bulbs.

4. When the great day arrives, take the plants out of the refrigerator, place them away from direct heat and out of direct sun. Keeping the bulbs relatively cool ensures a longer period of bloom.

   Forced tulip bulbs never come back, so compost them as soon as the flowers die.

   After the flowers of bulbs other than tulips die, cut off the flower head and allow the foliage to yellow and wither. As the foliage fades, keep the pots in the light, and continue to water if you want to put them in the garden later in the season. When they have completely died, cut the leaves off about 1 in./2.5 cm from the top of the bulb and stop watering. Take the bulbs out of the soil and store in paper sacks or canvas bags, in a cool dry place until they can be planted out in autumn. After a couple of years in the garden, they will once again begin blooming. No forced bulb, however, can be re-forced.

Refrigerator Bulb-Forcing

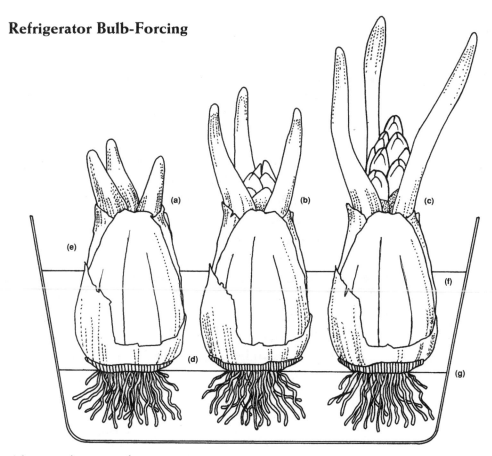

a) leaves only, not ready yet
b) flowerbud too small, not ready yet
c) most of flowerbud shows, ready to leave fridge
d) basal plate — the bottom of the bulb
e) 1/3 of bulb protrudes above soil (or pebble) level
f) soil (or pebble) level
g) correct water level for pebble-grown bulbs

Note: do not fridge-force bulbs if anyone in your house is apt to assume that **everything** in the fridge is edible.

CHAPTER 12

Throw Away Your Manicure Scissors: Lawn Care

Are you a slave to your lawn? Is your summer a purgatory spent mowing, watering and edging rather than drinking lemonade and reading novels? Put an end to this rigid behavior, this unswerving compliance to society's dictates. Think about it — do you really need a manicured lawn, an unbroken expanse of close-cut, weed-free, velvety-looking grass? Of course you don't.

Many North Americans have unquestioningly accepted the burden of lawn care, often without recognizing that the model they are unconsciously trying to copy is The British Lawn — a flat expanse of perfectly shorn green, green grass, unmarred by weeds, molehills or unsightly patches of winter-killed grass. If you want a British Lawn be prepared to spend hours watering, fertilizing, mowing, mowing, mowing.

Question: How can you create the ideal British Lawn?

Answer: Simply mow, water and roll it for four hundred years.

High maintenance indeed, and no fun for the Reluctant Gardener. British-style lawns will not thrive in the colder North American climate zones unless the gardener fiddles endlessly and uses copious amounts of questionable chemical compounds.

But, you say, if I don't pamper my lawn, the neighbors will walk by the house frowning and whispering. Let them. (Perhaps now is the time to admit that we have an attitude problem when it comes to lawns. We reckon it has something to do with our deep aversion to all forms of slavery.)

With one of them, her anti-lawn attitude is so bad that her husband does not trust her to cut the lawn. Strange things happen. The last time she mowed the lawn, thinking she was doing her over-worked husband a favor, he had hysterics for three days — not in anger, but in derisive, uncontrollable laughter. Unknowingly, when she was dragging the mower out of the basement, the height lever was knocked one notch higher on one of the left wheels. Well, your noble author pushed the mower around her double lot as fast as she could. In her haste, she did not notice the interesting pattern she was creating on the lawn. Not only does she not bother to mow in straight lines, but neither does she keep to a consistent mowing pattern. This in itself can create strange patterns. The uneven height adjustment made a normal mess worse. The front lawn looked as if it had been cut with (or by) a drunken mower. Later she tried to convince her husband to look at it artistically — the grass undulated in a most interesting way. He saw it, however, as ragged tufts of grass agonizedly heaving in random, wavy lines — seasick in other words.

Anyway, you now know the negative undercurrent beneath the solid information in this chapter. Your authors do, however, recognize the positive aspects of lawns. They are neat, no-nonsense, easy to lay out; simple, but time-consuming, to maintain; and effective foregrounds for flowerbeds, hedges, and shrub groupings. Lawns are also great for kids to play on.

Mowing

Mowing is the most frequent (all too frequent) chore, but there is no avoiding it. You could follow the example of one of our friends, who looks upon mowing as a walk in the park. She admits that it is a noisy, rather monotonous park, but this exercise in imagination carries her through the job. We also find that mowing is an excellent way to avoid being pestered — no one will interrupt you, for fear of being stuck with finishing the job.

Some lawn care specialists advise cutting your grass no higher than 1 in./2.5 cm. Balderdash! For one thing, you do not need to create a golf green. For another, the shorter grass is cut, the more it is stimulated to grow, the more you mow — a vicious circle. The shade cast by longer grass can stop some sun-loving weeds from sprouting, and will slow down the rate of water evaporation from the soil. Higher grass will also keep grass roots from frying during hot weather. So, cut higher, leaving the grass about 3 in./8 cm high. Some brave souls say 4 in./10 cm. All this is good news for the Reluctant Gardener who will not need to cut, weed or water as frequently as shorter-cut grass would require.

If the lawn turns yellow soon after cutting, you probably cut it too short and have thrown it into shock. Cut less off the next time. Also, if the mower blades are dull, the grass tips will turn yellow because the blades are being torn or ripped instead of sliced. Torn, frayed grass tips are open wounds, prime targets for insects and diseases. If you are using a rotary mower, you will never eliminate this problem completely — you can only keep the rotor blades sharp. Power mowers cut less sharply than reel mowers, however reel mowers cut too short. (For the differences in mowers, see Chapter 4.)

Mow grass only when it is dry and standing up straight. Wet grass blades bend over from the weight of water droplets, making it difficult to give the lawn a clean cut. If your lawn has clumps that are bent over or trodden down, just rake them up straight. If you leave the bent clumps, they will straighten up in the next few days after the mowing, making your lawn look ragged.

Before cutting, it is always wise to check the lawn for stones and twigs — they can give you a nasty bruise or cut when thrown up by a power mower. Also stones can damage the cutting blade. Wear stout shoes and eye protection — sunglasses will suffice — when mowing. You should also clean up dog and cat poop, too. It is not a pleasant experience to mow over it.

Grass feeds itself by absorbing sunlight through its leaf blades and then converting the products of this reaction into food. If there is not enough blade area (another reason to keep your grass high), the less food is produced, and the lawn becomes stressed and more susceptible to disease and insect attack.

Thick clumps or rows of long grass clippings must never be left on the lawn because they cannot work themselves easily down to the soil surface. They will just lie there, smothering the blades underneath. Rake them up, or, if the clippings are short, rake them evenly into the lawn. Some people avoid ever raking by using a grass catcher attachment on their mowers and composting the clippings.

A new introduction to the mowing world will help us resolve the problem of what to do with our clippings. Mulching mowers leave finely chopped clippings on the lawn. See Chapter 4 on tools for a fuller discussion of this attractive newcomer.

Watering

Watering is another maintenance chore. Water is becoming an expensive resource, especially in larger urban centers. It is a resource to be guarded, not squandered. So, here are some guidelines to help you use it effectively.

Deeply penetrating waterings are the best for optimum lawn growth. Depending on your soil type, this could mean about two hours of watering, so you can see, there is little point in standing out there squirting water around by hand for a few minutes. Deep watering encourages deep rooting, and deep grass roots sustain healthier grass. Water sparingly and you encourage a Bad Thing — shallow rooting. That is, grass roots stay near the surface where the water is. The roots dry out faster, as the top few inches of soil dry out faster. To test how deeply a watering has penetrated, cut a deep slice out of your lawn and take a look after an hour — then you can estimate how long to water. Grass usually needs about a 12 in./30 cm water penetration once a week.

Deep watering is not usually necessary until well into June. Before then, the soil has retained a lot of moisture from melted snow and spring rains. Higher cut grass also needs less watering, because high cutting promotes stronger, deeper root growth. When we reach the dry summer spell and it does not rain, your lawn may need a deep watering every seven to ten days. Sure signs that the lawn needs watering are: if it begins to turn brown; if the grass takes on a bluish tint; if footprints show in it after you have walked on it; or if the grass beings to wilt.

Some of us with bad attitudes let the lawn go dormant — that is, turn a bit brown — during a dry spell. Dormancy means the lawn has stopped growing above ground level, but the roots are still active. A good rain will snap the lawn into life again. Be sure to let your lawn dry out a bit between waterings, because overwatering can also cause problems. If you keep your grass and soil constantly moist you invite fungus and lawn diseases, root rot, and rank weed growth into your garden.

You probably will not want to stand out on the lawn, hose in hand, for these long periods of time. You will want to use a sprinkler. Most commercial sprinklers will do a good job. We have, however, a deep dislike for the impulse sprinkler. You know, the ones shaped sort of like a small revolver which you spike into the lawn. They spray water out in irregular bursts as they rapidly swing in half circles. The noise is infuriating. One of your authors is surrounded by this type of sprinkler. The noise is pitched higher than the lazy, nearly silent oscillating sprinkler. The rat-a-tat-tat bursts can be heard above normal levels of music or television programs. Do not buy these sprinklers unless you detest your neighbors. Buy a nice quiet oscillating sprinkler instead. A sprinkler which throws out a flat pattern of water (that is, the water is not thrown too high into the air) loses less water to evaporation. Elaborate and expensive in-ground sprinkler systems are only worthwhile if you are frequently away from home during the summer.

Morning or early evening are good times for watering lawns. In each case the sun will not burn the grass (the sun rays are magnified by the water droplets), yet there is still time for it to dry off before dark. Grass left damp overnight is more liable to get diseases. Also wind, which distorts the watering pattern, is less of a nuisance at these times of day. Just be sure not to water when the sun and temperature are high — hundreds of gallons of processed, paid-for water will be lost to evaporation.

Fertilizing

The next chore that many people associate with lawn care is fertilizing. The lawn care industry has traditionally fed the obsession for a perfect lawn by recommending the application of huge amounts of fertilizer, all season, every season. We do not believe this is necessary.

Really, why would you want to feed the thing — the monster will only reward you by growing faster and thus need to be mowed more often. If the soil under your lawn is healthy and full of earthworms, you need little fertilizer. You could put a light top-dressing of sieved compost, well-rotted manure, or topsoil on it for a nutritional boost. In fact, regular (once every year, spring or autumn) topdressing is the best thing you can do for your lawn. Many turf problems originate from a too-thin layer of soil beneath the grass. Regular topdressing — about as deep as your thumb is wide — is the only way to remedy this. The best lawns have a minimum 6 in./15 cm of topsoil beneath them.

Chemical fertilizers recommended for lawns are usually high in nitrogen (25-3-3, for example) and therefore create excessive and fragile topgrowth at the expense of root growth. As well, chemical fertilizers contain a high amount of chemical salts which can burn the lawn if not applied properly. The salts literally suck the moisture out of the grass plants.

Chemical fertilizers also kill off necessary soil life. Let earthworms be a lesson. They crawl away from chemically treated areas as fast as their little bodies can move.

Earthworms are needed as much in lawn soil as in garden soil, for a variety of reasons. Their constant burrowing and movement in and out of the soil aerates the lawn, providing oxygen for grass roots and soil microbes. Also, worms, after their earthy gormandizing, leave castings behind which are extremely rich in nutrients and thus good for the soil. Some species of earthworms crawl to the surface of the lawn and chew up grass clippings, leaving their castings. Do not rake the castings up — let them decompose into the soil.

Topdressing a Lawn — Correct Soil Depth

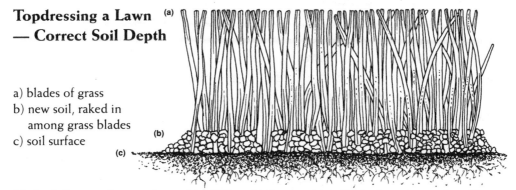

a) blades of grass
b) new soil, raked in among grass blades
c) soil surface

Method: Start with grass that is 3 in./7.5 cm high, or maybe a little shorter to make raking easier. Sprinkle soil or fine compost only as deep as your thumb is wide, and as evenly as possible. Rake the soil down between the grass blades to the soil surface. A thorough watering at this point will help wash the new soil down.

Decomposed organic matter feeds grass plants, aids in soil formation, and protects the lawn from disease and fungus attacks. The over-use of chemicals breaks down the structure of the soil itself over time, eventually sterilizing the soil by killing the micro-organisms. As well, chemicals leach down, through water action, deep into the soil, fouling our ground water, rivers, lakes and streams.

If you really feel your lawn needs a boost, buy a natural, organic fertilizer (sea products and liquid manure, etc.) mixture. A 3-2-3 natural fertilizer mix, for example, is quite enough once a year. Early September is the best time to fertilize. Fertilizing in spring is counter-productive, because the grass is still using its stored winter food and does not need more. Be sure to follow the instructions on the container in order to apply the fertilizer at the right concentration. If too much is applied, it will burn and kill the grass.

This will sound like radical advice, but please believe us when we say that the vast fertilizing programs you are used to hearing about are a recent phenomenon, and that, in the long run, they do much more harm than good.

Thatch

Another maintenance problem which can ruin a spring day is the removal of overly thick thatch. Thatch is an interwoven mass of grass roots, dead and living leaf blades, and other organic matter, which builds up on the surface of the lawn. If your thatch layer is more than 1 in./2.5 m thick, it should be removed. Thick thatch absorbs water and fertilizer and prevents air from reaching the soil. Insects and diseases love to multiply in it. As well, it retards grass growth and, in some cases, can suffocate new grass shoots. You can prevent thatch build-up by raking (a fan rake is less tiring and easier on your back) the lawn each spring as soon as the soil has drained. Raking after mowing helps, too. As well, if the grass is cut high and watered deeply, deep root growth will be encouraged, rather than surface root growth which helps produce thatch.

Aeration also retards the formation of thatch. To aerate your lawn simply poke holes in it so that air and water can penetrate. This also helps lessen compaction of the soil — roots have trouble pushing their way through overly compacted soil. A lot of plantain weeds in your lawn sometimes signal that the soil is compacted. You can rent power aerators which bring up cores of soil which look like the droppings of a very large bird. Rake these cores into the grass afterwards — they are great soil amendments. The simplest — remember that simple does not mean easy — method of aeration is to use a common garden fork. Stomp it into the lawn to a depth of about 6 in./15 cm, work it back and forth a few times, pull it out and move on until you have covered the entire lawn. A great way to spend your free time. But be comforted that soil compaction is seldom a problem in cold climates — frost heave takes care of it admirably.

Weeding

So we have raked, mowed and fed the worms, what's left? Weeding, that's what. Which brings us to herbicides, another aspect of the chemical onslaught fostered by the lawn care industry. By convincing us that a weed-free lawn is the only type to have, the lawn police have condemned us to chemical usage or hours, if you have been neglectful, of hand-weeding. Again you must ask yourself if you want a golf green or just a presentable splash of green in front of your flowerbeds.

We cannot in good conscience recommend the use of herbicides. They are toxic to you, birds, bees, and other nearby plants. Hand-dig what you can and do not worry if the lawn is not perfect. Instead, sit back and feel virtuous about not contributing to the pollution problem. A very pleasant feeling indeed.

We tolerate a weedy presence in our lawns. One of us has quite a liking for some of the weeds claiming to be lawn. Some weeds stay, others are dug out by hand. For example, fernweed, a type of yarrow, had spread, long before one of your authors had moved in, all along one side of her double lot. It has been allowed to stay. It is green, it is springy and if not mowed right away, it blooms with nice little white flowers. Dandelions are not allowed to stay because they are highly invasive — remember to get the *whole* root when digging them out. If a piece is left, a new dandelion will soon sprout. She gave up on clover and only rips it out when she is in the mood.

Do not worry about tall weeds, the mower will take care of these. Crabgrass, however, should not be tolerated. Pre-emergent crabgrass killers found in all garden centers are herbicides, and therefore not approved. Which leaves us with hand-weeding. Crabgrass is easy to identify: it is a whorl of coarse-looking grass lying close to the ground. Shove a trowel down beside it, and slowly tug it out while wiggling the trowel, loosening the roots. Or, you can wait until it blossoms, when the clump of grass takes on a purplish blush. Dig this up by the roots and do not compost it in case seeds have formed. As with all weeding, several years of conscientious work will eventually pay off and the amount of weeding will slowly diminish. The key, as always with weeding, is never to let seeds form.

Perhaps it is time to say a word about monoculture. Very rarely in nature will you find a vast, uninterrupted expanse where just one plant grows. A concentration of one species — a monoculture — is very vulnerable to species-specific pests. Thus, a lawn that is a mixture of a few weeds and grasses might resist grass-specific bugs and diseases better.

Insects and diseases

Another area of chemical misuse is the treatment of disease and insect infestations. A healthy lawn and soil will normally host a variety of insects, most of which do not intend to ruin your lawn. Many of them are beneficial. Even a healthy lawn, however, can harbor a few destructive insects, but usually these will not amount to much of a problem (bugs prefer unhealthy plants). One of the ways to combat destructive insects, other than maintaining a healthy lawn, is to attract birds to your garden. Birds eat amazing amounts of insects and are delightful to watch as well.

That is very nice, you say, but my lawn still has an infestation. What do I do? Well, it depends on the type of infestation. For example, one of the worst lawn destroyers is the *white grub*. Grubs are a young form of a variety of beetles such as the June beetle or chafer. These beetles lay their eggs on lawns, when the eggs hatch the grub emerges. It grows to about 3/4 in./2 cm long. Despite its small size, it can cause much damage — its favorite meal is grass roots. The grub slowly works its way through your lawn, munching at every step. If you see a dead or dying patch of lawn, grab the withered grass blades and pull. If you suddenly have a clump of rootless grass in your hand, your lawn has grubs. If the damage is slight, try to find the pests yourself — dig around with a trowel. There are some natural pesticides (rotenone, pyrethrum, and diatomaceous earth) which should be used in place of chemical ones. If the damage is extensive, contact a local environmental group to find out if there is an organic lawn care company in your area. Be warned. Many common lawn chemicals are not only damaging to the environment, birds, animals and bees, but harmful to you as well. Some enter your bloodstream through your skin or through inhalation. So do not hesitate to ask the lawn care people what exactly they are using, and do not be too quick to accept their assurances that their compounds are harmless.

Chinch bugs are another common lawn nuisance. These small black and white bugs cause grass to turn yellow, then brown. They are fond of deep thatch. Fight them by liberally spraying or sprinkling affected areas with a mild (40:1) solution of water and liquid dishwashing (not automatic dishwasher) soap. Then immediately spread sheets of newspaper over the area. The bugs hate soap, and in their desperation to escape, will cling to the underside of the newspaper. After fifteen minutes, peek to see if the bugs have surfaced. If so, scrunch up the newspaper and plunge it into very hot water to kill the bugs. Throw the newspaper into the garbage.

Lawn diseases are caused by one of a hundred different disease-causing fungi. Sometimes they are difficult to diagnose, and, if serious, should only be diagnosed by a professional. For example, if yellowish-brown spots appear on the lawn, they might be caused by a number of things: over-fertilizing, animal urine, compaction of the soil as well as fungal infestations.

Complete control is never possible. The disease-causing fungi are always with us, ready and waiting to gain a foothold. Sometimes a mild outbreak will go away by itself. When the lawn is stressed in some way, these organisms can cause damage. Fungicides are a short-term solution.

These chemicals may cure the disease, but kill the patient. Fungicides break the delicate balance between competing diseases, beneficial fungi-fighting organisms and the micro-organisms that keep the soil healthy.

One of the most common lawn diseases seen in our part of Canada is *gray snow mold*. White or gray patches appear on the lawn after the snow has melted. Lawn underneath a slow-melting deep snow cover is especially at risk. Rake the mold away or let the sun bake it off, or you have to dig the patch up and replant. Lush, overfertilized lawns are also prone to this disease.

So how to deal with the threat of disease? Keep the lawn and soil healthy by following the maintenance methods mentioned in the preceding pages. Be especially careful not to overwater. Deal with small damaged areas by digging down to a depth of 6 in./15 cm and throwing away the excavated soil — do not compost it, because the idea is to rid your lawn of any pests or diseases inhabiting it. Fill in with new topsoil and reseed. Patches smaller than a dinner plate do not necessarily need to be reseeded — let the neighboring grass fill it in. And never, never let trimmings or pulled-up weeds lie around on the lawn. Leaving leaves on the grass over the winter is also a sure-fire way to harbor and encourage the diseases and fungi that destroy a lawn. Be sure to rake throughout leaf-dropping season, so that the snow falls on grass, not leaves.

Our lawns have benefitted from scientific advances. In the last thirty years, a number of disease-resistant grasses have been developed and are now in commercial distribution.

QUICK REFERENCE LAWN CARE GUIDE — This summary is a perfectly adequate program for an established lawn. It assumes that there are no insect or disease problems.

- *De-thatching in spring, when the ground has drained dry;*
- *hand-weed dandelions and crabgrass as necessary;*
- *mow as needed, never shorter than 3-4 in./8-10 cm; gather and compost clippings or rake shorter ones into the lawn;*
- *water deeply as needed, mornings or late afternoons;*
- *topdress as often as you can bear to do it;*
- *in early September, fertilize lightly with an organic fertilizer.*

Seed vs. Sod

At some point in the life of your lawn, the turf will need to be repaired or replaced. There are two ways to go about this: using seed or using sod.

Seeding a new lawn is quite a challenge. Many people throw in the trowel and have it professionally done. The best time to reseed a lawn is late August, but mid to late spring is also a good time. Moderate warmth and moisture are the two main conditions which promote proper seed germination.

Choosing the grass blend will be the easiest part of reseeding. First of all, buy high-quality, disease-resistant seed (yes, it will be expensive) from a reputable garden center. It must be fresh, last year's leftovers will have a low germination rate. The mixture of seed types should be printed on the label. Often the bags of grass seed are labeled for dry, moist, sunny or shady locations, so choose wisely. Buy a grass mixture, not a single variety. Kentucky bluegrass and perennial ryegrass (turf-type) are commonly included in grass mixtures and do well cut high. Avoid mixtures with a high proportion of annual ryegrass. The seed germinates quickly, but it dies off during harsh winters. If your area has little rainfall, buy a mixture with a high percentage of fescue, which is drought, shade and cold-resistant.

No matter whether the area to be reseeded is small or large, the first step is to remove the old turf. Small patches can be trowelled up. Larger areas can be scalped by using a special sod-scraping tool which you can buy or rent. Insert the blade at root level and push it along, neatly severing the roots. Or consider renting a rototiller. Make several passes with it to break up the old lawn, then mix the sod thoroughly into the soil.

After the lawn has been rototilled, you should rake, breaking clods and smoothing the soil, until a level surface is created. Make sure that the level of lawn slopes away from the house, to keep surface water away from the foundation. This is the time when you decide whether or not you need to add topsoil. Dig a hole and take a look. Is there a good 6 in./15 cm of dark, rich-looking topsoil? If so, wonderful. If not, get a load of soil delivered and rake it level. Many lawn problems start with a skimpy layer of topsoil which the builders have hidden under the nice layer of sod that so pleases new home buyers.

See why so many people have their lawn done professionally? If you worked an animal this hard, you would have the Humane Society after you. Fortunately, the next stage is much less arduous.

For the next week or so, the ground should be thoroughly soaked by running sprinklers for two or three hours a day. This will settle the soil so any holes or unevenness will appear *before* you sow the seed. As well, any weeds that sprout can be hand-pulled. After you are satisfied that the ground has settled, no dips or holes were formed, and most of the weeds have been eliminated, load the spreader (see Chapter 4 on tools) with grass seed. (If holes and dips did form, fill them in and rake smooth.) You have, of course, measured the area to be seeded and bought the right amount of seed according to package directions. As well, you have correctly adjusted the setting on the spreader. Spread the seed carefully and consistently, so that the seed is distributed evenly across the ground.

Now cover the seeded area with a layer of soil about 1/4 in./.5 cm thick. Water immediately. The layer of soil will conserve moisture, keep the seed warm enough to germinate, and protect the seed from blowing away or being eaten by birds. Keep a sharp eye on the area. Weather conditions and your soil type will determine how often to water to keep the area evenly moist, but not soggy. If you are conscientious, you will be rewarded in a few weeks by the sight of a thin green haze which will soon grow into a vibrant lawn. Let the grass grow to about 4 in./10 before you cut it the first time. Take only 1/2 in./1 cm off it at the first cutting.

There must be an easier way, I hear you Reluctant Gardeners thinking. Well, there is, but you still cannot avoid the clearing, raking and earth preparation. Instead of seeding, however, you can buy rolls of sod from a reputable nursery or, if you have one in the area, a sod farm. Make sure the sod is the right type for your climate by asking at the nursery. Always be aware, however, of human perfidy and deal only with an established local company that will be there to complain to if necessary. Never buy any garden material from those seasonal corner-lot vendors who appear for a few weeks and then disappear.

Sod rolls are sold singly or in any quantity you need. Measure the area of your lawn and calculate, given the standard measure of sod rolls (usually 24 x 48 in./60 x 120 cm), the number you will need to cover the area. If it is a large amount, you might want to phone ahead and order and perhaps have it delivered. Sod is not light — your back will thank you the less you carry the rolls.

Have a look at the sod rolls immediately before buying or before the delivery truck leaves. The rolls should look fresh, the grass green and the soil layer moist. The soil should not be more than 1 in./2.5 cm thick. Do not buy yellow-looking sod — no telling what the problem might be. Check it for insects and grubs that might be hiding in the soil — whack it hard and see what crawls out. If you do not plan to lay the sod right away, be sure to keep it watered — never let the rolls dry out. It is best to use sod within forty-eight hours of buying it.

The ground level created for sodded lawns should be 1/2 in./1 cm lower than for a seeded lawn. This allows the sod to fit flush with the sidewalk. Begin laying the sods in a staggered pattern, as you would lay a brick wall, so that the end of one sod roll aligns with the middle of its neighboring roll. This will eliminate regular indentations. Also to avoid indentations, lay the ends and sides snugly up against one another. Because a sod roll shrinks as it dries, do not overstretch it or gaps will form between edges. But do not overlap the seams either. If you need to cut around a tree, steps, or flowerbeds, use a long-bladed, sharp knife. Old serrated bread knives work well. Save these pieces for filling in awkwardly shaped areas. If you are sodding a slope, lay the pieces of sod across the slope rather than down. Water will run down the joins and wear ruts in the new grass. After laying the sod, sprinkle topsoil into the crack between sod pieces.

Then roll it. You can rent a garden roller from rental companies. To increase its weight, fill the large steel roller with water to the weight you can manage. Push the roller carefully and consistently across the new sod. The weight of the roller will press the roots of the sod firmly into the earth. This will hasten the rooting process.

Thoroughly soak the sod. During the first month, never let it dry out. Sodded lawns usually establish themselves within two to three weeks — a seeded lawn will take that long just to germinate. Keep people off a newly sodded lawn and be careful when moving the sprinkler around the area. If you walk on a newly sodded, well-watered lawn, you risk leaving permanent footprints in it. Let the sod grow at least 4 in./10 cm tall before mowing. Set the mower at least 3 in./7.5 cm high. Any lower, and you risk the blade catching a corner of a piece of sod and yanking it right up out of the ground. We know. One of us did this, once. You would be amazed how far a big chunk of sod can fly.

Sodded lawns are a bit more expensive to create than seeded ones, but they establish faster and they are less prone to disaster — one missed watering and the newly germinated grass plants could keel over and die. Sod can be planted almost any time during the growing season to create an instant lawn. Sod also smothers most weeds before they can gain a hold in the freshly dug soil. As well, sod rolls are best used on slopes, where seed is very difficult to establish. The weight of watering often washes all that expensive seed to the bottom of the slope.

Lawn Alternatives

So what alternatives are there to the tyranny of the lawn? If the budget permits, hire a lawn care company to look after your lawn. Find a company that believes in natural, not chemical, lawn maintenance. There are a number of them springing up around the country. If that is not an option, you could build a deck. Plant a shrubbery. Or, you could lay paving stones, reducing the area to be mowed. Remember, though, that grass is a ground cover. If you accept a few imperfections and consider the fact that it can be walked on, you will see that it is a good ground cover. Besides, would you want your kids to grow up not knowing the magical scent of a newly-mown lawn?

Some anti-lawn types advocate a back-to-the-meadow approach, but this does not work well in the city. There are noxious weed laws, for one thing. Also, a meadow on your property will never look as good as it does in glossy photos. Wildflower lawns are beautiful in spring, but often turn yellow in summer with hardly a bloom to relieve the monotony of tall, waving grass, and tall grass is very difficult to cut. As well, even the most cared-for meadow will over time try to revert to forest. Therefore you must be vigilant and cut out all tree seedlings that appear among the tangled grass, flowers and weeds.

Obviously there are problems associated with each option. Concrete and paving stones can be hard-edged and ugly if used in the wrong places. They heat up the whole yard, unlike grass, which has a measurable cooling effect. Ground covers have drawbacks as well. Planting an extensive area with a ground cover can be expensive. Maintenance is not high, but it is not non-existent. If you have an area, say under a tree, where grass does not thrive, then a shade-loving ground cover may be just the answer. Ground cover lawns are not, however, places to romp and stomp on, to play games of tag, or cut-throat croquet, or even to take a simple stroll without causing some damage.

There is no simple solution. Unquestionably flowerbeds look fantastic when contrasted against a green, healthy lawn. You must decide what degree of lawn fanaticism you want to indulge in. How much time and effort are you willing to give to your lawn? It is up to you.

CHAPTER 13

It's May, Where's the Wheelbarrow? Seasonal Jobs

We find spring the busiest season, summer is often spectacularly lacking in jobs besides basic maintenance, and autumn brings along a hefty amount of work, but not quite as much as spring. Do not be surprised to see winter included in the list of work seasons. Winter is when you will be doing the work that saves you money, time, mistakes and aggravation later on — planning, in other words.

Please note that the how's and why's of all the jobs listed here are discussed more fully in the appropriate chapters.

Spring Jobs Part I: While There Is Still Risk of Frost

- Observe Rule Number One of spring gardening: do not walk on the soil until all the meltwater has drained away. Spring does not truly start until lawn and garden have drained and you can walk around on them without squelching.

- De-thatch the lawn.

- Pick up and rake up any and all debris left lying around from last year, particularly blackened, rotten vegetable matter (dead leaves, etc.) Ideally all vegetable matter should have been cleaned up last autumn, but there is always a little that escapes. Raking also helps to break up crusty soil to admit air and water. This debris can be composted if you are sure there is no road salt in it. Pick out candy wrappers, etc, too.

- Prune dead, diseased and damaged branches on shrubs and trees.

- Check trellises: are they sturdy; are cross pieces nailed securely; are any pieces rotting?

- Remove protective winter covering from roses in mid-April or when native trees leaf out, but replace covering at night if freezing temperatures threaten.

- Enjoy daffodils, crocuses, tulips, etc. Nothing needs to be done to them at this point.

- Dig up and prepare annual beds.

- Improve soil by adding organic materials such as compost and well-rotted manure. Either dig it in or apply it as a topdressing.

- Make sure lawn mower is oiled and sharpened. Begin mowing if necessary.

- Pull winter straw mulch away from perennials. This helps the soil to dry out and warm up. Set the pile of straw to one side. If freezing temperatures threaten, push the straw back into place for the night.

- If any perennials have heaved themselves out of the ground, push them back in with your foot by pressing firmly on the soil surrounding the plant.

- Lift and divide any overcrowded perennials when their shoots are about 2 in./5 cm tall.

- Plant container-grown shrubs (including roses) that you have just bought from the garden center and have hardened off, anytime from early to mid-May. Hardening off means setting them outdoors during above-freezing days, in order to allow them to adapt to life outside.

- Weed out plants which are definitely identifiable as weeds, otherwise leave them alone.

- Seed or sod lawns as necessary.

Spring Jobs Part II: After Danger of Frost Has Passed

- Plant annuals.

- Plant new perennials.

- Once your perennials and annuals are in place and well watered, apply straw summer mulch.

- One general fertilizing (10-10-10, 20-20-20, or 15-30-15) spread lightly on everything, except the lawn, will do fine.

- Continue weeding.

- Water as necessary.

- Mow lawn as necessary.

- Check climbers on trellises, make sure they are climbing where you want them too.

- Cut off all lilac suckers.

Summer Jobs

- When, and only when, the leaves of spring-flowering bulbs such as the daffodil, tulip and crocus are yellow and dead, clip them off level with the ground.

- Cut off all dead flowers.

- Stake taller plants as needed.

- Check for bugs and diseases.

- Mow as needed.

- Fertilize lightly once again in mid-August, excluding lawn.

- Continue weeding, especially before the weeds produce seeds.

- Water as necessary. Pay special attention to daily watering of hanging baskets and containers.

- Roses: cut off any suckers and leaves affected with blackspot.

- Check the bottom of your compost box to see if there is any usable material.

Autumn Jobs

- After mid September and before hard frost, plant spring-flowering bulbs.

- Prune cedars.

- Prune perennials as the foliage yellows off. Compost the trimmings.

- Lift and divide overcrowded perennials.

- Winter-mulch perennials after all foliage has died.

- Fertilize lawn (10-10-10, 20-20-20, or 15-30-15).

- Pull and compost frost-bitten annuals.

- Put roses and shrubs to bed for the winter.

- Make sure all climbers are firmly attached to their trellises.

- Take indoors any container-grown plants (such as geraniums or coleus) that you want to keep inside for the winter.

- Continue to be vigilant against weeds, bugs and diseases.

- Time for more soil improvement.

- Seed or sod lawns as necessary.

- Continue to mow and water as necessary.

- Rake and compost leaves.

- Some people plant shrubs in the autumn, but we think Reluctant Gardeners will have a little better luck (not to mention a better selection at the nursery) if they wait for spring.

- Make up pots of bulbs for indoor forcing.

- Check your garden furniture. Mend, paint and replace as necessary.

- Prepare mower for winter storage.

- Gather up other equipment that has spread itself throughout the garden.

- Order firewood so you will have a fire to sit beside while planning for next summer.

Winter Jobs

- Plan, plan, plan.

- Check out a stack of gardening books. Their pictures, descriptions and planting information are conducive to summer dreaming and helpful in your planning.

- Study our chapter on design carefully. Plan what to buy, where to plant it.

- A pleasant winter chore: on a warm, sunny day in January, go outside and clip a half-dozen twigs about 18 in./45 cm long from spring-flowering shrubs such as forsythia. Put them in water indoors. If your luck is in, the flowers will open.

- If you are out there digging snow anyhow, it does not hurt to throw extra snow, if it is not salt laden, over the top of perennial plants and small shrubs. This gives them a little extra protection against the cold. Be careful not to break shrub branches.

- We recommend that you not try to start seeds indoors. This is advanced gardening, and can be a very discouraging experience for Reluctant Gardeners.

CHAPTER 14

Hand-to-Hand Combat:
Weeds, Diseases and Insects

We hate to throw cold water on the happy garden picture we have been painting, but we feel honor-bound to say that once you begin gardening, even if only in a flowerpot, you will be constantly fighting weeds, insects and diseases. This fearsome threesome is an inescapable fact of gardening. No part of the plant is safe: insects attack buds, gnaw on roots, and as well attack leaves and stems by chewing, sucking and boring into them. Some weeds strangle the life out of plants and other weeds ooze toxins out into the soil to poison nearby plants. Fungal, bacterial and viral diseases can cause blackened leaves, deformed flowers and everything in between.

Why, you may lament, does Mother Nature put so many potential obstacles in the path of the well-meaning gardener? Why, indeed. Perhaps it can be condensed into one word — survival. Weeds, fungi, viruses, bacteria and insects, like all living things, are driven to survive, to multiply and perpetuate themselves. In a healthy garden, good living things are in balance with the bad. When the bad get the upper hand, trouble begins.

There is no total solution to the problem of pests. Complete annihilation is environmentally unsound, because a scorched earth policy is detrimental to ourselves, our gardens and ultimately our planet. Besides, you may win the occasional skirmish, but the war must be waged anew every growing season. Accustom yourself to degrees of control, take one gardening day at a time.

The key to living with the problem is knowledge — know a weed from a perennial, a beneficial insect from a ravenous vegetarian. The first line of defence in this war is a rich, healthy soil and hygienic gardening — clean up debris, clean your garden tools, destroy diseased plants. Healthy plants withstand and repel insect and disease attack better than ones struggling to survive in adverse conditions. A healthy soil, you may say, will also grow healthy weeds. Well, true, but good gardening practices will prevent their spread.

Weeds

What Is a Weed?

First discard that romantic notion that a weed is just a wildflower in the wrong place. There are many nasty plants lurking in the underbrush which are just plain ornery weeds. Take burdock, for example. Does any sensible person want to cultivate this difficult-to-eradicate, burr-bearing weed? Or would any sensible gardener welcome the creeping bellflower, a terrible weed unrelated to friendlier bellflowers, which slowly smothers neighboring plants, into the garden? Difficult to eradicate, its fleshy white roots seem to grow into the center of the earth.

Traditionally, weeds have been defined as plants that grow rapidly, are extremely adaptable to a wide variety of soils and conditions, are not bothered by the competition of nearby plants, and effortlessly reproduce themselves. Some gardeners might define a weed as anything they do not want in their gardens, but that keeps creeping in uninvited. Weeds, like ornamentals, are either annual or perennial. Annual weeds complete their life cycle in one growing season. They perpetuate by self-seeding, their seeds overwinter without any problem. Perennial weeds act the same way as other perennials — they survive the winter by going dormant and storing food in their roots. Their root systems are usually deep spreading and difficult to destroy.

In short, weeds are menacing, well-organized pests. They compete with our garden plants for available nutrients, water and sunlight. They offer room and board to a variety of insects and diseases, which is admirable, except these pests do not hang around their obliging weedy hosts, but wander off to wreak havoc in the rest of the garden. Some provinces have anti-weed laws which list the common noxious weeds. An anti-weed law usually states that listed weeds must be destroyed by the landowner. Ontario's Weed Control Act, for example, lists nearly twenty-five noxious weeds which either cause injury (such as poison ivy); weeds that harbor diseases which spread to agricultural crops (such as the common barberry); and difficult-to-control weeds which spread so widely that they reduce corp yield (such as the notorious Canadian thistle).

Weed Identification

Describing the many, many possible weeds which may invade your garden is beyond the scope of this book. Usually even the most sophisticated urbanite can identify dandelions, white clover and Canada thistle. Knowledge is the key — learn by observation the physical characteristics of the young perennials in your garden and the common weeds in your area. Compare an unknown plant with other plants in the flower border, if it matches a perennial it is not a weed.

Unfortunately your authors still make mistakes, even though they think they know their perennials. One year one of us gleefully destroyed a young delphinium and, to her great chagrin, coddled a fleabane weed. The other has parents who, every spring for years, nearly divorced when Dad weeded up Mum's oriental poppies, believing them to be dandelions. Now during spring madness when we are planning, planting and weeding and are the least bit unsure if a plant is a weed or a perennial, we wait until the young plant has leafed out a bit more before making a positive identification.

Help for the beginner and advanced gardener in identifying potential garden invaders is easy to find. Contact your agricultural department for weed-identification leaflets and booklets it may publish. These booklets are usually free or can be had for a nominal price. The library is also a good resource. See our book list in Appendix V.

Weed Control

Weed control is ongoing. Seeds are carried on the wind, birds drop seeds, seeds ride on the coats of cats and dogs and even on the clothes of weed-hating gardeners. Whether you are destroying noxious weeds or just the common garden varieties, the best way to control them is by pulling them out by the roots, smothering them with mulch or hoeing — that is, cutting the plant off at soil level. For all but the most persistent, cutting off the food supply shrivels the roots. Hoeing is, however, only effective if you have the room to manipulate a hoe between your garden plants.

Chemical solutions are, as we have continually noted, environmentally damaging. Indiscriminate applications of herbicides kill precious ornamentals, as well as weeds. Chemicals are only a temporary solution at best and we do not approve of their use.

Physical control is by far the best way to fight weeds on our small lots. If you weed the garden once a week while the plants are young and small, your task will be easier than if you allow the weeds to mature. The best time to pull weeds is after a rainstorm, while the soil is still moist. Digging dandelions, for example, out of a sunbaked lawn is no joke. Never, unless you are a horticultural masochist, let a weed go to seed, this will only multiply your weed problems. If you do not have the time to properly dig out seed-forming weeds that week, at least snip off the seed heads and put them into the garbage. In fact, it is best to get in there snipping when the flowers are still fresh, before they have had a chance to form even one seed. Never compost weed seeds, many of them survive the composting process only to emerge snickering at your stupidity and growing wherever the compost has been spread.

Perennial weeds should be dug out with the entire root intact. Be warned that some perennial weeds are so intent on living that any small piece of root left in the soil will immediately begin growing into a new plant. Sometimes, if the weed has strongly established itself, destroying it can be a daunting task. One of your authors has been battling creeping bellflower for years. Once she dug about three feet down trying, unsuccessfully, to uncover and destroy the full extent of one enormous tuber-like root and the plant's many branch roots. She never quite found every piece of root, so every year, the same job awaits her. Your other author had a similar battle with Chinese lantern (*Physalis*), which she planted on purpose in the perennial border.

 ————————————————————————

SOLARIZATION — No, sorry, this does not mean you can lay down your tools and go sunbathing. This is a new word for a practice your are probably already familiar with, and which is useful for eradicating dense weed invasions. It assumes that you own a patch of earth on which nothing but weeds is growing. You wish, not surprisingly, to destroy the weeds and plant something good. The solarization method is cheap, ecologically correct . . . the catch? It is a little time-consuming.

However, it is easy. Simply cover the area with black plastic. Shovel enough dirt over top to keep it from blowing away. Do this in the spring and leave it on for a full year. At the end of the year take up the plastic and begin enriching the now weed-free soil. Dig up and compost any dead weeds. The black plastic heated up the earth enough to harm the beneficial micro-organisms, so you will have to replace them. Do this by digging in as much compost as you possibly can — it will be full of beneficial nutrients and microscopic animal life.

 ————————————————————————

Diseases

Unfortunately, not only insects damage your plants. The garden is also threatened by a variety of fungal, bacterial and viral diseases. It is our experience, in our own gardens, that fungal diseases are the most common. Plant diseases cause discolorations, spots, rusty blotches, white or gray furry patches, black sooty spots, rotting growth on leaves and stems and, well, you get the idea. Be careful when diagnosing what seems to be a disease. Various soil deficiencies such as lack of magnesium or nitrogen can cause yellowing leaves. As well, frost damage, cold damage and lack of water can produce sickly symptoms which appear to be disease-produced. If you are not sure what is attacking your plant, it is best to be on the safe side and clip off the sick parts. Throw them in the garbage, never compost anything that looks ill and bug-ridden. Disease prevention includes insuring good air circulation around your plants, not walking through wet plants (you could be moving spores around) and picking up and composting debris.

Here are some remedies for specific diseases:

BLACKSPOT — a fungus disease of roses. Looks exactly the way it sounds, a nasty black spot on a rose leaf. You can try an organic fungicidal spray, but the only thing that really works is to trim off affected leaves the moment you see them and put them in the garbage.

BLIGHT — pray that your trees never catch fireblight or any other kind of blight. These bacterial diseases cause new shoots to wither and die, canker (rot) to develop at the base of leaves or stems, and on bark. Hideous chemicals do not work very well, so clip off the affected areas, cutting a good hand's width back from where good wood seems to begin. Throw what you clip in the garbage and disinfect the pruners with Javex or rubbing alcohol.

BOTRYTIS — A fungal disease also known as gray mold that can affect peonies among other plants. Leaf shoots wilt, buds turn black. At this stage try an organic fungicide. A badly infected plant — one whose stems and roots are rotting — should be dug up and put in the garbage, along with the top 2 in./5 cm of soil, to prevent further infection.

CANKER — see blight.

MILDEW — usually a mild fungal disease, if you catch it soon enough. Appears during hot, damp weather as a gray-white, dusty blush on leaf surfaces. Responds fairly well to organic fungicide, if you spray from the moment you see it until it is completely gone.

RUST — commonly seen on hollyhocks, the lower leaves become covered by red-brown spots. Use an organic fungicidal spray, being sure to spray the undersides of the leaves. Badly infected leaves must be trimmed off and put in the garbage. Plant breeders have produced many rust-resistant plants.

Insects

Terrible jaws fasten around a neck and — snap — its victim lies dead. Meanwhile, elsewhere, another sacrificial body quivers helplessly, imprisoned by the sticky bonds secured around it. Another victim is paralyzed and sealed into a small room. It waits in mute terror for the creature sharing the space to hatch, knowing it will then be eaten. Good heavens, have we suddenly strayed from the garden path into a horror movie? No, these are common scenes in your garden as the insect population goes about its daily round. No matter how high your own moral standards, your garden is a hotbed of sex and violence, where survival of the fittest and continuity of the species triumph over any other considerations.

We may shudder over insects' instinctive behavior but do not waste tears over the helpless vegetarian bugs tortured and eaten by blood-thirsty carnivores. Never forget it is the meek vegetarians who will devour your garden if they are not eaten up by kindly carnivorous insects.

Insect Control

The creepy-crawly world is divided into beneficial (carnivorous) insects and bad (plant-eating) insects, with a few in between. Unfortunately, it is sometimes difficult to tell one from the other — they do not wear white or black hats. Leaping into your garden with spray cans of insecticide blazing is *not* the answer — you could be killing beneficial insects at the same time as you kill nasty ones. Curb your urge to squish, poison or swat every insect seen in the flowerbed. Develop a more easy-going attitude to insect life. Our garden plots are small, and our livelihoods do not depend on the produce of these lots. Live and let live — without allowing the critters to take advantage of you by completely consuming your roses or petunias. The trick is to strike a happy medium, because insects are, and will be, always with us. Believe it or not, many of our crops and flowers depend on a host of insects to pollinate them, to set fruit, induce bloom, and transfer important genetic material.

The key is to know the enemy. Unfortunately, what we usually see is the after-effects of the enemy's presence, rather than the actual insect. We moan over the holes in our hosta leaves, the sticky webs on the coleus, the yellow, wilting leaves of the impatiens, and the rotting black stems on our begonias. We must be attentive if we are to catch the little dears eating, sucking and tearing the life out of our plants. Memorize your garden by simply observing it. This way you will catch problems before they overwhelm the garden.

When we know the enemy, we can then choose the most environmentally-sensitive method to rid the garden of the threat. Luckily out of the hundreds of thousands of different insect species in the world, only a few feast on your garden. You will probably meet no more than twenty insect species puttering around the garden, up to no good.

There are two major schools of insect killing: the squishing and the non-squishing, or chemical, approach. Your two authors agree on most horticultural advice, but they part ways over how to squish bad bugs.

One of your authors is a hand-squisher, delighting in hands-on extermination of a broad range of creepy-crawlies. She can get a dozen aphids with one pinch (they are poor runners and hang around in gangs). This method is ecologically correct, cheap, and good for her frustrations. She is careful to wash her hands after a bug-murdering session though: many bugs are sap-suckers, and she does not care to accidently ingest any potentially poisonous sap.

The other author would much prefer having a buffer between her and the bug to be killed — a trowel, the sole of her shoe, whatever. Quite understandably, she does not enjoy seeing the insides of an insect oozing over her fingers or mucking up her favorite gardening gloves. She bears in mind the fact that a strong spray of water, or a soaking with 1:40 pure soap-and-water solution, or a spray of ecologically-correct insecticidal soap will rid her plants of many a bug.

Whichever method you choose, be sure to pursue the bugs persistently. A day or two of backsliding on your part, and they will regain their toe-hold.

A common destructive insect is the *aphid*. Usually the aphids you will see are soft-bodied, tiny and green, however, you may see a few more of the other 2,000 species, which may be pink, yellow, black or transparent. Aphids are not loners, but cluster in large groups on buds and on new plant growth. They are also sneaky — be sure to examine the undersides of leaves. They suck the fluids out of plants, stunting the plant, and if allowed to persist, eventually causing its death. Lady aphids give birth to hundreds of babies every ten days without any assistance from the male. Obviously, if not checked, aphids could take over the world. Happily, birds and ladybugs love to eat aphids. The ones they miss can easily be squished or sprayed with a variety of organic mixtures — see our extermination recipes on pages 257-261.

There are a multitude of *borers*, the larval form of beetles or moths, which attack woody plants. They often look like brown, green or white caterpillars or grubs. Often the only warning you have that they are busily tunneling through your garden plants is small piles of sawdust near tree trunks or plant stems or caught in the bark. If your trees and vines are healthy, the borer may pass by. However, if it spots a tree or plant weakened by insect attack, poor soil, drought, etc., that plant will be earmarked for attack by the observant borer. When mowing the lawn, be careful not to bash holes where borers could then enter the bark of trees or shrubs. Kill a borer by sticking a thin wire into its hole, neatly skewering it.

Caterpillars of all types and sizes often creep through the garden, eating any vegetation in their path. These adolescent forms of moths and butterflies eat large holes in leaves. A common caterpillar, the *cutworm*, lives on the surface of the soil during the day, emerging at night to feed on plant stems. It is easy to identify cutworm damage. The stem seemingly breaks at ground level and falls over — the stem has been "cut." Tender, young shoots are especially vulnerable.

Cutworms can be thwarted by sticking two toothpicks on either side of a stem of a seedling or by mounding up crushed eggshells around the stem. If you are into crafts, make circular, 3 in./8 cm cardboard collars and place them around stems of young threatened plants to ward off the cutworm. However, this seems like a lot of work for the Reluctant Gardener and does not, in our experience, work very well.

In early spring, one of the most visible caterpillars is the *tent caterpillar*. It is aptly named, for it constructs dense, web-like "tents," usually between two thin branches on trees and shrubs. Crabapples seem to be especially tasty to these nasty creatures. Destroy the webs whenever you see them. If the webs are consistently broken open when the caterpillars are young, they will probably die because they need to shelter in the tents at night until they are full-grown adults. Some gardeners burn the webs with a candle flame or a small propane torch, such as you might have around the house for plumbing repairs. The caterpillars will fry in a couple of seconds, so there is no danger of setting the tree on fire.

Earwigs are unmistakable. Small, brown, with a pair of curved pincers on the back end of their hard-cased bodies, earwigs are a persistent pest. They eat everything, including each other. Earwigs are difficult to control, because they have no fixed address and roam neighborhoods at will, eating, eating, eating. One year they were so bad in one of our gardens, we could almost read a newspaper through the holes in the dahlia flowers. Fortunately, they go in cycles, usually one bad year and three not-so-bad years. They can be squished, trapped or drowned — your choice.

Japanese beetles are terrible plant destroyers. In their larval form, as white grubs, they feed on plant roots, seriously weakening a plant, eventually killing it. These grubs are often found feasting on your grass roots. Adults, small reddish beetles, chew flowers and leaves. They especially love roses. A keen entomologist once timed a Japanese beetle and found that it could devour half a rosebud at one sitting.

June bugs are also a serious pest, both in larval or grub form and in the adult stage. They are large, brown, hard-bodied flying beetles often found knocking on screens and darting around porch lights in the summer. Sometimes cats are obliging enough to catch and eat them for you. The white grubs live in the soil and do a lot of damage gnawing on the roots of perennials and grass. Hand-picking and dropping them into a jar of soapy water kills them. They are attracted to yellow, so you can make a variety of traps using yellow cards covered with sticky substances.

Leafhoppers, small and green, feed on developing buds, severely diminishing the amount of bloom on a plant. They are difficult to see, but when you brush against plant leaves, they hop mightily. Spray them with soap-and-water or with insecticidal soap.

Leaf miners are larval forms of a variety of insects. After the insect lays its eggs on stems and leaves, the eggs hatch into larvae, which immediately tunnel into leaves. The miners live happily inside the leaf tissue, between the upper and lower layers of the leaf. Their presence is unmistakable. Many varieties cause white trails to form on leaves, a delicate tracery of their internal travels. Cedar bushes infected by leaf miner have brown-tipped leaf clusters. Less energetic species of leaf miners prefer to hollow out large rooms in one place rather than travel throughout the leaf. Spray three times in May with an organic insecticidal soap, then twice more in the first half of July.

Plant or leaf bugs, such as the *four-lined bug, harlequin bug, tarnished plant bug* and various other bugs eat ragged holes in a wide variety of plants. Be sure the bug you are planning to murder is actually eating the plant. We again remind you that the good bugs are difficult to distinguish from the bad.

Spider mites, or *red spider mites*, the bane of the indoor gardener, are also a persistent outdoor pest. Mites are nearly microscopic, but the observant gardener knows to look on the underside of leaves and at the join of leaf to stem for the mite's delicate webbing. If the mites are allowed to settle in, affected leaves will turn yellow and drop off. If you do not take immediate steps, mites can multiply rapidly and turn a healthy plant into a defoliated, stunted, web-covered mess. Fortunately, insecticidal soap or a garlic spray usually deals with them.

Spittlebug nests are easy to spot. The nests, on the stems of a number of garden plants and trees, look like foamy clusters of tiny bubbles. The worms hide in their frothy nests, safe from predators and dry weather. They damage their host plants by sucking the sap or fluid out of its leafy victim. If you investigate one of these wet lairs you will find a small worm, sometimes two, in the center. Squish it.

Scale is what it sounds like — a brown oval insect which looks like a hard, brown scale or barnacle attached to a stem or leaf. Some scale are wooly and white. Scale insects are quite mobile and move from place to place on a plant, hunkering down to suck the life fluids out of any tasty morsel they come across. Scale insects are specialized. Some only want to savour orchid leaves, others like woody ornamentals. Scale, with difficulty, can be controlled by rubbing them with denatured alcohol. Large trees must be treated with dormant oil spray. Buy the kind without lime sulphur and follow directions carefully.

Slugs — yeech — we hate slugs. They are repulsive, mobile gray blobs which leave slimy trails behind wherever they crawl. On the West Coast especially, slugs are huge, snail-like creatures as large as, shudder, your thumb. They are night feeders who enjoy most plants, but seem to zero in on young leafy plants, hostas and lettuce, for example. If you decide to hunt them down, wait until early dusk and then arm yourself with a flashlight and a salt shaker. If you score a direct hit with a few grains of table salt, their little bodies shrivel right up.

Thrips unfortunately are so small you do not know they are hiding between petals and in the folds of leaves until you see the damage. They feast on new shoots and developing buds of many plants, especially day lilies and gladioli. Their gormandizing causes dirty brown or silver streaks to appear on leaves and flowers. Try spraying with insecticidal soap.

Whitefly, a small white fly, is the scourge of greenhouse and indoor plants. However, they wreak havoc in the garden when they escape outdoors in the summer — luckily they cannot survive winter outdoors. If you shake a plant and a small white cloud drifts away from the leaves, your plants have whitefly. They usually feed on the undersides of leaves, and seem to enjoy a wide variety of container plants, such as fuchsia, and vegetable garden plants, such as tomatoes. Spray with insecticidal soap. They are attracted to yellow, so some gardeners fill yellow bowls with soapy, but not bubbly water, which they drown in.

Extermination Recipes

As we have already made clear, we are strong believers in non-chemical warfare in the garden. Do not be shocked by the terminology, it is a battle for the survival of your roses, grass and cedars. You cannot win the war, but you certainly can even the odds. The first line of defense is preventive. Build up a fertile, organically rich soil. Healthy soil supports healthy plants which will be better able to ward off damaging infestations of insects and disease. Clean up the garden, compost rotting vegetation rather than leaving it lying in the garden, as it is a drawing card for all sorts of bad insects. Buy the disease-resistant plants, shrubs and trees plant hybridists have been so busy creating. Marigolds, garlic and mint, planted throughout the garden, repel a number of insects due to their offensive, to the insect nose, odors and fluids. (If you decide, however, to plant mint, put it in a container. Mint is invasive and can overpower a garden if not contained.) If your neighborhood cat population is low, encourage birds to nest in your garden by putting out a birdfeeder. They are great insect eaters. Scare away pigeons and grackles, however, as they sometimes eat leaves and flowerbuds.

If these preventive measures are not effective, then consider a more aggressive approach. Many of the larger insects can simply be hand-picked by the gardener. If you see a bug munching away on your favorite hydrangea, simply pick the thing up and drop it in a jar of soapy or very hot water. If you are reluctant to touch it, place the open jar under the leaf and scrape the bug off, with your trowel, into the water. If this is still too close for comfort, cut the leaf, bug and all, off and let it drop into the jar. When you unearth a grub, give it a good whack or stab with your trowel. You won't have to touch the loathsome creature, and the force of the blow will drive the severed grub down into the soil so you do not have to look at its oozing carcass. You can use this same no-touch, no-see method on caterpillars and other large, slow-moving insects, by first knocking them to the ground. Touching insects, not the leaves, with a rag dipped in kerosene, kills them almost instantly. Small, slow insects such as aphids, in small groups, can be squished between gloved fingers, unless you think you would enjoy murdering them bare-handed. Large, soft-bodied insects, however, can make a gory mess on your gloves or hands when they are squished. Some insect innards are poisonous, so wash your hands when you are done.

The gardener can also use various traps and barriers. There is a sticky trap available in some garden centers which is simply a yellow piece of paper or plastic (yellow seems to attract a number of insects) covered with a glue. A number of flying insects such as aphids, whitefly and gnats home right in on the yellow glue-card. When the card is filled with glued-on insects, put it in the garbage. Some insects prefer red, so try one of each color. Make your own with colored cardboard and a thin film of motor oil.

All is not fair in love nor war, and insect trapping is no exception. You can buy traps baited with an insect's specific pheromone (sex hormone). Lust-filled insects make the proverbial bee-line to their doom. Lured to their death by the attractant, the sex-crazed insects crawl into a glue-filled bag or stick to a glue-treated card.

A do-it-yourself trap for slugs is the famous saucer of beer. Slugs seem to crawl happily to their deaths and drown in the beer. It was believed that slugs were an alcoholic race, fatally attracted to the brew. Some enterprising gardener has discovered, however, that it is not the beer, but the yeast in the beer, that is the attraction. Those of you who do not want to sacrifice a bottle of beer in the interests of horticulture can use the new non-beers (that is, the no-alcohol type) to the same advantage. If you do not want to spend money on the critters, mix up a yeasty drink. According to the April 1991 issue of *Organic Gardening,* slugs will be attracted to a mixture of 1 cup/250 mL water, 1 teaspoon/5 mL sugar and 1/4 teaspoon/1 mL yeast. Set saucers of the mixture near the plants that slugs crave. Pour the contents out every day or so, depending on how many slugs have drowned, around threatened plants. Evidently many insects are repelled by the presence of their own dead comrades and will steer clear of the tiny corpses.

Slugs and earwigs are attracted as well to other types of traps. Some gardeners set out grapefruit rinds, tipped slightly up on one side, around the garden. Both earwigs and slugs, nighttime feeders, will crawl inside these beckoning domes to sleep off the effects of their nighttime revels. Earwigs, which like close, dark places, can also be trapped in crinkled-up newspapers, slightly opened matchboxes, inverted flower pots, etc. You must empty these traps every day either into a pail or jar of soapy or hot water, or throw them into a bag and then into the garbage. Squish the beasts if you want to be really sure they are dead. If you forget to empty the traps, the beasties will simply saunter out the next night and eat a little more of your garden.

Diatomaceous earth, usually sold as "Perma Guard" or "Fossil Flower," is the fossilized skeletons of single-celled algae-like organisms which lived thirty million years ago. These skeletons are now found in fossilized beds which have compacted into soft, chalky rock. This rock is ground up into powder, packaged and sold. The gardener sprinkles a thick barrier — about as deep as your little fingertip is wide — of the stuff around threatened plants. When any soft-bodied insects, such as slugs, foolhardily try to crawl over it, the razor-sharp, microscopic shards pierce their bodies. Sometimes sharp sand will serve the same purpose. Unfortunately, diatomaceous earth can harm worms, which are beneficial. Also do not inhale this powder or get it in your eyes — wear a mask and goggles.

Bacillus Thuringiensis, sold as "Dipel," "BT," and "Thuricide," is a pathogenic bacterium that makes bugs sick when they come in contact with the stuff and eventually kills them. It is mainly toxic to the caterpillar stages of moths and butterflies. There is still some question as to whether or not it harms other beneficial insects.

The gardener who has a wood fire can use the wood ashes as an insect deterrent. Sprinkle ashes around the base of plants to repel cutworms, beetles, mites, aphids and slugs. Be careful that the ash does not actually touch the stems, for it may make them rot.

There are a number of home-made sprays the desperate gardener can make in the blender. You have your choice of ingredients. A mixture of puréed, strained, garlic and/or onion and/or hot pepper mixed with water, then sprayed on plants and insects, will reduce the attack of sucking insects such as mites and aphids. If made with hot pepper, it can deter deer. It can also be sprayed on plants to prevent mildew and other fungal diseases, as well as on those infected, in the early stages, with leaf spot, rust and spore diseases. For obvious reasons, never get this stuff in your eyes, but if you do, splash them with cold water.

Non-detergent soap dissolved in water (40:1, water:soap) controls many insects including aphids, whiteflies, leaf miners and spider mites. If you do not want to mix up anything special, try blasting infected plants with a forceful spray from the garden hose to unseat these tiny marauders. If you feel particularly lazy, buy a commercial organic soap spray, such as Safer's Insecticidal Soap, often found in garden centers.

If you have an old blender and a strong stomach you can grind up dead larvae and beetles in the blender, mix with water, strain, then spray affected plants. The smell of dead insects scares the living away from your plants.

When using any of these sprays, be sure to coat every part of the plant, the stem and undersides of the leaves, everywhere. Contact sprays only work if they hit the insect directly. After spraying, check every few days to see if any of the pests have returned. Many of these insects not only have very short reproductive cycles, but also their eggs are usually not affected by the spray. Normally it is best to spray in weekly cycles until you are sure all insects have been killed.

A number of toxic biological sprays, composed of rotenone, ryania, pyrethrum, and nicotine, are often sold over the counter. While these are not as harmful to the environment as the synthetic chemicals used in many commercial insecticides, biological toxins are not to be used indiscriminately. Because they are nerve toxins, they can kill the beneficial as well as the harmful insects. Some can make humans feel ill after exposure. Synthetic pyrethrums are also on the market, but do not use them because they are not biodegradable. We do not recommend biological sprays except as a last resort when all else has failed. As well, we never recommend the use of some of the common garden poisons that are available such as chlorpyrifos, carbaryl, diaxinon, malathion and dimethoate.

Another means of insect control is to take advantage of the killing instincts of beneficial insects. Spread out the welcome mat for a number of these insects, such as dragonflies, which eat mosquito larvae, and ground beetles, which eat tent caterpillars and other larvae.

The well-loved ladybug eats aphids for breakfast, lunch and dinner. If you see a ladybug sitting around doing nothing, gently pick her up and carry her to a favorite rose bush or other perennial and let her feast on aphids.

One of the many beneficial insects killed by toxic sprays are bees. Bees not only pollinate the flowers of many ornamentals, fruits and vegetables, but also feed on soil insects and millipedes.

Damselflies and spiders are great insect eaters, as are a number of wasps.

Hornets are beneficial because they eat many caterpillars, but their sting does not feel so beneficial.

So you can see, pest and weed control is not straightforward, and there is no neat solution, only unrelenting vigilance.

The best you can hope for is a balance — a bit for the insects, a bit for the weeds, and hopefully, a pleasing garden for yourself. You should welcome the chance to pit yourself against these age-old enemies. After all, what forms a common bond between gardeners but their tales of gardening wars? You will be able to hold your own in any social situation with stories of your battles with earwigs, your ingenious traps, or the summer's spine-tingling tangle with bindweed.

This is a contest for domination, in which you are pitting yourself against the elements, against every dirty trick Mother Nature can throw at you. To survive, use your common sense and creativity. Throw away the poisonous herbicides and insecticides. Roll up your shirtsleeves and don't be afraid to get your hands dirty.

CHAPTER 15

Old Savvy for New Gardeners: Garden Lore It Took Us Years to Accumulate

We all accumulate bits of lore on various topics as we go through life. It helps compensate for wrinkles and gray hair. However, it seems to take a long time to acquire lore and no time at all to get the wrinkles and the gray. In view of this, we have compiled an alphabetical list of useful and interesting gardening information to give you a head start.

Bird Feeders

If you love to feed the birds, but hate to tidy up sprouted birdseed in the lawn, use cracked or coarsely ground corn instead — it does not germinate.

Cats

You can spend a lot of money on chemical animal repellents that are environmentally suspect and, in our experience, never work. Here are two ways to prevent cats using your flowerbeds as their private toilets. Our favorite method is sticking lots of little twigs between 6-12 in./15-30 cm tall into the soil where the cats want to, er, dig. Because the flowerbed becomes a cat obstacle course, they will leave it alone. Spreading chicken wire mesh over the beds works fine in early spring, until new growth appears. This is a more expensive method than the twigs.

Eventually, some fool will tell you to plant catnip (*Nepeta cataria*) in a corner of your yard to lure your own cats to use that one spot as their toilet. Never do this. All it does is attract every cat for miles around.

Dripline

What is this dripline gardeners talk about? Like the equator, it is an imaginary line. Picture the crown of a plant — the big bulky spread of branches and foliage. Draw an imaginary line around its circumference. Now move that circle down to sit on the ground. This is the dripline. It is useful because it shows you where the most actively feeding roots are located. The other kind of dripline is one directly under the edge of your roof — water runs off the roof and digs a long, narrow trench, usually washing away anything planted there. This is why eavestroughs were invented.

Fast Growing = False Friend

Watch out when you see the phrase "fast growing" in a nursery catalogue. This sounds wonderful to the impatient beginner, but it often means that the plant grows rampantly, year after year, far beyond the bounds of the space allotted to it. An example of this is Siberian or Chinese elm, *Ulmus pumila*, sometimes grown as a hedge in cold-winter areas. One of your authors has neighbors who are the unhappy proprietors of such a hedge. They are out there at least twice a summer, every summer, pruning away (and bundling up) several feet of new growth all along its length.

Gardening in the Real World

Totally problem-free plants do not exist. There is always a trade-off. When hybridists bred square tomatoes for ease of shipping, they wound up creating dry, tasteless fruit. If the plant breeders ever come up with a truly black rose, it will doubtless be terribly susceptible to mildew. Life is like that, and so is gardening. Resign yourself to this fact — it is easier on your stress level. We have tried, however, to ease the sting of the unpredictability of gardening by winnowing our selections of plants in this book down to those with only one or two drawbacks, rather than the nine or ten that some persnickety plants have.

Be prepared to host a bit of plant disease now and then, and even a few bugs. Many bugs are beneficial, and should not be killed. The sad fact is that the only way to have a totally pest-free garden is to use a barrage of

How to Keep Cats Out of Your Garden

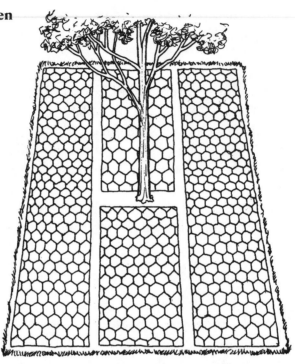

In spring (before perennials sprout and annuals have been planted) or in autumn (after perennials have been clipped and annuals have been pulled up) lay chicken wire over the earth. Cats do not like to walk on it. Autumn-applied mesh can be left in place all winter and do spring duty.

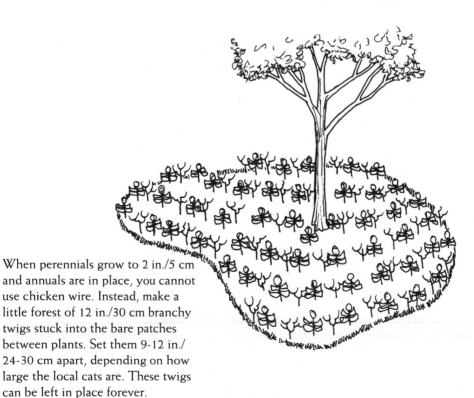

When perennials grow to 2 in./5 cm and annuals are in place, you cannot use chicken wire. Instead, make a little forest of 12 in./30 cm branchy twigs stuck into the bare patches between plants. Set them 9-12 in./ 24-30 cm apart, depending on how large the local cats are. These twigs can be left in place forever.

chemicals damaging to the environment. The health of the planet outweighs our desire for a pest-free garden.

Despite all our good intentions, death in the garden is inevitable. Sometimes an undetected disease has weakened a plant to the point that it dies during a winter that, ordinarily, it would survive. Sometimes an especially cold winter or one with less snow than usual comes along, killing normally hardy plants. So never take it as a personal rebuke if something you nursed along turns up its toes. It is all part of gardening.

Grafts

Many woody plants are grafted. This means that a tough, cold-hardy rootstock has been joined to a cutting (scion) from a more tender, sometimes prettier, plant in the same family. Grafting makes it possible to grow a tender plant in a hostile climate. Such plants may experience

Grafted Plants

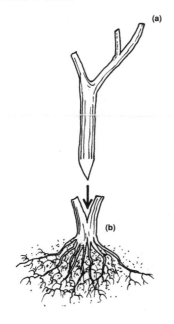
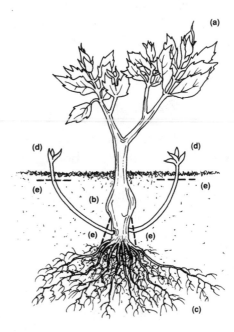

a) tender but pretty scion that will produce the flowers you want

b) the understock, usually a hardier plant of the same family as the scion

a) crown of desired plant (scion)

b) graft or bud union. In cold-winter areas this is placed beneath the soil. The site of actual join between the two original plants always turns into a knobby bulge.

c) root stock. Same family as the desired plant, but hardier

d) suckers

e) sites of cuts to remove suckers

considerable winterkill, but if the graft union survives, new growth will sprout from it in spring. The catch (there is always a catch) is that growth may also sprout from the rootstock. This growth, called a sucker, often is a much less attractive version of the desired stock and should be cut off, or the sucker will steal food and water from the tender plant. If removal is neglected, suckers can take over the whole plant, and choke it. Very energetic people will dig down to where each sucker grows from the root, and cut there. Real people will snip it off a little below soil level. Method #1 is more horticulturally correct, but life is short and there are limits to what one can be expected to do in the garden.

Greenthumb, Ms. or Mr.

Find the local Ms. or Mr. Greenthumb — the best gardener on your street. Keep an eye on what she or he does, then do the same yourself. Since this gardener lives on the same street, the soil is probably similar to yours, and the garden certainly gets an identical amount of rain. Walk by the house when the gardener is out working in the (fabulous) flowerbeds and sort of dawdle. When he or she notices you, say something nice about the garden. The gardener will, if you are lucky, immediately adopt you, and tell you everything you want to know.

Hardiness Zone Map

Reluctant Gardeners should familiarize themselves with plant-hardiness zones. Many gardening books, garden center plant lists and mail order catalogues note the appropriate zone for each plant described. Often this will be a terse "hardy to zone 2" or just "2." Don't panic — all you have to do to understand this number is to check a copy of the plant-hardiness zone map to see where your garden lives. The climate zones were identified after various factors affecting a plant's ability to survive winter (the lowest winter temperature, length of frost-free days, summer rainfall, etc.) had been crunched together in a complicated formula. The numbering begins at 0 (the coldest zone) and goes higher as the climate becomes milder.

The numbers on the Agriculture Canada map do not correspond exactly to the zonal ranges of the U.S. Department of Agriculture plant-hardiness map, so Canadians using the American map must double check, as must Americans using the Canadian map.

However, for simplicity's sake, our book does not use numbered zone references. Most of the plants we have recommended will survive temperatures of -22°F/-30°C, and are well worth trying if temperatures occasionally go to -40°F/-40°C.

Houseplants

Most indoor plants benefit from a summer out of doors. Introducing them gradually to the increased light levels is the key to avoiding disaster. No matter how bright your growlights or how sunny your window, outdoor sunlight is much stronger. So take your housebound treasures outdoors when temperatures are steadily above +50°F/+10°C and put them in the shade. After three or four days, move them to an area that gets a few hours of direct sun each day. Then to full sun, if that is appropriate for that particular plant. Houseplants such as areca palm, dracena, and philodendron, which need low light in the house, should remain in the shade all summer. Because they are in pots, houseplants should be watered every day.

In autumn, bring them in before frost — except for azaleas, which need a few nights of light frost to set flower buds. Do not panic if a plant drops a lot of leaves soon after being brought back indoors. This is a natural response to readapting to reduced light levels. Indoor light levels can be boosted by placing the plants under growlights (plain old inexpensive warm white fluorescents work fine) run by a timer, set for 12 hours of light, 12 of dark.

Kids and Gardens

Many people find it pleasant to spend time in the backyard with growing children. Some gardeners find that it makes sense to give the children their own stake in the family garden. We suggest the following plants for children to grow:

Give them some Russian Mammoth sunflower seeds, which are available at most garden centers. Plant around the second week of May in full sun. These friendly giants are fully described in Chapter 6 on annuals.

Remember those October newscasts, telling you about the winner of the agricultural fair's pumpkin growing contest? Most of the winners were grown in full sun from seeds of the 'Atlantic Giant' pumpkin, available from Stokes Seed Co., 39 James St., Box 10, St. Catharines, Ont., L2R 6R6.

Scarlet runner beans not only grow easily from seed, but also make a most attractive vine. You can eat the beans if you pick them young. If the weather is hot the vines will, however, produce mostly flowers and no beans. Plant in mid-May in sun or light shade, in front of a trellis of some sort. When the seeds germinate they heave the soil impatiently out of their way in a let's-get-going manner. Many bean seeds are chemically treated, so never let a child touch them with bare hands, let alone put them in their mouths.

Monoculture

An old piece of gardening advice says to find out what grows best for you and then grow lots of it. This sounds enticingly simple to the Reluctant Gardener, but we regret that we cannot endorse it. A concentrated planting of one plant invites an invasion of that plant's pests. For example, one of your authors had a clump of orange lilies. They were lovely and trouble-free, so she bought some red ones. Then pink ones. Then yellow ones. Then white ones. Now she spends half her life picking lily-eating bugs off the plants. The moral of this story is: a varied planting reduces the damage insect and diseases might cause.

Poison Ivy

If you want to be rid of poison ivy but do not want to use chemicals, you will need to practice a combination of weeding and mulching. In spring or autumn, when the soil is moist, simply pull the weeds out. Get as much root as you can. Be sure to wear rubber gloves and old clothes. If the roots are too tough to pull, clip the plants off at ground level. Put the greenery into a plastic bag and close it tightly when you are done, then put it out in the garbage, *never* in the compost. Even dried-out plants can make you itch. Do not let your gloves or clothes touch anything until they have been thoroughly washed. Cover the area with a thick mulch (black plastic is appropriate, but hideous) to exclude light — this part is important, because it discourages re-sprouting. You will need to repeat this procedure over several years.

Public Gardens

If you are fortunate enough to live near a public garden, go visit it. Few other places offer such a good look at so many plants you might want to grow. Think of giving them a cash donation, too — what with falling budgets and rising plant theft, they have a difficult time surviving.

Rocks

If you have a garden area that is always chilly, why not work a largish mass of rocks into your design? The rocks will not only collect and hold warmth when the sun shines on them, but they will later radiate this warmth for you to enjoy after dusk. They become, in effect, solar collectors. Similarly, a hot spot that lacks shade is not the right place for a concrete or stone patio. Apart from the discomfort of sitting somewhere so hot, it will heat up the adjacent house. Put the patio somewhere else. Or, construct a wooden deck — elevate it a little off the ground so that breezes will pass underneath.

Salt in the Soil

More homeowners and communities are using alternatives to salt for de-icing streets and sidewalks, but we still have a ways to go. Salt can damage lawns and gardens. Salty snow accumulated during the winter melts in spring, and carries the salt down into your soil. Spring rains usually flush the salt farther down by mid-May, so do not worry about your annual beds. But what about perennials and shrubs? Try adding sand to your soil to promote drainage in areas where salt is a problem. Do not pile salty driveway snow clearings on top of plantings. In areas which may be liable to salt damage, use salt-tolerant plants such as honeylocust, potentilla, lilac, dogwood, smoke tree, hawthorn, oak, Russian olive and juniper.

Seeds

The Reluctant Gardener does not start plants from seed. It is just too tricky. The only exceptions are noted in the section *Kids and Gardens*.

Tetanus Shots

Once, one of your authors mentioned to her doctor that she was a mad gardener. The doctor promptly told her to stick out her arm for a tetanus shot, saying, "Dirty stuff, dirt."

Wild Plants

Never, ever dig up wild plants and transplant them to your home garden. Many wild species are endangered these days, and we do not want to diminish the numbers of these native flowers, shrubs and trees. Besides, most of these transplants would die anyway, because their wild environment is very specialized. It is unlikely that the home gardener would be able to reproduce it.

CHAPTER 16

The Absolute Minimum You Can Get Away With and Still Hold Your Head Up in the Neighborhood

Your authors are both passionate gardeners who have difficulty believing that anyone would really, truly hate to garden. However, we are also women of imagination, and have done our best to put ourselves in the shoes of such people. We both loathe housework, so when writing this chapter we pretended we were giving instructions for housework. This produced a suitable "Oh, please, anything but that" frame of mind. Here is what we came up with;

Soil

We are sorry, but we insist that you enrich your soil. Even the smallest collection of plants needs decent earth to grow in. Please read Chapter 2 on soil, paying close attention to composting. The bottom line for soil repair is to add all the compost or well-rotted manure possible.

Fertilizer

Over the last two or three decades, too many gardeners have become fertilizer-happy, applying the stuff every time they turn around. Believe us when we say that one or two stingy applications will suffice. A 10-10-10, 2-20-20 or 15-30-15 fertilizer applied twice — once in June and once in August (lawns in September only) — is enough.

Flowers

"Absolute minimum" is a relative term. Some people think they *must* have a few flowers, some do not. There is no shame at all in a completely flowerless garden. For those who wish to include a mild show of flowers in their minimalist yard, we recommend annuals — rather than perennials which are more work.

Minimalist gardeners do not have flowerbeds, as such. What they have are one or two nice little edges of annuals around the base of shrubs, the base of the house wall, or beside paths.

For a sunny spot: marigolds are the most problem-free, sun-loving annuals we can think of, although geraniums are certainly in the running. Of the commonly grown, sun-loving annuals we specifically warn you *against* petunias, because of aphids and mid-season pruning needs, and *against* pansies, because they require constant deadheading to keep them blossoming.

For shady areas: impatiens or begonias are the most problem-free. Do not grow coleus because too much deadheading is required.

Annuals in Containers

It is nice to putter around a few container plants at the end of the day — watering and deadheading can be calm, pleasurable activities. We do realize that containers are a little extra work, because of the need to check them for water *every day*. However, if you have a pot or two of geraniums, which thrive in dry soil, you need only check them every second day for watering. Containers are *not* for people who go away a lot.

Roses

The true minimalist gardener does not even consider growing roses. The sort-of minimalist will attempt rugosa roses or the non-climbing Explorer roses. People who would rather eat dirt than garden in it, never, but never, grow hybrid teas, grandifloras, floribundas. They also never grow climbing roses.

Shrubs

The least troublesome shrub you will ever come across is cedar. Prune in early spring or late summer — your choice — but only if the shrub threatens to become too big for its location. Cedar makes a wonderful hedge. All it asks is a little sun and some water now and then.

Two obliging flowering shrubs, with minimal pruning needs, are lilac (large) and pink spirea (small).

Trees

The selection of a tree or trees is a major decision. You really should read the whole of Chapter 9.

Garden Flooring

For most people this automatically means grass, but it does not need to be so. Consider installing a large deck or patio. Or, you might want to carpet your garden floor with ground cover. Once the ground cover is established, it will take less maintenance than grass, although it does need to be kept weeded during the first couple of years.

A good, fast-spreading ground cover for partial shade is goutweed. However, it is very invasive, so make sure it is not close to desirable plants that it might choke out. Wood violets will quickly cover up a shady area, too. For sunny expanses, try annual portulaca (it reseeds itself if it is happy). Also for sun, try creeping thyme.

Bulbs

If you really want bulbs in the spring, plant daffodils. They are extremely hardy, rodents do not eat them, and they come up again year after year. Grape hyacinth and crocus are fine, too. Just remember that you *must* allow the foliage to ripen. Do not plant tulips, which cannot be relied upon to bloom again after the first year or two, especially in colder areas.

Lawn

Diehard lawn lovers should realize that a happy lawn rests on at least a 6 in./15 cm layer of good soil or there will be nothing but trouble. De-thatch the lawn in spring, remembering to wait until spring run-off has drained away and the lawn does not squelch when you walk on it. Never mow it shorter than 3 in./8 cm. Water only when the soil is a little on the dry side, but when you do, water deeply enough so the soil is moistened 12 in./30 cm down. Never over-fertilize. A weak application of organic fertilizer in September will do fine. Topdress lightly with sieved compost or well-rotted manure once every year or two.

Bugs and Diseases

They are always present, even in the smallest gardens. The bare minimum preventive action is to keep your yard scrupulously tidy in the first place, that is, *never* leave rotting greenery lying about. Another important rule is to grow a good mixture of different plants.

Many plant-infesting bugs will curl up and die if you squirt them directly with an organic insecticidal soap, which is ecologically correct and widely available. You can make up a batch of your own. A 40:1 mixture of water and dish-washing (not automatic dishwasher) liquid soap works well. Heavy-duty insecticides are not the answer.

The easiest way to treat diseased plant material is to clip away the affected part of the plant and dispose of it in the garbage.

Weeding

Unfortunately, weeds are always with us. Once a week you should pull up all weeds that have crept into the garden or that hid from you the last time you weeded. Ignore them at your garden's peril. They have no inhibitions and no shame about moving in and elbowing out all your ornamentals. We warn you away from chemical herbicides, which are dangerous both to your ornamentals and you. Why not apply a summer mulch? See Chapter 3 on general garden maintenance for more information.

We hope you do not find this list discouraging. A few flower-filled containers, a small patch of lawn, a small flowerbed should not take much of your time — maybe, depending on the size of your lot, an hour a week. We do feel obliged, however, to warn you that gardening can sometimes grip you like a persistent fever. Last year the small bed of marigolds sufficed, this year, well, you reason, why not enlarge the bed with a flowering shrub in one corner, a clump of daylilies in another. . . . Watch out, the Reluctant Gardener is reluctant no more.

Appendix I — Allergies

Sneeze and wheeze, sniffle and blow. What does a gardener do upon waking up one fine morning with the first allergy of his or her life? What happens when a gardener marries an allergy sufferer? Or gives birth to one? Compromise, that's what — no stranger to married or family life. We are not allergists, but we are sneezers, and here are a few tricks that have worked for us.

One good compromise that works for a friend of ours is this: all the flowering, pollen-making, scent-producing plants go in the front, for the neighbors to admire. All the non-flowering plants — those grown for their foliage — go in the back, where the family sits out.

If you have allergies, wear a face mask while gardening, especially when mowing the grass. A lot of pollens and molds that have settled on the lawn are kicked up by the mower.

Never bring cut flowers into the house if you have allergies. One of us, who has only mild inhalant allergies, had a fit of near-terminal sneezing when she brought a big vase of flowering nicotine into the house.

Some plants, such as cedar, juniper and euonymus, contain resins that may give you contact dermatitis. One of your authors developed quite a painful rash on her cheeks after brushing her hands across her face after planting two small variegated euonymus shrubs. Other plants with this potential are chrysanthemums, tulips, tulip bulbs and daisies. Be suspicious of anything with hairy or sticky leaves or stems. Wash immediately with soap and lots of running water if your skin tingles after touching a plant. If it hurts enough to worry you, see a doctor.

People plagued by allergies should be especially careful never to use herbicides or insecticides, because of the potential for a big-time reaction. If you are considering using any of these, or using a fungicide to get rid of, say, powdery mildew (which could affect mold-sensitive people), consult your allergist.

Appendix II — Smart Lifting

Neither of your authors is exactly a spring chicken anymore, and we have both had our bad-back battles to deal with. But do we stop gardening? Not on your life. Instead, our movements in the garden have come to resemble a sort of horticultural t'ai chi, with our weight-bearing moves thought out beforehand and executed slowly. Here is what works for us and what should help you avoid a sore back:

- You have heard it a million times before, you are hearing it again here: lift with your leg muscles, not your back muscles.

- A doctor told one of us once, "Do whatever you like, just keep one knee bent while you do it." It works amazingly well.

- Never twist and turn as you lift. Who are you, Chubby Checker? Put that bucket of manure in front of you, not to one side.

- Never lunge and lift. Bring the bucket close to you.

- Two trips are better than one trip. If a full bucket is too heavy to be carried without a lot of grunting and groaning, make two trips.

- If you are doing something that requires a full squat down onto your haunches, forget squatting — kneel instead.

- Stand up slowly. Fanny comes first, head comes up last. Saves your back and reduces dizziness.

- When shoveling, use your foot to jab the blade into the dirt. Using your arm and shoulder muscles over and over for this purpose will have you in pain in no time flat.

- When raking, do not lunge and reach and twist. Instead, step a little closer to the spot you are working on.

- To get rid of a spadeful of dirt, do not twist at the waist and toss. Use your feet to change the direction you are pointing.

- Buy and use kneepads. Yes, we know they look tacky. Who are you trying to impress, the worms?

- Vary your jobs. No one says you must weed the whole bed all at once, then shovel that entire pile of dirt waiting over by the garage. Weed for five minutes, shovel for five, admire the flowers for five, then back to work deadheading chest-high roses for five. Get it?

Appendix III — Common Latin Names Translated

We were both writers before we were gardeners, and have always been charmed by some of the Latin words used in botanical nomenclature. We think many of them would make wonderful, dog, cat or people names. "Pour little Humilis, she is so shy." Lanata the poodle. Auriculata the basset hound.

Here are a few Latin terms you may meet during your gardening life, especially at the garden center:

alba – white
alpinus – alpine
angustifolia – narrow-leaved
argentea – silver
atropurpurea – dark reddish purple
aurea – gold
auriculata – has ears
barbata – bearded
biennis – biennial
borealis – northern
centifolia – many-leaved, usually said of a many-petaled rose
cilians – fringed
compacta – compact
contorta – twisted
damosa – bushy
decumbens – lying down

eximia – distinguished
floribunda – flowering freely
gracilis – slender
heterophylla – leaves have different shapes
humilis – low-growing
lanata – wooly
musculata or *meleagris* – spotted
moschata – musk-scented
nana – dwarf
obtusa – blunt
palustris – from a swamp
pinnata – shaped like a feather
saxatilis – living among rocks
tormentosa – hairy
vegetus – has vigorous growth

Appendix IV — Dry Gardening

Over the last few years, many of us have realized that water is a resource that must be as carefully tended as our forests and wetlands. Plants tolerant of dry conditions tend to have gray leaves, or succulent (thick) ones, or narrow ones, or hairy ones. Ornamental grasses do well in dry conditions, as do poppies (*Papaver* and *Eschscholzia*), because of their long taproots. Most herbs are happy in dry soil. Other plants that we have mentioned in our YES! list which can grow in dry conditions are:

Annuals

- dusty miller
- geranium
- portulaca
- sunflower (Russian mammoth)

Perennials

- black-eyed Susan
- dianthus
- euphorbia
- flax
- gaillardia
- hen and chicks
- liatris
- mallow
- monarda
- periwinkle
- creeping phlox
- purple coneflower
- all sedums
- yarrow

Trees and Shrubs

- pea shrub
- cotoneaster
- euonymus
- gingko
- hawthorn
- locust
- mock orange
- common ninebark
- oak
- Russian olive
- sand cherry
- serviceberry
- spirea
- viburnum

Appendix V —
Selected Reading Material

Magazines

Canadian Gardening (130 Spy Court, Markham, Ontario, L3R 5H6)

COGnition (Canadian Organic Growers, Box 6408, Station J, Ottawa, Ontario, K2A 3Y6)

Harrowsmith (7 Queen Victoria Rd., Camden East, Ontario, K0K 1J0)

Organic Gardening (33 East Minor St., Emmaus, Pennsylvania, USA 18098)

TLC . . . for plants (1 Pacific, Ste-Anne de Bellevue, Quebec, H9X 1C5)

Books

Andrews, Brian, *Northern Gardens*, Lone Pine, Edmonton, Alberta, 1987.

Bennett, Jennifer and Turid Forsyth, *The Harrowsmith Annual Garden*, Camden House Publishing, Camden East, Ontario, 1990.

Buckley, A.R., *Canadian Garden Perennials*, Hancock House Publishers, Ltd., Sannichton, British Columbia, 1977.

Calkins, Carroll C., *Reader's Digest Illustrated Guide to Gardening in Canada*, Reader's Digest Association, Montreal, Quebec, 1979.

Campbell, Stuart, *Let It Rot! The Gardener's Guide to Composting*, Garden Way Publishing, Charlotte, Vermont, 1975.

Cole, Trevor, *The Ontario Gardener*, Whitecap Books, Vancouver, British Columbia, 1991.

Cullen, Mark, *A Greener Thumb: The Complete Guide to Gardening in Canada*, Penguin Books, Markham, Ontario, 1990.

Cullen, Mark and Lorraine Johnson, *The Real Dirt: The Complete Guide to Backyard, Balcony and Apartment Composting*, Penguin Books, Markham, Ontario, 1992.

Damrosch, Barbara, *The Garden Primer*, Workman Publishing, New York, 1988.

Franklin, Stuart, *Building a Healthy Lawn*, Storey Communications, Inc., Pownal, Vermont, 1988.

Harris, Marjorie, *The Canadian Gardener: A Guide to Gardening in Canada*, Random House, Mississauga, Ontario, 1990.

Harris, Marjorie, *Ecological Gardening: Your Path to a Healthy Garden*, Random House, Mississauga, Ontario, 1991.

Hart, Rhonda Massingham, *Bugs, Slugs, and Other Things*, Storey Communications Inc., Pownal, Vermont, 1991.

Kline, Hilary Dole and Adrian M. Wenner, *Tiny Game Hunting: Environmentally Healthy Ways to Trap and Kill the Pests in Your House and Garden*, Bantam Books, New York, 1991.

Lima, Patrick, *The Harrowsmith Perennial Garden*, Camden House Publishing, Camden East, Ontario, 1987.

Patterson, Allen, *Plants for Shade and Woodlands*, Fitzhenry and Whiteside Ltd., Markham, Ontario, 1987.

Philbrick, Helen and John, *The Bug Book*, Storey Communications Inc., Pownal, Vermont, 1974.

Riotte, Louise, *Secrets of Companion Planting for Successful Gardening*, Garden Way Publishing, Charlotte, Vermont, 1977.

Rubin, Carole, *The Organic Approach to Home Gardening*, Friends of the Earth-Canada, Ottawa, Ontario, 1989.

Shewchuk, George, *Rose Gardening on the Prairies*, University of Alberta, Edmonton, Alberta, 1988.

Index

Printed and bound in Canada by
Best Gagné Book Manufacturers